The Lilas of
ॐ The Sons of Shiva ॐ

Ancient painting of Shiva and Parvati with Ganesha and Kartikeya.

ॐ Sri Ganeshaya Namaha! ॐ

The Lilas of

The Sons of Shiva

Narrated by

Vanamali

Aryan Books International
New Delhi

THE LILAS OF THE SONS OF SHIVA

ISBN-10: 81-7305-342-1
ISBN-13: 978-81-7305-342-9

First Published in **2008** by
ARYAN BOOKS INTERNATIONAL
Pooja Apartments, 4B, Ansari Road, Darya Ganj, New Delhi-110002
Tel.: 23287589, 23255799; Fax: 91-11-23270385; E-mail: aryanbooks@vsnl.com

Computer Typeset and Printed in India at
ABI Prints & Publishing Co., New Delhi

DEDICATION

ॐ *Poornamadam, Poornamidam,*
Poornath, poornamudachyathe,
Poornasya, poornamadaya,
Poornamevavashishyathe

That is full and this is also full,
When the whole is removed from the full,
Fullness alone remains

To
My beloved grand-daughter
POORNA
With all my love

FOREWORD

By His Holiness Sri Shivarudra Balayogi Maharaj!

No Hindu ritual or Spiritual Exercise begins without an invocation to Lord Vighneshwara, the remover of all obstacles. Remembering Swami Kartikeya as the Deva Senapati is also equally important.

Saint Devi Vanamali is very humble and sincere. Her life is dedicated to the service of humanity in whom she sees her God. She is doing a wonderful service by adopting a village and helping the children to get educated amongst other services. I was touched by her simplicity. To go and sit in her Ashram on the banks of the beautiful Ganga in Rishikesh is always a wonderful experience for any spiritual seeker.

She has knitted this book titled "The Lilas of the Sons of Shiva" so beautifully. This is helpful for devotees who follow both, the path of *Bhakti* and Knowledge. She gives a deep insight into the concept of Lord Vighneshwara, Lord Kartikeya and Lord Dharma Shasta. Her work is Universal and would be helpful for people in all walks of life.

We wish long life to Devi Vanamali and may humanity be benefited by her services.

With love and blessings,

Shivarudra Balayogi Maharaj
Shri Shivabalayogi Maharaj Trust
180-C, Rajpur Road, Rajpur P.O.
DEHRADUN   UA 248009

CONTENTS

ॐ

Vigneshaya Namaha!

INTRODUCTION I

The Rishis

ॐ *Ajam, nirvikalpam niraakaaram-ekam,*
Niraanandam aanandam advaita-poornam,
Param nirgunam, nirvishesham, nireeham,
Parabrahma-rupam Ganesham bhajema

We worship thee O Ganesha! Who art the unborn, the absolute and the formless,
The essence of bliss, yet beyond bliss.
The indivisible and the infinite, the Supreme without attributes and desire,
The very form of the transcendental Reality – Brahman

— *Sri Ganesha-Sthavsam*

In order to understand the stories of the gods, it will be good to go into
the history of the *Sanatana Dharma,* or the ancient law of righteousness, as the
Hindu religion was known.

This most ancient religion rests upon a vast canon of Puranas, Vedas and
Agamas that include both revealed scriptures as well as those, which are the
result of the inspiration of the ancient sages. The Puranas belong to the second
category and contain an encyclopaedia of sacred wisdom. Scientists and Western
oriented philosophers are only just beginning to appreciate the deep psychological
and metaphysical wisdom preserved and transmitted in the form of puranic
lore and legend. This tradition maintains that there was once a period when
there lived a class of highly evolved souls in India called *rishi*s or *munis,* who
had the gift of inner vision and were able to see the past, present and future.
They could go to the realms of the gods and demons, the demigods and the

ॐ

titans of our mythological lore and describe the events that went on at that time or would take place at a future time.

Let us try to take a glimpse at the Age of the *rishi*s – the Vedic Age. The Vedas are the most ancient record of human wisdom known to man. The modern age has suddenly discovered their potential and a lot of interest is now centred on them. But unfortunately very few care to find out about the life of the *rishi*s who were the immediate cause of their coming into existence. Of course it is a fact that they did not care to reveal anything about themselves. However it is possible to glean something about their lives and ideas from the Vedas themselves. So let us try to find out their secrets as far as possible.

These seers or sages or *rishi*s were superior to the gods. They existed before the gods. In fact they were the ones who brought the gods into existence. They were the supreme creators! Vasishta, Marichi, Angiras, Pulastya, Pulaha, Kratu and Atri were the seven great *rishi*s – the *sapta rishi*s – who were the mind-born sons of Brahma. Later on two more, Brighu and Daksha, were added to the list of the sons of Brahma. They are called Vedic seers because they saw the hymns of the Vedas. They were not the only ones who saw or heard the hymns of the Vedas. Many other names like Visvamitra, Gautama, Bharadvaja, Agastya, Jamadagni, Kausiki and Markandeya are found in the Vedas. These Masters were not just Indians even though they were born on the soil of India. They were Super Humans. In them, human evolution reached its zenith. The rest of the history of the human race is a decline from their superior heights.

These spiritual giants strode across the Indo-Gangetic plain long before the dawn of historic time. They were the sublime expressions of the perfect human being. They were the crown and cream of Nature's evolutionary cycle. Modern man has only recently begun to envisage the possibility that such specimens of humanity can exist. These men were really supra human, superior even to the gods. No one knows how old they were. They were ancient. They had the power to choose the hour of their departure from this world. It is said that some of them like Markandeya, continued to live in the eternal snows of the Himalayas, unseen by any human eye. In fact one of them known as Bhogarnatha still exists and we will be taking up his story in the portion on Kartikeya. It is because of the power of their *tapasya* (austerity), that the world continues to retain its integrity. They had extraordinary powers. They could control the elements, travel with ease in astral worlds, cover vast distances rapidly through the sky without any aircraft, catch sound and light waves in their minds and see what was happening miles away as if on a TV screen. Their look could cut through rocks and drill holes in metals and they could have anything they wanted just by formulating a wish in their minds.

Yet strangely enough these men had no desires. They did not wish to conquer or control, they were content with whatever nature provided, they did not yearn to possess more and more for the simple reason that they possessed the wish-fulfilling cow of plenty in their own minds which was capable of granting their every desire. Having found the secret of all existence they continued to live only with the one desire, which was to serve the rest of creation. *Loka-samgrahamevaapi* – this was their creed – "For the good of the world!" They needed no commandments to keep them to the right path for they were the very embodiments of all commandments, of *dharma* or the cosmic order!

The age of the Vedic *rishi*s is amazing for this one thing. They had so much of mental power that they could materialize or create anything they wished. Yet we find that they did not bother to conquer countries or control others or make palaces and edifices that would last forever. They did not seek to carve in stone or wood or make effigies or temples or in anyway try to immortalize themselves in this world even though they were perfectly competent to do so if they wished. They made themselves known exclusively through their words. They have left nothing else. They left no chronicle of their achievements, nor images that might have survived the course of time. They knew that this world was only as real as the morning mist and would melt with the rising of the sun. The sun of their consciousness was at its zenith and they did not desire the trifles of the world.

We see from the Vedas that these *rishi*s were capable of anything that the mind could conceive. The Vedas describe fabulous palaces, gardens, divine beings and events. The *rishi*s could travel with ease to other planets and create all sorts of fantastic things including modern devices such as aeroplanes and even atomic bombs. The only instrument they needed or used was their mind. Using mental power alone, they were able to discover many things in the field of astronomy, physics, astrology and medicine. Their predictions in the field of astronomy and astrology have been proved to be true only in the last millennium. Before that nobody could even understand what they were talking about. Only modern computers can verify their mathematical calculations. No human brain is capable of it even today.

Worldly success meant nothing to them. The goal of human life was not to make a comfortable and easy life for oneself in this ephemeral world but to find one's true Self. That was the only treasure worth striving for. Everything was available to one who had found this jewel. Human life is fleeting and human beings spend the best part of their lives searching for happiness in the external world. The *rishi*s were convinced that this happiness lay within them and the only duty that was incumbent on the human being was to find this source within, which was the core of their being and the very source of all life! The strange thing was that the one who discovered this source no longer craved for the baubles of the world even though Nature was only too eager to bestow her priceless treasures on such a person!

This is the strange story of the Vedic *rishi*s. No other civilization except perhaps the present one, has reached such heights of knowledge but unlike this culture that craves for material wealth, they deemed all the knowledge of the external world to be secondary and to be used only as an aid to the discovery of the true Self. All they needed was their little grass huts or *ashrams* situated in the middle of jungles, where wild animals roamed unafraid. Everyday was a new day. They never stored or hoarded for the next day. Everyday they made a fire into which they poured their oblations. They had a few cows that supplied the butter and *ghee* for their oblations and they cultivated the land only to the extent that they needed. Nothing engraved on stone and marble remains to tell the tale of their incredible life.

Then how do we know about them is the question? The Vedas – which are the greatest and most ancient collection of the wisdom of the human being, contain their thoughts, which as has been said before, were the greatest gift they could give to humankind. The Vedas are said to be without beginning – even though Westerners with their zeal for tabulating each and everything have placed them in a chronological niche. In India they are known to be *anadi*, without a beginning and therefore without an end. That is why the Hindu religion is known as the *Sanatana Dharma*, the eternal law of righteousness, which has always existed and will always continue to exist, till the end of time. The Vedas have no authors. Yet many of the hymns and *mantra*s are connected with the name of one of the *rishi*s. Why is this so?

The *rishi*s claimed no authorship for them. According to them the hymns existed as vibrations in the *akasa* (ether) from the beginning of time. Vibrations create sounds. These sounds always exist in ethereal space. Only those with ears, which have the power to hear these subtle sounds, will be able to hear them. The ability of the dense radio receiver can well be acquired by sentient beings. In fact we can do much better. Just as electromagnetic waves are converted into sonic or sound waves, cosmic vibrations can become audible to our ears. *Tapasya* or austerity is what gives us this power. Immersed in *tapasya* it is said that the *rishi*s saw the hymns. Hence they are called the see-rs and the Vedic hymns are known as *sruti* or that which has been heard. Each of the hymns has the name of one of these *rishi*s attached to them. He was the one who saw that particular hymn and that is how we even know their names.

These words of theirs are the source of the culture of India. This spring is not meant for India alone but it is the heritage of the world, meant for all those thirsty for spirituality. The Hindu way of life has existed almost unchanged to this present day because it has been fortified and permeated by the thoughts of these great Masters even though much of it could not be grasped by the following generations. But since it has the stamp of absolute Truth, these thoughts have left an indelible mark on the Indian mentality. This can be felt even today by those who have cared to go deep into the thoughts of the sages as expressed in the Vedas. Those who read them are filled with a feeling of awe.

As has been mentioned before, the sages came before the gods and they proclaimed that everything including the gods stemmed from one single truth that they called Brahman – the Absolute Consciousness. The Absolute alone is Real, inasmuch as THAT is the only thing, which is imperishable, changeless, steadfast and eternal. "Unreality", is the transitory, the ephemeral and the elusive. By this classification, the world is unreal, since it is transitory. The world is thus known as *Maya*. *Maya* can be called an art or an artefact or something that is an appearance and has been produced at some point in space and time. *Maya* is the display of forms. It can also be called an illusion, trick or jugglery.

One of the great couplets of the Vedas says,

"Lead us from the Unreal to the Real,
From Darkness to Light,
And from Death to Immortality."

By death was not meant the death of the body but the death of the super-imposed ego, which claims that it alone is real. This ego identifies with the impermanent body and wavering mind and is only another creation of that self-same mind which has infinite tricks at its command. When that identification ceases, the Self, which is always immortal, shakes off its cloak of mortality and melts into the Truth of its immortality.

This then was the thought that obsessed the minds of the sages – that they were conscious. "Consciousness" precedes and pervades everything. Consciousness is that unique manifestation which needs nothing but itself. To become conscious of "Consciousness" is to become Brahman. The sages were the first to penetrate this Absolute Consciousness and to become "That" or Brahman. Human beings are also capable of becoming "That". The gods alone are not able to do so and thus it is said that they are jealous of humans and strive to hinder those who endeavour to become "Brahman". This is why people who practice intense *tapasya* find that many obstacles are placed in their way by the jealous gods.

We consider the world to be solid and real but to the *rishi*s, this was not so. The world's existence is sometimes manifest and sometimes submerged in *pralaya* or dissolution. It is ever being composed, decomposed and re-composed. The only reality that the world can claim to have is that of some type of continuity in eternity. But the *rishi*s were above this world play. They realized that the universe is a derivative of the mind. That is why they called it *Maya*. It is only in the twentieth century that the Newtonian fiction of solid matter was blasted by Einstein's Theory of Relativity. The modern world is slowly coming to recognize this fact but this was already known to the *rishi*s from the beginning of time. Nature itself is only a backdrop for this mind. Everything that happens, happens within the mind. Everything, including this limited mind has emerged from some super mind – Supreme Consciousness, so the only duty imposed on the human being is to discover that Supreme Consciousness. This can be done only through *tapasya* – intense austerity. The word *rishi* implies a friction that unleashes heat. *Tapas* acts on the immobile mind and produces both light and heat. Shut up in the cages of their minds, the sages vibrated with the heat of *tapasya*. This was their main activity. When the mind concentrates on a thing, *tapas* feeds it and its profile will emerge perfectly formed.

Creation itself is only an idea or thought in the mind of the Creator. This being the case, creation is not a blind mechanical force as Darwin suggested and survival of the fittest is not the only factor that prompts evolution. He forgot that the continuity of life could be had only if the mother sustains the infant in its helpless state and this factor, which sustains the child, is "love". Had the value of co-operation and love not been expressed in life, there would have been no evolution and no life. So, contrary to Darwinian thought there is a survival of the helpless aided by maternal love, which is more basic than the survival of the fittest. In dramatic opposition to the mechanistic Darwinian mind was the mind of the *rishis*. They cultivated the sensitive parts of their brain so that they could penetrate into the esoteric secrets of life. Unfortunately there is an atrophy of these parts of the brain in the modern age, which is what is encouraging the young to senseless destruction and violence leading to chaos and total annihilation.

Tapas was the method the *rishis* chose to activate this part of the brain. The mind is focused constantly on an object or objective, disregarding physical comfort, heedless of hunger and thirst, sleep and rest. This can only be done with humility and total surrender to God. They knew that despite our best efforts without the grace of God we can achieve nothing.

Having found the source of their true selves, having discovered the well of happiness within themselves, their compassionate hearts were anxious to share this wisdom with posterity and thus they passed on this precious knowledge to their disciples and their descendents. It was originally an oral teaching handed down from generation to generation. The Vedic *mantras* have maintained their purity because they have power only if they are correctly intonated. Their purity was zealously guarded. In order to preserve their purity a separate caste was made. This was the Brahmin caste who are the descendents of the *rishis*. To this day all Brahmins have the family name or *gotra* that proclaims them to be the descendent of one particular *rishi*. Initially the only job of the Brahmin caste was to see that this supreme wisdom was kept intact and preserved for future generations. They were the custodians of this ancient wisdom and they were committed to handing it down safely from generation to generation. The world owes a debt of gratitude to this caste for it was due to them that the Vedas have been preserved in their purity through the centuries. Initially every Brahmin had to personally experience the truth of the Vedas and become Brahman. Only then was he qualified to be called a Brahmin. But with the passing of the years people were unable to keep to the strict discipline, which was entailed in the Vedic culture, and eventually all they could do was to memorize the hymns like parrots. Even this was good enough since they were able to hand it down to their descendents. But as in a radio, a slight change in tuning gets a different station. To get the desired station we have to have perfect tuning. The sages were well aware that there would be a decline in the memories as well as the spiritual calibre of their descendents and they took very special care to see that the memorization was perfect and at least the sounds would remain unchanged with the passing of the years. The *swara* or pitch of the sound had to be perfect in order to get the perfect result. Any change in the chanting of the Vedic *mantra*s produces a different effect. This is why they stipulated that the *mantra*s should be learnt only by listening to the chanting by a competent *guru* who had himself mastered the technique and was perfectly tuned to the reality implied. Reading from a book will not give the desired effect.

The word *mantra* means that which by repeated chanting and meditation has the power to liberate us. It is the duty of the Brahmin to chant these *mantra*s repeatedly and correctly so that the necessary vibrations are created again and again, resulting in his own well-being and the well-being of the world.

The Sanskrit language that the *rishi*s spoke is called *Devanagari* – the "language of the gods". The alphabet contains all the sounds that the human tongue is capable of making and these sounds have amazing vibratory power that can create an effect on an intuitive level even when repeated only in the mind and are not even audible to the physical ear. Thus the sounds would be decipherable only to the evolved person. But even one who is not fully enlightened, which is the case of the majority of the people today, can chant them even though in a parrot-like fashion. However, because of the vibrations created by correct intonation, the Vedic *mantras* will produce the desired results even though the person may not know the meaning. The effect produced by the sound is all-important. The meaning is secondary. However, if we can understand their meaning also, obviously their effect will be more potent.

The sages moreover were masters of grammar and syntax as they were masters of everything else and they took particular care to see that the language would remain unchanged through the centuries. They devised a system of complicated recitations from very early times in order to preserve the purity of the word, sound, intonation, pronunciation and accent. Their grammar reached its supreme expression in Maharishi Panini. Many grammarians who came after him were convinced that they had invented generative grammar until they came across his work. Then they came to realise that Panini's treatise on grammar was so perfect that it eclipsed theirs as well as all the others that had come before them. In four thousand aphorisms or *sutras*, Panini analysed the phonology and morphology of Sanskrit. This ensured the pristine purity of the language. This is why the Vedas are still being chanted today, in the same manner as they were chanted during the time of the *rishi*s. The tone in which they are chanted, is the same from the Himalayas in the north down to Kannyakumari, in the southern tip of India. This is the thread that runs through the fabric of Hindu society and holds it together.

It is interesting to note what Hindu mythology has to say about the birth of these sages. In the Hindu trinity, Brahma was the creator. He is not to be confused with Brahman or the Absolute. The seven sages were Brahma's children. They were all mind-born. They knew only the meaning of *tapasya* or austerity as has been said before. The normal means of generation at that time was not sex but *tapasya*. That is why the sages are said to be mind-born. Propagation through sex did not exist. Brahma was dissatisfied with this type of creation and he made the first man and woman – Manu and Shatarupa. From then on creation proceeded through the normal channels of sexual intercourse. Sex and asceticism though apparently opposites are actually the two different methods of creation. The *rishi*s knew only too well the generating power of the creative mind – of asceticism or *tapasya*. But they knew nothing of the creative power of sex.

Brahma insisted that his mind-born children – the seven sages or the *sapta-rishi*s – should marry the daughters of the patriarch – Daksha and understand the meaning of sex as well as they understood the meaning of *tapasya* or austerity. They agreed to marry and procreate children as demanded by Brahma. In fact the Brahmin caste as has been said before, can trace their lineage back to one or other of these sages. After marriage the sages found to their consternation that a woman was occupying their hitherto solitary beds. With great naturalness they discovered what they were supposed to do in order to procreate. What they hadn't expected was the pleasure they got out of the act. This pleasure seemed as acute as the bliss they enjoyed during certain states of meditation. After due cogitation they came to the conclusion that "sex was the *tapasya* of the ordinary human being". It existed so that the world could exist. If they withdrew into themselves and became immersed in *tapasya* alone the world would wither and die. *Tapasya* took them back to the "Formless" from whence they had come and sex brought them down to the world of forms.

The chronological age of the *rishi*s is impossible to gauge. Their lives seem to have spanned across three of the *yugas* – *Krita, Treta* and *Dwapara*. The compassion and love they bear to this land – the land of their origin – is inexhaustible. They have chosen to incarnate themselves even in this *yuga* – *Kali Yuga* – the Age of decadence and strife in order to upkeep the Eternal *Dharma*. Proof of this is the great number of known and unknown Masters and *gurus* who have taken birth in India, age after age. These Masters are continuing to incarnate right up to the present age. To mention only a few names – Ramakrishna Paramahamsa, Rama Thirtha, Rama Das, Ramana Maharishi, Chandrashekara Saraswati, Sri Aurobindo, Paramahamsa Yogananda, Sri Mukteswar, Sri Shivarudra Balayogi, Shirdi Sai Baba, Sathya Sai Baba, Neeb Karoli Baba, Nityananda Maharaj, Mata Anandamayi, Amritanandamayi Amma and a host of others have all taken birth in the soil of this blessed land. Even the gods seem to have an interest in keeping alive the *Sanatana Dharma* or this eternal way of life as given by the *rishi*s in the Vedas. As is said in the *Srimad Bhagavad Gita*, whenever this *dharma* or teaching went into a decline many *avatara*s of Vishnu, like Rama and Krishna came down to the world in order to uplift it.

During the Vedic Age and for a long time after it, this knowledge was just a homogenous cloud that would have been lost with the passage of time despite all the precautions that they had taken to ensure that it would never be lost.

The Puranic Age or the age of the Epics came after the Vedic Age. This is the age of the gods. The birth of gods is shrouded in mystery. Who are these gods that dominate the whole of Indian mythology? Their numbers are astronomic. They are supposed to be thirty-three crores of gods. The Puranic seers, like Vyasa were as great as the Vedic *rishi*s. It is due to their compassion that we can even begin to understand the esoteric meaning of the Vedas.

The *Itihasas* like the *Ramayana, Mahabharata,* etc. are integral parts of the Hindu religion as are the Vedas and Upanishads. The *Skanda Purana* calls them the *atman* or soul of the Vedas. The *Narada Purana* calls them the *saara* or essence of the Vedas. The *Vayu Purana* declares that one cannot appreciate the Vedas and Upanishads if one has not read the Puranas. They are called Puranas because they are of ancient origin (*purakaala*). They also complement the knowledge of the Vedas.

The great sage, Vyasa or Veda Vyasa was the author of the *Mahabharata.* He is known as Veda Vyasa because he compiled the vast amount of verses of the Vedas. During his time the infinite hymns of the Vedas were scattered in the minds of many people. Some had been totally lost and only 1180 *shakas* or sections of the Vedas were available. He was the only one who had learnt all the 1180 Veda *shakas*, which had come down from ancient times and existed till the end of the *Dwapara Yuga.* He could master them only due to his yogic powers and the power of his *tapasya.* He collected and compiled this vast knowledge and made them into four different divisions, which were easier to memorise. Each of these divisions was taught to one of his four disciples, thus ensuring that they were preserved for eternity. The descendents of these disciples had to memorise only one division and that made it easier for them. The four books of the Vedas, which are available to us now are called *Rig Veda, Sama Veda, Yajur Veda* and *Atharva Veda.* The *Rig Vedic* hymns are conducive to worship and prayer, the *Yajur Veda* accents the ritualistic portions, the *Sama* hymns are musical in form, and the *Atharva* hymns contain *mantra*s designed to protect people from dangers, illness and enemies.

Vyasa is also the author of the eighteen Puranas, which contain stories of all the gods and the great *avatara*s of Vishnu. In fact he is the one who gave

a form to the formless Brahman so that the normal human mind could conceive
and understand. Vyasa is said to have begged the Lord to forgive these two
transgressions – one in having defiled the formless by giving it a form and
secondly by giving it a name by which it was further defiled by being repeated
by countless tongues. Yet it is due to his kindness that the generations that
came after him were able to conceive of the form of the deity. Vyasa declared
that that which is formless could take on any form. In fact all forms are basically
His form. The human mind is incapable of contemplating on the "formless"
so many types of forms have been given by the Puranic sages which would
help it to fix itself on the "unformed". Many, many paths of yoga have been
advocated by them so that the common man who has no time and not much
inclination to go after the things of the Spirit may be induced to take up this
all-important activity which is really essential for a fulfilled life.

The two great epics or *Itihasas* of our country came in the Puranic Age.
Sage Valmiki was the author of the epic called the *Ramayana* and sage Vyasa
was the author of the *Mahabharata*. The literal meaning of *Itihasa* is - "thus
must we live".

An *Itihasa* has to explain all the four goals of life – *Dharma*, or virtue and
righteousness, *Artha,* or the acquisition of wealth, *Kama*, pleasure, and *Moksha*
or liberation from the mortal coils. The *Ramayana* is the very first poem to
be written in the world. It is the story of Sri Rama who was an *avatara* of
Vishnu and it is a book that has influenced the life of this country to the greatest
extent. It has also spread to many outlying countries like, Thailand, Burma and
Indonesia. Sage Valmiki was a contemporary of Sri Rama so it is almost a
first-hand account of the history of that age.

The *Mahabharata* contains one *lakh* of couplets (*slokas*). But Vyasa was not
content with this and went on to compose four more *lakhs* of *slokas* and these
constitute the eighteen Maha Puranas or the major Puranas. The *Mahabharata*
has been called the fifth Veda and contains the essence of all the scriptures.
It is really an authority on the history of Indian culture and religion. In it is
found a part of the life of the great *avatara* of Vishnu, Lord Krishna. Vyasa
was his contemporary. The great advice of Lord Krishna to Arjuna known
as the *Srimad Bhagavad Gita* is found in the middle of this enormous book
containing eight thousand and eight hundred verses.

they operate. All the different planes of existences are manifestations of that inexhaustible, original and eternal well of "Being" which is the play of *Maya*. Thus *Maya* is personified as the world-protecting feminine, maternal side of the Ultimate Being and stands for the loving acceptance of life's tangible reality. She is the creative joy of life. She herself is the beauty, the ugliness, the enticement and the seduction as well as the suffering, sacrifice, death and devastation that are a part and parcel of the experience of the world. She teaches us to accept life as it is and to surrender to the Supreme by which alone we can hope to overcome both her fascination as well as her repulsiveness. She is the divine womb from which all creatures emanate, both wonderful and terrible. Parvati was the incarnation of this Divine Mother and Shiva, the embodiment of the Absolute. Their play is the play of the *Purusha;* the Supreme Soul enfolded in *Prakriti*, the Divine Mother who is known as *Maha Maya* – the great illusion.

"Nothing enchants the mind more than the existence of the outside world, of something that resists it and will not obey. Pampered by its own omnipotence, its own capacity to connect and identify with everything, the mind needs an obstacle, at least as big as the world to oppose it. To pursue this world and conquer it is a challenge that alone can thrill and uplift the mind. This pursuit has never stopped and will never stop because the world cannot be conquered by the mind. It cannot even be understood by the mind so long as it is made into an object. The only way to conquer it, is to realize that it is a subjective phenomenon and this is the object of all *sadhana* or spiritual practice."

Enthralled by our pitifully small ego-self we fall a prey to the blandishments of the world and revel in that which is unreal. The aim of Hindu religion has always been to cut the knot that binds us to these false ideas and enable us to discover our true identity. All the mythical tales about the various gods contained in Hindu mythology are meant to display the wisdom of the Vedic seers and to reveal it in a popular and more understandable form.

Gods don't have ordinary births like human beings. The birth of the three sons of Shiva is no exception to this rule. Shiva is the supreme ascetic, the *Mahayogi*. Yet he is the one who has produced the three most popular gods in the Hindu pantheon. How could he beget sons, is the question which rises in the mind of most people. The answer is that he didn't beget sons from either of his wives – Sati or Parvati – but two of his sons, Kartikeya and

Shiva, Parvati, Ganesha & Kartikeya on Mount Kailash, Pahari Painting.

The need to follow *dharma* or the cosmic law is what is stressed in bo these epics. This is the way in which the Puranic sages sought to preserve truths of the Vedas and popularise them so that the common people co comprehend and follow the advice and thus make their own lives perfe

Shiva is said to be the Destroyer in the Hindu Trinity. But the word 'shi means the auspicious one. How can we combine death with auspiciousne According to Hindu teachings death is not death in the sense of a passing aw into non-existence but simply a change into a new form of life. He who destro therefore actually causes beings to assume new phases of existence. Shiva really a re-creator. A pot breaks and returns to the mud from which it w made. Now it is ready for the potter to re-cast into a new mould and a ne form. Thus Shiva also gives an opportunity for beings to be born in new form Thus he is known as the auspicious one.

Shiva has always been the most mysterious of all the gods. His norm to be extreme in all things. He was either steeped in asceticism or locked eroticism. He was the anti-*brahminical* god, totally oblivious of the rules an regulations stipulated in the laws of the Vedas. It was only much later th he was given a place in the Vedic rituals. He despised nothing and nobod Nothing was beneath his consideration. Hence his followers called the *gana* are seen to be a motley crew consisting of the defamed and the despise most of them deformed and ugly. Yet he loved them all as his own son He was the god of the *asuras* as well as the outcaste and the lowly. His for as well as his behaviour was totally beyond the pale of the accepted mod of behaviour in the Vedic society. The gods always tried to get him out his seclusion and draw him into the world of sex and procreation. But foiled them at every turn even though apparently giving in to their deman

It was to help the gods that the divinely beautiful Parvati, who was t incarnation of the Divine Mother herself, loved him and wooed him a persuaded him to marry her. She alone was able to recognize and appreci his perfection.

We have seen that the world is *Maya* or illusion. The *Maya* of the go is their power to assume diverse shapes by displaying at will various aspe of their subtle essence. But the gods themselves are the products of a grea *Maya*. This *Maya* produces not only the gods but also the universes in wh

Dharma Shasta were born from his seed. However, Ganesha who is supposed to be his eldest was not born from him. He was the creation of Parvati, the divine mother, made out of her own body. This is one of the miraculous stories connected with Ganesha's birth that we will be going into.

Though most people know of Ganesha and Kartikeya, very few know that Shiva had a third son called Dharma Shasta. He was born of both the great gods of the Hindu pantheon – Vishnu and Shiva. The story of Shasta will be taken up in the third portion of this book.

I meditate on the one-tusked son of Lord Shiva,
Who is the Lord of Yama, the god of Death.
He is graceful with lustrous teeth,
He is eternal and his form is inconceivable by the mind,
But he dwells always in the heart of yogis,
And is the destroyer of all miseries.

— *Sri Maha Ganesha Pancharatnam*

Hari Aum Tat Sat.

ॐ *Anantaaya Namaha!*

"Even ordinary, unenlightened human beings express the Infinite Consciousness more fully than animals. The devas or gods have their existence above the human level. However even they are less evolved than the rishis and spiritual masters. A spiritual master has reached the pinnacle of evolution. Evolution ends when we reach endlessness. These beings have submerged in the ocean of existence, consciousness and bliss and have no trace of ego even while they exist in the human body. However many of them continue to help their disciples from the astral plane.

Human beings who have achieved some measure of self awareness have a duty to uplift creatures on a lower level of evolution. Kindness to animals helps them to increase their spiritual unfoldment. It also helps us to attune ourselves to the source of all love."

ॐ

Vigneshaya Namaha!

INTRODUCTION II

Anantarupa

THE PURANAS

Anantarupa, ananta naama,
Adi moola Narayana

Narayana is the root cause.
He has endless forms and endless names.

As we saw in part one of the Introduction, the *rishi*s were able to explore the depths of their Being through the process of *tapasya* and discover the Supreme within them. Having discovered this they were anxious to share this deep esoteric secret with everyone else. There are tremendous difficulties in communicating this revelation in terms of ordinary language. This is due to the limitations of the human mind and intellect. The intellect is the most powerful and versatile instrument known to us. Scientists make use of it to price open the mysteries of the universe. It has led us to split the atom and reach the moon but when it comes to discovering the truth of our innermost Self, the intellect is confounded. It can analyse any object and discover the reality underlying it. It is a highly efficient instrument for objective study but the *rishi*s realised that it is sadly inadequate when it comes to subjective analysis. When the Self itself becomes the object of study, the intellect is powerless to surmount its inherent weakness and is unable to analyse itself. The fact is that the Self is the torch which lights up the intellect, so how can it see itself? In all other fields of investigation the investigator is different from the object of investigation but here the investigator himself is being investigated. How to surmount this difficulty was the question that faced the sages. Sugar can never know the taste of tea. It can only dissolve in the tea and "become one with it".

The *rishi*s decided that the intellect had to be made subtler so that it could apprehend subtle realities and not merely gross entities. In the state of deep meditation the intellect becomes so subtle that it dissolves like the sugar into the subject of its investigation which is the very Self within. Thus the intellect's search for the Self ends in a glorious experience of the Divine rather than a comprehension of it.

This amazing experience, as can be imagined, could not be communicated in terms of ordinary language and be made comprehensible to all. Therefore we find that the great *Advaitic* truths of the *rishi*s were encoded in the books knows as the Upanishads, which come after every Veda. In these books many methods of meditation were given as well as other techniques that would develop the student's powers of concentration. This would help to make the mind single-pointed and the intellect more and more subtle. With the passage of time there was a decided decline in the desire of the human being to discover these subtle truths within him. The intellect was totally preoccupied with discovering millions of facts in the outer world. This of course is a never-ending process but it keeps the intellect busy and that is what it wants to be. Moreover the general theme of the Upanishads was too abstruse for the casual reader to comprehend and therefore people were not eager to follow this path, which was really an esoteric teaching given by a teacher to his disciple. The Upanishads were normally in the form of a teacher-student conversation in which the *guru* pointed out the goal to the disciple and gave him a certain amount of advise on how to reach it. This was all that he could do. The final leap had to be made by the disciple himself. In the conquest of Everest, the guide can only take you up the slope or show you the path and tell you of the pitfalls and perhaps even give a few hints about methods, but the final attempt has to be made by the climber himself.

The Upanishads use terse language to point out the direction to the student. They help only those who have an intellectual and spiritual bent of mind that is capable of grasping subtle, subjective truths. They need deep study by serious seekers and continuous and sincere practice before they reveal their secrets. Such seekers are few and far between in the annals of history. What was to be the fate of the remaining majority? The *rishi*s did not believe in the redemption of the few alone. Their hearts overflowed with love for the whole of creation. They wanted everyone to be saved.

The great mystery about the human mind is that even though we long for Truth, our first reaction to this Truth when told by the sages is one of hostility and fear. Thus the *rishi*s adopted another method. This way was opened by the *Puranic rishi*s. They created a device to circumvent the opposition of their listeners to the simple yet shocking truth of who they were in reality. For this they created "stories"! It is common to oppose a truth but impossible to resist a story! Vyasa was the greatest of the *Puranic rishi*s and he dramatized these revelations of the Upanishads and wove stories around them, which could become familiar and understandable even to the poorest intellect. In fact even children could appreciate them. Vyasa declared that if you listen carefully to a story, you would never be the same again. The story would worm its way into your heart and break down the barriers you have erected between yourself and the divine. Stories have a way of slipping through your defences and tearing open the fences you have made round your heart!

Worship of divine forms is part of the practical aspect of Hindu spirituality. The Upanishads open us to the path of knowledge and the Puranas lead us to the path of devotion. Both these paths lead to the same goal, the liberation of the mind from its social and biological conditioning and its expansion to unlimited freedom. Many of the Puranas depict the war between the negative and positive aspects of the mind in its relentless struggle to expand to the unlimited freedom of the divine. These aspects are known as the *asuras* and the *devas*.

God implies unconditioned freedom. He has the freedom to assume any form he likes. To limit him to one form alone is the failing of the human mind. The universe of innumerable forms is an expression of God's freedom to take on any form he chooses. The word paintings of Vyasa have given us graphic details of the forms of the various gods, which have provided a fund of spiritual wealth from which generations of Hindus have derived their inspiration.

The ancient *rishi*s discovered that the material world and its evolution was controlled by a subtle spiritual energy called *prana*. In lower forms of life, evolution is a mechanical process but in the human being there emerges the possibility to consciously cultivate this spiritual energy in order to get an evolutionary thrust. That is to say the human being can consciously direct his energy in order to evolve. Biologists are only now coming to be aware of this exciting possibility of what they call selective evolution. The *rishi*s knew it long ago but it was not their method to write long treatises on such abstruse subjects. Instead they resorted to symbols and parables that could be better understood by the common man. The Hindu scriptures are full of such symbols, analogies and allegories. These have been shaped through abstract conceptions of the external environment and are very scientific in nature. The Vedas actually proclaimed a long time ago, the findings of quantum physics that there is no such thing as matter. There are only force fields of time and space that can be observed in varying intensities. Thus an atom in not a bit of matter. It is a time-space-energy force field of a particular intensity.

Shiva and his sons are all aspects of the great electromagnetic forces that control life. Shiva is the source of all energies. He is the nuclear energy underlying the subatomic particles. At the very core of matter, Shiva whirls in his cosmic dance as Nataraja.

This was the poetic vision of the seer. Modern physics has shown that the rhythm of creation and destruction is not only manifest in the turn of the seas and the birth and death of all living beings but also in the vast density of inorganic matter. Each and every subatomic particle does an energy dance of the pulsating process of creation and destruction. Shiva Nataraja's dance is then the dance of the subatomic particles. Our ancient spiritual truths are in complete accord with modern scientific discoveries.

Einstein's ground shaking formula, $E = MC^2$ means that matter is nothing but condensed energy. So matter evolves out of the energy of the cosmic dance of Shiva.

The Puranas are studded with stories of an amazing variety of gods and goddesses who are dynamic representations of the Truth as represented in the Vedas. These stories are not fairy tales but reflections of the revelations of the *rishi*s. Thus the Puranas came to be written, couched in mysticism since this was the only way in which this great esoteric secret could be communicated. The human mind is conditioned by names and forms from birth onwards. The Puranas are like abstract paintings that suggest a different dimension to the mind and enables it to comprehend the intangible ideas, which are expressed in these forms.

Professor Eliade declares, "Images, symbols and myths are not irresponsible creatures of the psyche. They resound to a need and fulfil the function of bringing to light the most hidden modalities of our being."

Vyasa saw the totality of Nature – both her outer physical phenomena as well as her inner invisible psyche. The symbols of the various gods and Ganesha in particular are the visible signs for expressing the invisible. One who meditates on these symbols will be able to penetrate the subtle psychic presence in them and thus come to a comprehensive view of the totality of the cosmos. Such a person will also be able to dive into the recesses of his own psyche and get higher spiritual experiences. This is the truth underlying all the so-called idols and often-bizarre forms as in the case of Ganesha. They translate the Infinite in terms of the finite and the spiritual in terms of the material. These symbols thus help us to concentrate better during meditation. By fostering our faith in the symbols and forms of the deities we can establish a rapport between the deity and us, which will help to draw us closer to the Supreme.

Thus, many Puranas were written and the Truth was photographed from different angles and from various standpoints so that it could be appreciated from diverse intellectual levels. In this unique way, the *rishi*s succeeded in getting the incomprehensible Supreme, reflected in the liquid poetry of their Puranic literature and created a myriad forms or altars for worship which would be suitable for different personalities. These forms were evolved in the super conscious state of the *rishi*s in an attempt to give the common man a glimpse into the Truth, which was ever blazing in their hearts. The mind of man has to learn to focus on some form that inspires him, before proceeding to the formless. This is the experience of almost every seeker. Lord Krishna tells Arjuna in the *Bhagavad Gita* that worship of God with form is superior to worship of the formless, simply because it is easier to practice.

It is imperative to create ideals of perfection for a society in order to help it to evolve to higher states of consciousness. Only then will true devotion be evoked in the heart of man. This process of lifting oneself to one's ideal is accomplished by unflinching devotion to that ideal. Human beings are created in different models and with different personalities. It is impossible that all of them can follow just one single path and thus gain liberation. This psychological truth was well known to the *rishi*s who provided many different paths designed to suit every type of temperament and personality. But the insistent message underlying all their words was that all of these forms led to the same truth.

Lord Krishna says in the *Bhagavad Gita*, "Whatever form my devotee worships with faith, I enter into that form and make his faith firm so that he gets from that symbol all that he desires."

Hari Aum Tat Sat.

"The devas or gods are naturally much higher on the scale of evolution than the ordinary human. However they can hasten their own evolution by helping human beings. They thrive on our love and give us more energy if we offer them our love and devotion. If they feel unloved or ignored they withdraw their protection from us. This is why it is important to offer worship to the devas.

The Bhagavad Gita says 'Worship the gods and the gods will cherish you. Thus fostering one another you will attain the Supreme Truth. Pleased by this attitude of self sacrifice, the gods will bestow upon you all that you desire. One who takes from them without giving something in return is verily a thief'.

Thus all of us need to worship the gods for our own well being as well as the well being of the world."

ॐ

Sri Mahaganapathaye Namaha!

BOOK ONE

Ganesha

Twameva pratyaksham tatwamasi
Twameva kevalam kartaasi,
Twameva kevalam dhartaasi,
Twameva sarvam khalvidam Brahmaasi
Twam sakshaat-atmaasi nityam

O Lord Ganapati,
You alone are the visible manifestation of
the essence of the words, "That
Thou Art".
You alone are the Doer,
You alone are the Creator and the sustainer.
You alone are the destroyer.
Verily you alone are all this – idam sarvam –
in creation because you are Brahman.
You are the eternal atman in bodily form.

— *Sri Ganapati Atharva Sirsha*

Five-faced Ganesha (Illus. done in ancient Kerala mural style using only vegetable dyes by K. Suresh).

CHAPTER ONE

SUMUKHA

Historic Concept

Lambodaraya vidmahe
Mahodaraaya dhimahi,
Tanno danti prachodayaath

I contemplate on the one with the big belly,
I invoke the one with the huge stomach,
May the tusked one guide us on the right path.

— *Ganapati Gayatri (Agni Purana)*

ॐ

Adi Shankaracharya was the great advocate of the Advaita system of Hindu philosophy. Even though this is purely a monistic viewpoint of non-duality, Shankara was a mastermind who was a fitting descendent of the *rishi*s of old. He knew how difficult it would be for the common man to grasp his *Advaitic* system and therefore he unified the various factions of Hinduism under the *Advaitic* fold. He consolidated the different forms of worship of the various gods into a six-fold system known as the *Shanmata*. These six systems are known as *Vaishnava, Shaiva, Shakta, Shouraya* and *Kaumara*. They are respectively the worshippers of Vishnu, Shiva, Devi or Shakti, the Sun and Kartikeya. The sixth system is known as *Ganapatya* and these are the worshippers of Ganesha or Ganapati. All these had their basis in the Vedic tenets. This was done in order to ensure that all factions would progress in the right direction within the realm of their own chosen deity and eventually come to recognize the oneness of the Supreme Truth from which all of them are derived and into which they would ultimately merge. This was the greatness of Adi Shankarachaya.

The book on the life of Adi Shankara mentions six sects of *Ganapatya*s. Those who worship Maha Ganapati come under the first group. Maha Ganapati has ten arms, is of crimson colour, and has the goddess Shakti beside him. The second group worships Haridra Ganapati with a brilliant golden complexion, having four arms and three eyes. The third group worships Ucchishta Ganapati who is very powerful. They are the left-handed worshippers of Ganapati who do not follow the Vedic rules. Their rituals are conducted secretly, in lonely places. They chew betel leaves and eat the *prasadam* (offerings) without cleaning their mouth. Other sects consider this most unholy. The remaining three sects are known as Navanita, Swarna and Santana. They follow the normal Vedic tenets.

The *Ganapatya*s picture Ganapati in various ways – as the Lord of the five elements, as the *saguna* (with form), manifestation of the Supreme, as the sound of *Aum* and so on. They consider the form of Ganapati to be an amalgamation of all other gods. In the mystic body of Ganesha, the naval is Brahma (the creator), the face is Vishnu, the eyes are Shiva, the left side is Shakti, the right side Surya and the soul is *ananda* or bliss. In fact in him all the other systems are fused. The *Shaivites* worship him as the son of Shiva, the *Shakta*s worship him as the son of Parvati or Shakti, the *Kaumara*s worship him as the brother of Kartikeya, and the *Vaishnavite*s worship him as the one who removes all obstacles in their worship.

The *Bauddha*s (followers of Buddha) maintain that one of the names of the Buddha was Vinayaka. They say that Buddha himself gave the mystic *mantra* of Ganesha called the 'Ganapatihridaya' to Ananda, his favourite disciple. When Buddhism spread to other countries the concept of Ganapati was taken along with it.

Ganesha worship has existed along with *linga* worship which was existing from the time of the Mohenjadaro and Harappa civilizations, as can be seen from the seals.

Chronologically speaking the first Sanskrit text ascribed to the *Ganapatya* system comes in the *Rig Veda*. It is known as the Ganapati Suktam and begins with the words, *Utthista Brahmanaspate.*

Gananaam twa ganapathim havamahe,
Kavim kavinam apamashravashtamam.

Jyestarajam, brahmanaam brahmanaspata aa na.
Shrunvanoothibhi seed saadanam

"O Ganapati!
You are the seer of seers, unrivalled in wealth,
King of kings!
Principal of principals!
Hear us and take thy place, bringing with thee all enjoyments.
We sing in praise of Him who is the essence of omkara."

The *Ganapati Upanishad* says, "You alone are the visible manifestation of the essence of the words, 'That Thou Art'. You alone are the doer; you alone the creator and the sustainer; you alone are the destroyer. Verily, you alone are all this, because you are Brahman. You are the eternal Atman in bodily form." The *mantra* of Ganapati is given as ॐ *Gam Ganapataye Namaha*!

The Atharva Sirsam comes in the *Atharva Veda*. It is called the *Atharvana Upanishad*. The *Atharvana Veda* describes many magic rites and incantations invoking ghosts and spirits and thus Ganesha was at first allied to this group and was known as a malevolent deity. When Ganesha rose to be a deity in his own right, a new Upanishad was made for his worship after the pattern of the *Atharvana Upanishad* and it was called the *Maha Ganapati Upanishad*. This Upanishad starts with the invocation: ॐ *Namaste Ganapathaye,* which means, "Salutations to Lord Ganapati".

In the *Baudhayana Grihya Sutra* (4th century AD), the leader of the troops is mentioned as being elephant faced – *hastimukha*. He is also designated as Vignesvara (Lord of obstacles), and "Bhuta Natha", "Master of Spirits".

The *Brihat Samhita* refers to a god who is elephant faced, *gaja mukha*, with a huge belly and only one tusk. He is described as being the Lord of the hordes of Shiva – carrying an axe and radish in his hands. However in this scripture Ganesha is mentioned at the end of the section on gods, after the description of Yama, the god of death. At that time he was considered as a minor deity of the Yaksha clan with only two hands. *Manu Smriti* describes him as the god of the aboriginals.

The *Yajniki* or *Narayanatya Upanishad*, which forms the last and tenth part of the *Taittiriya Aranyaka*, mentions some *gayatri mantras* referring to Mahadeva

Rudra and also to Vakratunda and Dantin, both well known names of Ganesha, thus establishing his relationship to Shiva.

Chief among the Puranas that relate stories about Ganesha are: *Brahma Vaivarta Purana, Mudgala Purana, Shiva Purana, Brahmanda Purana, Ganesha Purana, Varaha Purana, Bhavishya Purana* and *Skanda Purana.*

Many temples have *mahatmyas* written about Ganesha and the most famous is the Vinayaka Kshetra in Orissa and the Gajaranya Kshetra in Trichinapoly.

A *Ganesha Bhagavatam* and a *Ganesha Darsam* are also given in this manuscript. The latter is composed of eight hundred *sutras* that give the philosophy of the *Ganapatya*s to the full. It describes Ganesha as the supreme Brahman. The style is adapted from the *Brahma sutras.*

Next come the *Tantras.* Every book of rituals of the *Tantras* has a chapter on Ganesha. One of the most famous amongst these is the *Sharada Tilakam,* by Lakshmana Desika (10th century), the *Tantra Sastra* of Agamavagisa Krishnananda who was a contemporary of Chaitanya Mahaprabhu, and the *Mantra Mahabhodhi* by Mahidara from the 14th century. The *Tantras* also give classifications of the different forms of Ganesha.

The word *gaja* can mean elephant, origin or goal in Sanskrit. The word *ga* means goal and *ja,* means origin. The word *ajam* means unborn. It indicates the Supreme Brahman that has never come into existence for the simple reason that IT always existed. *Gajam* means both elephant and earth. Thus Ganesha with the head of an elephant symbolises both the Supreme and the finite.

Gaja as we have seen, means elephant and *nara* is man. As a combination of *Gaja* and *Nara,* Ganesha is identical with the Brahman in both his *nirguna* and *saguna* aspects or the Supreme as conceived of, with form and without form. The word *gaja* can be further split into *ga* and *ja. Ga* signifies the Supreme which *yogis* experience in their sate of *Samadhi* and *ja* is that from which all beings were created.

It is interesting to know what the word *gana* means since it comes in all Ganapati *mantra*s. It comes from the root, *gan* which means to count. *Ganya* means limited and *aganya* means unlimited or infinite. *Ganya* includes the whole of manifold creation – everything that the human intellect can comprehend and even beyond that. Therefore Ganapati is the Lord of all the finite things that we can imagine. He is also Ganyaapati – Lord of everything in creation.

The *aganya* or Infinite has taken on a finite form as Ganesha, in order to uplift humanity out of these finite forms. *Gana* also means category and Maha Ganapati is the master of categories. He guards the first approach to life.

The present day concept of Ganesha is a synthesis of pre-Vedic and Vedic thoughts and accommodates all the other sects in Hinduism. His personality is a complex one of sagacity, shrewdness, patience and self-reliance. He has all qualities that can overcome obstacles and difficulties both material and spiritual. This is the secret of his popularity since everyone wants success whatever be the field of their choice.

Mounjikrishnajinadharam,
Nagayajnopaveethinam,
Baalenduvilasadmoulim
Vandeham gananaayakam.

"I bow to Lord Ganesha,
Who is clad in a deer-skin,
And wears a snake as a sacred thread,
Who is adorned with the crescent moon on his forehead."

— *Sri Ganashtakam*

ॐ *Gam Ganapataye Namaha!*

"I worship the one-tusked Lord Ganesha who is the destroyer of the darkness created by obstacles, who makes the lotus face of his mother blossom as if he is the sun, And who grants all the desires of his worshippers."

— *Sri Ganapati Stotram*

ॐ

Ekadantaaya Namaha!

CHAPTER TWO

EKADANTA

Concepts of Ganesha

ॐ *Mahotkadaaya vidmahe,*
Vakratundaaya dhimahi,
Tanno Danti prachodayath

We devote our thoughts to the huge-bodied Lord.
We meditate on him who has a curved trunk.
May the tusked one guide us on the right path.

— *Agni Purana*

Originally Ganesha's worship was not recognized by the upper classes. He was the god of the aboriginals and the *Sudras*. This was because he was first considered to be a malevolent deity. The *Bhagavat Purana* mentions *Vinayakas* along with *Dakinis, Kushmandas, Bhutas* and *Pretas* who were all malevolent spirits. Perhaps Ganesha was first worshipped out of fear since he was the one who created obstacles and had to be propitiated before people could start anything. So he was first worshipped as a guardian deity. Even today most Hindu homes especially in the South consider it auspicious to keep an idol of Ganesha in front of the house to ward off evils and obstacles. Afterwards he was elevated to the position of being a bestower of gifts to his devotees. From being the creator of obstacles he became the remover of obstacles. Later on he was elevated to the position of a super god. Thus Ganesha's evolution was from tribal god to super god.

His ideology spread to neighbouring countries like Burma, Thailand, Cambodia and Indonesia. It also spread to places like China, Japan and Mongolia. Recently a figure of Ganesha was unearthed in a village in Bulgaria along with figures of Buddha and Mahavira. Images of Ganesha have been discovered in excavations in Central America and Mexico. There he was known as Virakosa.

A metal plate depicting Ganesha holding a quill in his hand for writing the *Mahabharata* was found in Uristan in Western Iran.

Rock caves of Japan and Thailand have also revealed Ganesha images.

The Buddhist monks who went to China introduced the doctrine of the *mandalas* of the two parts known as *Vajra-dhatu* and *Garbha-dhatu*. These became very popular both in China and in Japan. In Japan he was called Vajra Vinayaka and had a dual form, one male and the other female known as Kangi and Ten. The Japanese also called him Vinayaksa or Sho-ten. Japanese consider these figures to have great spiritual import and worship them in secret. The worship of Ganesha in China and Japan was no doubt due to the influence of *Tantric* Buddhism.

The Chinese thought of him as a massive dragon whose physical immensity depicts his irresistible force. To some Chinese he is Kuan shi t'ien or Ho Tei, the large bellied god of happiness. To the Polynesians he is God Lono. In South India and Sri Lanka he is known as Pullayar – the noble child. The Tibetans call him Ts'ogsabdag and Burmese worship him as Maha-Pienne. In Mongolia he is called Totkharour Khagan, and in Cambodia, as Prah Kenes. The Greeks called him Janus and sought his blessings at the start of any venture.

His cult spread to Mongolia through Tibet. The Tibetan monk Hphagapa carried Mahayana Buddhism into Mongolia in the 13th century and converted even the emperor Kublai Khan. To the Mongols, Shiva's main manifestation was that of Maha Kaala and it was natural that Ganesha should become popular there. It is said that Kublai Khan's father was childless and was asked to pray to Ganesha, and Kublai Khan was born as a result of his prayers. According to the legend of his birth, the father, Hphagapa is said to have invoked Ganesha who carried him in his trunk to the top of Mount Meru. He showed him the country of Mongolia and said, "Thy son shall subjugate this whole country", which of course proved to be true. The dancing form of Ganesha is to be found among the five hundred gods of Nar-than. He is shown sitting on the mouse that holds the jewel of plenty called the *chintamani* in its mouth. Ganesha's four hands hold the axe, radish, a bowl of sweets and the trident.

Some images of Ganesha ascribed to the Gupta period are found in Afghanistan. Some recent ones were also found in Cardez and removed to Kabul where the Hindu residents worship them. One is of a standing figure with a muscular torso. The trunk appears to be broken and the broken tusk is indicated on the left. There is a close fitting coronet both round the head and the neck. He wears a snake as the sacred thread.

Another interesting marble image of Ganesha was found at a place called Sakar Dhar near Kabul. It is again a standing Ganesha. The left tusk is broken and he has the usual snake in lieu of the sacred thread. His two lower arms are resting on the heads of the *gana*s who are looking up at him with great devotion.

A large number of Ganesha's idols are found in Nepal. Two of them in Kathmandu are unusual as they both show a rat under each foot. Both have only one head but one has four hands and the other has sixteen and both embrace their Shaktis.

Heramba is the most popular form of Ganesha in Nepal. In this he is shown on his vehicle, which is a lion and has five heads, ten hands and on his lap is his Shakti. Another interesting Heramba Ganesha is now in a museum in Munich and this shows a rat under one foot and a lion under the other.

A few images of Ganesha have been found in Western Tibet where he was looked upon as a powerful guardian against demons and evil spirits. His image was placed above the main entrance to Tibetan temples, including Buddhist temples. This is basically a Hindu tradition. Here you find his female form known as Gajanani.

He was most popular in Khotgan. A number of bronze tablets and painted wooden panels were discovered in a stupa in Endare. In the rock temples of Bazalik, there are several frescoes in which his figures were exposed. He is usually shown seated with six arms holding the sun and moon banner. The interesting feature here is that the trunk resembles the snout of a wild boar more than the trunk of an elephant.

In Sri Lanka we find an image of Ganesha sculptured on a pillar in the Shiva temple at Polonnaruva. He is seated and has four hands in which the lower left holds the *modakam*. In the Subramania temple at Kataragama, which is supposed to be the birthplace of the legendary Mahavatar Babaji, Ganesha has an independent temple and is worshipped even by Christians and Muslims.

Burma is essentially Buddhist and follows the Pali canon. However, Hinduism had penetrated into Burma long before Buddhism during the Gupta period (5th and 6th centuries). A number of Ganesha idols have been found in south Burma. His idols were carried by the traders who went out of India since he was the one who would remove all obstacles. There are two interesting idols in the Rangoon Museum. One shows him to be seated in *padmasana* with six arms.

Thailand came into contact with Hinduism at a very early period. Several statues of Ganesha have been found in Ayuthia or Ayodhya. The famous Hindu temple of Bangkok also has an interesting statue of Ganesha. He holds a broken tusk in his right hand and a manuscript in his left, which is no doubt meant to be the *Mahabharata.*

India had made connections with Cambodia at a very early date. A Brahmin called Kaundiny is said to have gone to the coast of Cambodia and established a kingdom there. He Indianised the country completely and many figures of gods and goddesses are found there. The *Mahabharata* was known to Cambodia as early as the 6th century. So they knew of Ganesha from that time onwards. Here also a number of Ganesha figures have come to light. One temple at Prasat Bak was dedicated to his worship. He is popularly known as Prah Kenes in Cambodia. He is never shown as bulky and pot bellied. He is usually sitting cross-legged and has two hands. The trunk is almost straight and curled only at the tip. He is bare to the waist and has the snake as a sacred thread. One of his most remarkable images is in a private collection. He is sitting in a cross-legged posture. He has two hands and four heads and wears a tall conical headgear.

There is an unusual temple of Ganesha in the Shiva temple in Central Java. Here he sits with the soles of his feet pressed together like a child. In Kuala Lumpur the Kottamalai Pillayar temple in the busy street of Puduraya is very small but considered to be very powerful and is the most popular Ganesha temple in Malaysia.

The religion of the earliest known N. American Indians was an offshoot of the *Sanatana Dharma.* This can well be seen from their rituals and symbols. Ganesha's oldest symbol, the *swastika* was one of the central motifs used in their designs by American Indian tribes and is still seen in their beautiful blankets and pottery.

The most famous *swayambhu* (self-created) *murtis* of Ganesha are found in Kashmir where there are three famous though formless idols, which have attracted pilgrims from ancient times. One is near the village of Ganesbal with the river Lidar on its right bank. Another rock in Kashmir is at the foot of the hill, Hari Parvat near Srinagar and is known as Bhimaswamin. The most famous is the one on a cliff along the Kishen Ganga known as Ganesh Gati.

Lord Ganesha does not have many temples in India that are solely dedicated to him. The reason is that he is believed to be a god who is to be worshipped first for the removal of obstacles so he is given a prominent place in all other temples. Although his idols are found everywhere there are not many highly decorated and exclusive temples to him like there are for Vishnu, Shiva, Durga and Kartikeya.

Three temples that are exclusively for him are the Ganesha temple in the Uchi Pillayar kovil at Trichy. This large temple is also known as the rock fort temple and is built on a hilltop and commands a breathtaking view of the city and of the river Kaveri.

Another large Ganesha temple is the Pillaiyarpatti temple near Karaikudi in Ramanathapuram in Tamil Nadu. In New Delhi there is the Siddhi Buddhi Vinayaka temple in Vinaya Nagar.

In India, many images of Ganesha have been found dating from the twelfth century onwards. Excavations at Sanchi, Udaigiri, Khandgiri, Ellora, Aurangabad have unearthed many idols. A 7th century figure of Ganesha has been discovered in Seliundam in Andhra Pradesh. The oldest image of Ganesha traced to the Gupta period of the 5th century has two hands and was found in Bhumra. He is seated and wears a chain of bells. The largest figure of Ganesha in South India is in Chidambaram temple. It is a huge monolith painted red. The image of a reclining Ganesha has been excavated in Dholbaha in Punjab.

There is a very unusual depiction of Ganesha in the Mara mandir near Jaipur. He has been shown along with his consort in an curious dancing pose. Normally we do not expect such heavy bodied individuals to dance and there is no such reference in any of the Puranas. However, this whole sculpture gives an aura of hilarity and joy.

A five-headed Ganesha mounted on a lion resides in Nagapattnam. At Vellore Ganesha is enshrined as Valampiri Vinayaka with his trunk turned to the right. This is considered to be very auspicious. The Mukkuruni Pillayar inside the Meenakshi temple in Madurai is ten to twelve feet tall. The word *mukkuruni* refers to a large measure of rice, weighing about twenty kilos. The priests cook a huge *modakam* or sweet ball for Ganesha using this measure. In Madurai he is also worshipped as Vyaghrapada Ganeshini, which is a female form having tiger's feet.

We find that this feminine form of Ganesha called Ganeshini is found in many places. It is possibly of *Tantric* origin and came in the Medieval period. The name Ganeshini does not appear in classical texts whereas the feminine name Vinayaki occurs in some Jain texts.

There is another Ganeshini sitting in *sukhasana* (cross-legged) pose in the Shiva temple of Suchindram near Trivandrum in Kerala. Two more female forms of Ganesha are to be found, one in the 10th century temple dedicated to sixty-four *yoginis* (female *yogis*), in Bheraghat which is a village near Jabalpur and another one in Tanumalaiaswami temple in Suchindram.

Agajananapadamarkam,
Gajananamaharnisham,
Anekadantam bhaktanaam-
Ekadantamupasmahe!

"I worship the one-tusked Lord Ganesha,
Who makes the lotus face of his mother,
Parvati blossom as if he is the sun,
And grants all the desires of his devotees."

— *Sri Ganashtakam*

ॐ *Gam Ganapataye Namaha!*

ॐ

Kapilaaya Namaha!

CHAPTER THREE

KAPILA

The First Form

ॐ *TatKaraya vidmahe,*
Hasti mukhaya dhimahi
Tanno danti prachodayath

I know the mysterious Lord,
May his elephant face guide me,
May the tusked one guide us on the right path.

— *Maitrayani Samhita*

In the alphabet of symbolic forms devised by the *rishi*s, Ganesha forms the first letter. He is the most popular and most beloved of all the gods in the Hindu pantheon. Even the votaries of all the other gods have to pay obeisance to him before starting *puja* to their own special deity. Hindus start all sacrifices and religions ceremonies, all serious compositions, and even worldly affairs of importance with an invocation to Ganesha. Few books are begun without the preface of "Salutations to Ganesha". He has to be invoked at the beginning of all *yagya*s (fire sacrifices) also. In South India you will find a small temple dedicated to this beloved and charming deity, at every street corner so that everyone can make a quick prayer to him on their way to work. He represents the power of the intelligent will unfolding the spiritual life from out of the world of matter. Scientifically speaking he is the god of gravity, which is at the base of all ordinary existence.

Ganesha is very easy to contact so he is the gateway for all seekers who want to enter into the most ancient religion of the world. One who wants to be a Hindu must supplicate Ganesha. He is the one who will admit you

into the Hindu family. Unless you worship him you cannot establish a relationship
with any other god. He is the Lord of all beginnings, and guides the practical
aspect of our life in a way that will best fulfil our needs. He is Lord of the
*gana*s who are the subtle creative powers and elements that cause diversity and
create obstructions in the universe. It is only by contacting Ganesha that these
obstacles can be removed. He removes obstacles not only from our physical
life but also from our spiritual life and thus aids the progress of life from
the lower forms to the human. When one takes the wrong path he places
obstacles in our way. Thus he is both Lord of *karma* (action) and Lord of
dharma (righteous behaviour). Like an elephant going through a forest and making
a way for the rest to follow, he goes ahead and removes obstacles so that
his devotees can proceed without any hindrance.

Ganesha represents the foremost initiating spiritual power at every stage
of evolution. At the time of the emergence of the universe, he represents the
power of Brahman as symbolized in the sound of ॐ. The universe of forms
emerged from this initial sound vibration and the consciousness that was latent
in matter turned into various forms culminating in the human being. The figure
of Ganesha symbolises the idea of the emergence of life from earth and the
unfoldment of consciousness from matter. His dual form of animal and human,
indicates a sublime theme, which points out to us that we too can aspire to
a supramental level even though we have evolved from the animal. Thus the
apparently ludicrous figure of Ganesha mounted on a small mouse is actually
a representation of this theme and meant to give an impetus to the human
being to realize his own inner divine potential. Only very few gods have this
blend of animal and human. Apart from Ganesha, three of the *avatara*s of
Vishnu have this combination. Varaha Murthi has the head of a boar, Narasimha
has the head of a lion and Hayagriva has the head of a horse. These figures
as well as the strange figure of Ganesha seated on a small mouse are not mere
figments of imagination but contain within them a scientific truth, which relates
to the very nature of evolution and the means for expanding the human
consciousness in order to express the divinity within.

He is the son of Shiva and Parvati. Shiva stands for Brahman and Parvati
for *Shakti* or the creative force of the Brahman. The sound of *pranava* or
ॐ is said to be the first cause of the universe of forms. The Sanskrit letter

ॐ resembles the head of an elephant with an upraised trunk and the Tamil letter "ॐ" gives the impression of an elephant with a downward trunk. In fact in all Indian languages even though the alphabets vary there is an amazing similarity in the case of the letter representing "ॐ". One of the names of Ganesha is Vakratunda, which means the one whose trunk is curved. This curved trunk has great esoteric significance. Sri Muthuswami Deekshithar described the face of Ganesha as *pranava- swaroopa-vakrathunda,* the one whose trunk is in the very form of *pranava* or the primeval vibration which causes the sound of ॐ. If we look closely at his figure when the trunk is turned to the right we will notice that his whole face has a strong resemblance to the letter "ॐ". This is what Parvati saw in the picture hall of the gods and that is why she chose an elephant head for her son.

The most striking thing about Ganesha is his elephant head. Let us find out the esoteric reason for this. The elephant is the largest amongst the vegetarians of the animal world. In fact it is the most powerful and massive creature on earth. Despite its size it has a sophisticated social life. It is also loving and affectionate. It is long-lived and vigorous with a large brain and an excellent memory. The horse, giraffe, cow, zebra, rhinoceros, ape, dolphins and a few others are lifelong vegetarians and friends of man. Animals who are feared by men and beasts alike are all predators and eaters of flesh. No one fears a gentle vegetarian. This is perhaps one of the reasons that the elephant came to be chosen as the most auspicious symbol for the ancient Aryans. Therefore it was considered to be a royal animal not only because of its strength and size but also because of its intelligence and prodigious memory. Since it is a vegetarian it is a symbol of auspicious power. It has the positive and propitious strength of the vegetarian whose mind is naturally directed towards the holy and not the brute strength of the meat eating lion or tiger. It is a spiritual symbol in both Hindu and Buddhist literature. In India the elephant is considered the most auspicious omen one can see at the start of a journey so in most houses a figure of Ganesha will be kept at the gate so that the traveller can bow to him before proceeding on his journey. It is also believed that the presence of such a divine symbol at the front of the house will ward off all negative energy. Hence the worship of Ganesha is given top priority by the followers of all other gods.

Many reasons are given in the Puranas to show why Ganesha had an elephant's head. Once the celestial sage, Narada asked Lord Vishnu the reason for this.

Vishnu replied, "The sage Durvasa, who is noted for his short temper once gave a celestial garland with miraculous powers to Indra, the king of the gods. The goddess Lakshmi was said to reside in this garland. However Indra stupidly threw the garland away and it fell on his elephant's head. This is the head, which I got for Ganesha when Shiva cut off his head. Thus it is ordained that Lakshmi will always be with him. He will be filled with prosperity and have a great intellect and many super-normal powers. All those who worship him will get the same benefits."

The *Brahmavaivarta Purana* gives this version. Once Shiva was chasing some demons across the sky and accidentally struck Aditya, the sun god and made him fall from his chariot and lose consciousness. By this act he incurred the wrath of the sage Kasyapa, who was Aditya's father. He cursed Shiva that his son would lose his head. This is the reason why Ganesha's head was cut off by Shiva's trident. However since Ganesha was fated to get the head of Indra's elephant, filled with glory, the decapitation was a blessing rather than a curse.

Ganesha's figure is said to have sixteen characteristics. He is dwarfish in stature, has a round body, hidden ankles, a pot belly, curved trunk, elephant head, bald head, large flapping ears, small round eyes, elongated nose, black teeth, smoky grey complexion, is apparently greedy, is nude and carries a water pot. This is the basic form but there are countless variations. All his names are connected with these characteristics. Considering his funny figure it's strange how popular he has become.

Many other atttibutes are shown in many of his forms. In some he carries a water pot, a stylus, which stands for knowledge, *trisula* or trident, a drinking cup and skull bowl which are attributes of Shiva and Parvati, his mother and father. He also has Vishnu's accoutrements like the lotus and bow and mace as well as the discus and conch. He carries sheaves of different kinds of corn, condiments, sugar cane, parched rice and cooked foods with different delicious tastes.

There are supposed to be ninety-one different figures of Ganesha available in India today. All of them have the above basic details with small variations.

Normally he has only one head, but we also find idols having two, three, four and even five heads. Sometimes he is standing, sometimes sitting, dancing and even crawling. Usually he has only four hands but some figures depict two, six, eight, ten, and twelve and even fourteen hands, all carrying different symbols. He was seen to have only two hands when he was a malevolent deity but he became four-handed when he became a super god. Twenty-one of his forms have four hands; four have eight hands and another four have ten hands. There is a sixteen-handed form called Vira and a twelve-armed one called Uddanda.

As a rule Ganesha is seen with only two eyes but two forms out of thirty-two have three eyes. He is supposed to have fifty-seven symbols in all. To the uninitiated his figure may look ridiculous but to the Hindu it is adorable. In fact the first *mantra* in his list of names is Sumukha – the one with a pleasing countenance.

The complexion of his body is of great significance. It is generally said to be red like the hibiscus flower or the vermillion dot that is put on the forehead of all Hindu women. Out of his thirty forms, fifteen are blood red, four are white, four are golden coloured, two blue and the rest yellow, black and vermillion.

Normally in most of his poses we find that one foot is touching the ground and the other is lifted and placed on his thigh. This suggests that the middle path is the one that is most suitable for human evolution. The foot touching the earth suggests that the human being has to live an active life in the world as said by Lord Krishna in the *Bhagavad Gita* and the lifted foot tells him to beware of indulging too much in the earthly life.

His many powers and personalities are shown in his different forms. As Bala Ganesha he indicates the possibility for growth in spirituality. As Nritya Ganesha he shows dynamic and harmonious activity.

An elephant's trunk is the most amazing instrument known to man. Human ingenuity has not been able to devise such an instrument. It is capable of lifting huge logs of wood as well as of picking up a microscopic pin lying on the ground. Hence his trunk is a symbol of his great dexterity and versatility. The fact that Ganesha's trunk is curved shows that it is active. It is not just hanging straight down. It is ready to remove every obstacle on the path of his devotee. Normally in his idols the trunk is turned either to the right or to the left and rarely hanging straight down. These positions have a deep spiritual significance and are not chosen at random. The idol in which the trunk is turned to the right is capable of giving *moksha* or liberation from the coils of life. It is a symbol of the mind's spiritual progress through the path of the sun or the path of light. When it is turned to the left it is normally found nuzzling the *modakam* or sweet ball, which he carries in his left hand. This figure is capable of granting all that we desire from the material world. When the trunk is hanging straight down it indicates the path through which the primeval force of the *Kundalini Shakti* is supposed to travel.

The form of Ganesha is closely connected with the *chakras* (psychic centres) and the *nadis* (astral tubes) of the body. His left side corresponds with the flow of the breath called *Ida* and the right side represents the *nadi* called *Pingala*. The *Kundalini Shakti* is the coiled-up power of the divine mother at the base of the spine in the *chakra* known as *Muladhara*. Ganesha is the presiding deity of this *chakra* and sits in the psychic lotus of this *chakra*. The element "earth" is predominant in this *chakra*. The *Kundalini Shakti* wakes up only when Ganesha's grace is given. Thus he is the presiding deity of the evolutionary energy of the *Devi Kundalini*, potent with infinite powers and remains with us throughout our evolution, life after life until we attain liberation.

A Tamil classic praises Ganesha thus: "The notes made by the anklets of the lotus feet of the Lord are as cool as sandal paste."

Gandha is the Sanskrit name for smell and sandal paste. It is the *tanmatra* or essential quality of the earth element. The red lotus indicates the *Muladhara Chakra*, which is the seat of the earth element in which Ganesha is the presiding deity.

He is a counterpart of Saraswati, the goddess of learning and fine arts and is the presiding deity of a special class of musical instruments – mainly percussion instruments. He is looked upon as the guardian deity of all musicians who play on percussion instruments. They always repeat a well-known prayer to him before starting their music concerts. All dance recitals start with a prayer to Ganesha and like his father, he is also known as the master of dance. He is described as having played on the *mridanga* or a special type of drum when Shiva danced in ecstasy before Vishnu at the birth of the Ganga.

His symbol is the *swastika*, which is also the symbol of the *Muladhara Chakra*. It represents the sun and the cycle of life. *Su* means well-being and *asti* means "it is". Hinduism uses the right-armed *chakra,* which is considered to be a most auspicious sign in India and is usually found outside houses. However, the Nazis had no idea of its esoteric significance and used the left-armed one, which symbolises evil and is used only in black magic rites.

Gajavakram   Surashreshtam
Karnachaamara   bhushitam,
Pashangushadharam   devam,
Vandeaham   Gananaayakam.

"I bow to Lord Ganesha,
Who is the noblest of all the gods,
Who is embellished with ears like fans,
And who carries a lasso and a hook."

— *Sri Ganashtakam*

ॐ *Gam Ganapataye Namaha!*

"One should ever worship for one's peace of mind that delightful Lord Ganesha whose body and clothes are white,
Who has been worshipped on the shore of the Milky Ocean with white flowers, sandal-paste and jewelled lamps.
Who is the first to be worshipped by both gods and humans,
Who reposes on a jewelled throne holding the noose, and a lotus flower in his hands,
Who bestows boons and ensures the safety of all,
Upon whose forehead reposes the crescent moon,
Who has three eyes and who ever dwells in the company of Lakshmi, the goddess of prosperity."

— *Sri Ganapati Stotram*

ॐ

Gajakarnakaaya Namaha!

CHAPTER FOUR

GAJAKARNA

Attributes of Ganesha

Ekadantaaya vidmahe,
Vakratundaaya dhimahi,
Tanno Danti prachodayaath

We devote our thoughts to the one-tusked Lord.
We meditate on him who has a curved trunk.
May the tusked one guide us on the right path.

— *Ganapati Atharva Shirsha*

Hinduism caters to all aspects of an individual's nature therefore it accepts that there are four goals in life which are prompted by our desire for righteousness, our desire for wealth, desire for love and finally our desire for liberation. Ganesha's four hands stand for these four *purushartha*s or the goals of life, which are known as *dharma, artha, kama* and *moksha*. The middle two, which pertain to material life, are also given a proper place in the life of the human being. It will be noticed that they are hemmed in by *dharma* or righteousness on one side and *moksha* or liberation on the other. If our desire for wealth and love are guided by righteousness, they will lead us to *moksha* or liberation.

Ganesha's two tusks represent duality or the pairs of opposites in life such as pleasure and pain, sorrow and joy and so on. But Ganesha is known as Ekadanta or the one with only one tusk. His right tusk is broken. This shows that the man of perfection is not under the sway of these opposites. He has consciously broken off from this world of duality. He is very often seen to hold this tusk in his right hand like a pen, denoting the creative capacity of the man of wisdom. The right side normally denotes Brahman or the changeless reality and the left, the creative power of *Shakti*. The broken right tusk indicates that the man of perfection is permanently established in a state of Brahmic consciousness. The unbroken left tusk shows that he is also actively fulfilling his role in society.

There are many stories about how he got only one tusk. Parasurama who was a disciple of Shiva went to Kailasa. At the door to the inner apartments, Ganesha barred his passage, as his father was asleep. Parasurama insisted on going in and Ganesha obstructed him strongly. When he tried to push his way through, Ganesha started to fight and seized Parasurama with his trunk and twirled him so that he fell down senseless. On recovering Parasurama threw his axe at Ganesha. The latter recognized it as his father's weapon, given to Parasurama by Shiva, and received it with all humility upon one of his tusks which became severed.

Parvati was highly incensed at this and was about to curse Parasurama when Brahma appeared and appeased her indignation. He promised her that her son would be worshipped before all other gods.

Another story in the *Skanda Purana* describes his encounter with the demon called Sindura or Gajasura who had an elephant head. During the course of his fight with the demon, he broke off one of his tusks and used it as a weapon. The broken tusk is symbolic of the shedding of the ego. The single tusk indicates the non-dualistic aspect of the mind when it merges with the *atman*, thus effacing the phenomenal world. In the story of Gajasura, it should be noted that the demon as well as the God had elephant heads. The esoteric meaning of the story is of Ganesha curbing the elephant-headed demonic ego by breaking off one tusk and thus focusing on the *atman* within, with his single pointed tusk.

Another story claims that Ganesha broke off one tusk in order to use it as a stylus when he became the scribe for Vyasa. This story will be narrated later. The esoteric interpretation of the one tusk also shows single-pointed attention to whatever is being done. This is a very important aspect for anyone who wants to accomplish an important job.

His two feet stand for *siddhi* and *buddhi,* who are his consorts. *Buddhi* is discriminating knowledge, wisdom and sagacity. *Siddhi* is success, fulfilment and attainment.

He has exceptionally large ears. That is how he got the name Soorpakarna, which means having ears like winnowing baskets. They resemble a type of flat basket that is used in India to sift the chaff from the grain. Of course all elephants have large ears that act like antenna to receive all possible sounds. He gets transmission from all sides and is thus able to gauge every situation. He makes a decision only after having gathered all possible information. Hence Ganesha's large ears help him to winnow all the information received and keep only that which is essential. In an esoteric sense, he can sift the chaff from the grain – discern the real from the unreal, like the proverbial swan, which is supposed to be able to separate milk from water when both are mixed together.

His big belly is meant to be a symbol of the whole universe. All the events of the world emerge from the cauldron of his belly. No power in the world is capable of subjugating him. He who has mastered his mind has mastered the world. A circle is an accepted symbol of the universe. It describes the completeness or fullness of everything. His huge belly also signifies his capacity to digest all the information received through his highly sensitive ears and trunk.

He has small eyes. This shows his ability for making minute observations. He has great powers of observation and can ferret out the truth through any camouflage. His benign but steady look sees everything – both good and bad – in the object viewed. Very often he is seen with a third eye, which is the symbol of the higher faculties. Though he is born from the earth, he lives in eternity.

All Brahmins have to wear a sacred thread across their left shoulder. This is a symbol of their caste and the fact that they have been invested with a large amount of responsibilities like chanting the *gayatri mantra* and looking after the spiritual welfare of the public. Normally this is made out of three strands of cotton thread.

These three strands stand for the Ida, Sushumna and Pingala, which are the *nadis* or subtle paths of psychic energy through which the *Shakti* of the *Kundalini* rises. The unawakened *Kundalini Shakti* is often compared to a coiled-up serpent. In fact it is commonly known as the serpent power.

It is possible that one of the reasons for his using a snake as a sacred thread is to denote that he is the presiding deity of the *Kundalini Shakti* in the *Muladhara*

Chakra and is thus the custodian of the mystic serpent power. It also indicates his deep compassion for all creatures even those that are considered dangerous and feared by most people. His father Shiva too has great love for snakes and even wears them as ornaments.

When Gajanana set out to vanquish Vighna, the spirit of obstacles, the gods equipped him with their own accoutrements and weapons. Shiva gave him the crescent moon and the bow and arrows, Brahma, the sacred thread, Vishnu, the conch and discus, Indra, the thunderbolt, Varuna, the noose, and Yama the cudgel. Kartikeya gave him a spear and Kubera, a jewelled pot. Lakshmi gave sheaves of corn and sugar cane to him. Thus Gajanana had the appurtenances and weapons of all the gods.

However his main weapons are those used by the elephant trainer to subdue an elephant. One is the rope or *pasa* used to bind the pachyderm and the other is the *ankusa* or goad used to prod him to walk faster. Ganesha uses the noose for controlling the senses that run hither and thither like unbridled horses and will lead to our downfall if left uncontrolled. The noose in Ganesha's hand symbolizes the reins of discrimination by which we can control the senses. The goad is generally used by mahouts to control elephants on the rampage. Our passions can be compared to mad elephants and the goad alone can subdue them and bring them to heel. Under their sway a man becomes a mad elephant and can commit any atrocity. The rope also signifies the passions that bind us to material life and the goad has to be used to prod us into giving up these attachments. The noose and goad also denote his all-pervasiveness and grace. He can throw the noose and lasso at anyone, however far they might be and bring them directly under his care. Even evildoers are not shut out of his all-encompassing love. The goad is used to prick them and bring them to heel. In an esoteric sense, the bow stands for the mind, the noose for the will, the goad for the intellect and the arrow for the power of action.

Very often he is seen with a half moon on his head, which he has inherited from his father. The moon on the forehead ensures that the brain is always calm and cool whatever the circumstances. The moon is always supposed to have a cooling effect.

He wears a pearl necklace with one hundred and eight beads. The pearl is the symbol of affluence combined with purity. It also has a direct connection with the moon. The number, one hundred and eight has great significance in Hindu mythology. All *japa malas* have hundred and eight beads. It is believed that the normal person breathes 10800 times in twelve hours. Each bead when chanted with a *mantra* gives the effect of 100 counts so we can cover the whole day with one round of the *japa mala*. His jewelled crown represents this many-spleandoured universe that we live in.

Other things that are associated with Ganesha are his favourite food articles. *Modakam* or the sweet ball is definitely his favourite and has to be offered to him at all his important functions. In fact the word *modakam* means that which gives joy. It also denotes *jnana* or supreme wisdom that confers bliss. It reminds us that bliss is within the reach of all of us. It does not lie outside us but within us. The fact that he holds it in his hand indicates that he is capable of giving this bliss, the real sweetness of life that only the enlightened can savour. The rat also holds a small sweet ball and looks at Ganesha pleadingly as if asking his permission to eat it. This sweet ball held in the paws of the rat represents earthly joys that the spiritual seeker can enjoy if he places them under the control of his higher self. His natural impulses need not be suppressed but only sublimated. Sugar cane is another of his favourites. This of course denotes his identification with the elephant.

Three animals are connected with him – the elephant, the snake and the mouse. He has the head of an elephant with only one tusk and he wears a serpent either as a girdle round his waist or as a band across his shoulder and his mount is a mouse. All these composite aspects go to make up him most adorable of all deities in the Hindu pantheon.

The fact that the insignificant mouse is shown as his mount is the most enigmatic portion of his figure. A mouse is a creature of the earth and has its existence in burrows and holes in the ground. Its body and head touch the earth most of the time. It cares only for the satisfaction of its palate. The fact that Ganesha rides on it denotes that the liberated man keeps his worldly desires completely under control.

Consciousness according to Indian belief is ingrained even in the grains of sand. It turns into intelligence after passing through the rudimentary forms. The mouse is a fitting symbol for this. It has a primitive intelligence encased in ignorance and is thus restless, avaricious and worried. On the other hand, the elephant is the symbol of strength and wisdom. It indicates the strength and power lying hidden in nature and also arouses reverence in us. The figure of Ganesha on the mouse thus suggests that the human being has both characteristics within him. The elephant is normally calm and composed. It is a majestic creature with immense potential power. The rat on the other hand is a restless animal, constantly running here and there in its frantic quest for food. The human being has the power to be calm and majestic with an ever expanding consciousness stretching to the infinite but he continues to be a rat and rush about in the "rat race" of life, fighting and squabbling over trivialities. These two animals symbolize the two stages of consciousness, the primitive and the expanded states. The human body as in the figure of Ganesha is in between these two and connects them. Thus his whole form paints a graphic picture of the immense possibility of the human being to reach the hitherto unattained heights of consciousness. Evolution of life so far has not meant an evolution of consciousness but the evolution of the equipment to express higher states of consciousness. Despite his latent ability to attain super consciousness, the human being continues to live the life of a restless, frightened rat, concerned only with his material needs. The figure of Ganesha mounted on the rat encourages us to focus our energies in finding the supreme goal of life.

The elephant is the largest of the vertebrates and the mouse the smallest and they contrast sharply with one another. One can trample the other to death. There is an esoteric meaning to this also. The Lord takes care of and loves even the smallest of his creations and is even prepared to use this little creature as his vehicle thus raising him to a high status. Another meaning is this. There are two ways of overcoming obstacles. One can trample over them like an elephant or one can find small holes and chinks through which one can slip in unnoticed like a mouse and gain the same objective with less damage.

Again the rat is a creature that is always looking out for means of survival in the material world. Ganesha brings it under control and curbs its destructive power. The rat is a symbol of the mind with its endless craving and seeking for sustenance from the material world. Ganesha is the one who curbed the *asura*, "Trishna" or the thirst for material enjoyments. He has to be invoked to curb this tendency of the mind to consider that only the things of the world will satisfy it and make it discover a new world of the spirit by which its inordinate thirst for objects will be tuned down to the thirst for the divine alone. This will happen only when it realizes once and for all that the divine alone is capable of satisfying it.

The traditional meaning of the mouse is that it stands for *kutarka* or perverse arguments. Everyone in a high position knows the difficulty of having to face perverse arguments that stand in the way of any enterprise. So Ganesha rides on this and keeps such arguments under control.

Only two of his figures as Vijaya Ganapati and Srishti Ganapati are seen to be riding a mouse. It's the *Matsya Purana* that declares for the first time that a mouse is an essential part of the image of Ganapati. The *Ganapati Upanishad* describes how he conquered the *asura* Gaja Mukha who changed himself into a huge mouse. Ganesha subdued him and used him as a mount.

The *Taitirya Upanishad* descries the fight between Agni, the god of fire, and the other gods. Agni disappeared into the earth and later assumed the form of a mouse. This mouse was presented to Shiva who in turn gave it to his son Ganesha who had no vehicle of his own.

Gajananam bhuthaganadisevitam,
Kapithajambuphala charubhakshanam,
Umasutam shokavinashakarakam,
Namaami vigneswara padapangajam!

"I salute the lotus feet of Lord Ganesha,
who has the face of an elephant,
And is the son of Uma (Parvati),
Who is served by all beings,
Who relishes sugar cane and other fruits,
And is the destroyer of all grief."

— *Sri Ganashtakam*

ॐ *Gam Ganapataye Namaha!*

ॐ

Lambodaraaya Namaha!

CHAPTER FIVE

LAMBODARA

Birth of Ganesha

Tat purushaya vidmahe,
Mahadevaaya dhimahi,
Tanno Danti prachodayaath

We devote our thoughts to the That Supreme Person,
We meditate on him who is the great Lord.
May the tusked one guide us on the right path.

— *Narayanopanishad*

There are many stories connected with the birth of Ganesha, which are all very interesting. Vyasa, the author of the Puranas was a master storyteller and he has given these many vantage points from which we can view the birth of this most delectable god. Stories serve as pools in which the reflection of Reality can be caught. Too much intellectualism spoils the whole story. The subtle essence of truth can only be caught through a web of allegories, symbols and stories. These stories have to be read with the sensitive heart of an artist and not with the critical intellect of the scientist. If we read them with a childlike innocence they will open our hearts to a vast vista of mysticism and romance for which the human heart actually craves.

Some modern children are most argumentative and try to show off their scientific knowledge and keep saying, "How is that possible?" But the parents will say, "Don't ask too many questions. Just accept the story as it is."

However the modern mind, which was highly scientific in the last century, is now slowly veering to the mystical and the incredible. Look at the popularity of books like "The Lord of Rings" and "Harry Potter". The sages realized long ago that the mind of man is always wanting to look for a truth beyond the apparent reality which is revealed to him by his five senses and these type of stories help to release this pent-up longing buried deep in the human heart for the mystical, the magical and the unbelievable.

The *Linga Purana* says that Ganesha was born as a part of Shiva out of Parvati's womb. The reason for this birth is given here.

The gods held a meeting in order to find the answer to a question that had been troubling them for a long time. All the good works that they wanted to get done through the agency of good and pious people were being constantly blocked from all sides by a demon called Vighnasura, whereas all the unholy acts performed by the demons seemed to succeed. They approached Shiva and begged him to solve their problem. The Lord agreed and cast his loving glance at his consort, Parvati, whereupon an effulgent form manifested itself in front of them. It was a child with the face of an elephant, holding a trident in one hand and a noose in the other. The hearts of the gods were filled with joy. Parvati was overjoyed and bedecked him with clothes and ornaments.

Shiva took him in his lap and said, "You have incarnated in order to fulfil the desires of the gods and put obstacles in the path of evil doers. May the endeavours of the evildoers always fail. All those who want to propitiate me or Vishnu, Brahma or Devi, will have to worship you first. If they don't do this they will meet with failure. The divine child, Bala Ganapati now created the *vighna gana*s (obstacles in the form of *gana*s) and agreed to do as his father wished. Thus he was called Vigneshvara, Lord of obstacles as well as the one who removes obstacles. He creates them if the time is not right and removes them when success is assured.

A similar version is found in the *Varaha Purana*. The gods and sages approached Shiva and begged him to create a being that would put obstacles in the way of evildoers and remove obstacles from the path of the good. Shiva gazed lovingly at Parvati and out of his look was born a radiant, handsome youth possessing all noble qualities. However, Parvati disapproved of this Being that was created without her participation. She cursed him that he would become ugly, have an elephant's head and a potbelly. Shiva countered the curse and said that he would be known as Ganesha, son of Shiva and leader of his host of *gana*s. He declared that in all endeavours, success and failure should stem from him alone, and that he should be invoked first in all rituals.

According to a South Indian version, Ganesha was born of Shiva and Parvati when they had assumed the form of elephants and were roaming around incognito in the forest. Thus he was begotten with an elephant's face.

In the poem known as "Manasamangala" it is said that once Durga (Parvati) appeared as a milkmaid in front of Shiva. He became enamoured of her and spent the night in her company. Ganesha is supposed to have been born from this divine union.

The great hymn to the goddess Lalita comes in the *Brahmanda Purana*. In this is given a beautiful version of Ganesha's birth. Lalita had manifested herself at the behest of the gods in order to kill the demon, Bhanda. At one time during the battle, Bhanda's general crept into Lalita's camp and inscribed the "Jaya Vighna Yantra" on a rock. This was a magic figure, which would induce laziness and sleep. All the warriors in Lalita's army started to yawn and fall asleep. The only two who were still vigilant were her chief generals called Dandanayaki and Mantrini. They immediately reported the matter to Lalita. She is supposed to have smiled and gazed adoringly at her husband Kameshwara (Shiva in the form of the Lord of Love). Out of the interlocking of their gaze was born the brilliant form of Gajanana, with an elephant's head and ten arms. Having bowed to his parents and received their blessings, he went into the camp and discovered the *yantra* and smashed it to bits. He then entered the fray and routed the army of Bhandasura. Lalita was so pleased with him that she granted him the boon that his worship should take precedence over all other deities in all rituals.

The *Brahmavaivarta Purana* gives another account of his birth. Shiva and Parvati had been married for a long time and Parvati was very anxious to have a child. Shiva advised her to undertake the vow known as the Punyaka. This is a vow undertaken to propitiate Lord Vishnu. It should be started on the thirteenth day of the bright fortnight of the month of *Magha* (Jan/Feb) and continued for a year. Everyday one thousand Brahmins had to be fed and worshipped with flowers, fruits, vessels, gems, gold and clothes. Parvati was told to undertake a life of complete inner and outer purity and fix her mind on Vishnu alone. Sanat Kumara, one of the four boy sages, was her priest.

The ritual was performed on the banks of the Ganga. All the gods and sages arrived at the spot to participate in this wonderful function. After completing the ritual, Parvati wanted to give Sanat Kumara, the officiating priest, some *dakshina* or fee for having performed this work. Sanat Kumara made an unexpected demand. He wanted Lord Shiva himself to be given to him as *dakshina*! Parvati was aghast and didn't know what to do. She offered him numberless gifts, all of which he refused. If the priest left without a *dakshina*, the effects of the year-long vow would be annulled. Lord Vishnu to whom the vow was being done, advised her to give away Shiva and then take him back by offering the priest one *lakh* of cows. She agreed to this and gave away her husband and concluded the vow in a befitting manner. After that she offered a *lakh* of cows to Sanat Kumara who said he didn't want any cows and preferred to keep Shiva.

Parvati was heart broken since she couldn't bear to be parted from her Lord even for a minute. She prepared to immolate herself and prayed to Lord Krishna before doing so. Krishna appeared before her and at his vision her sorrows disappeared. Seeing this, the gods were emboldened to approach Sanat Kumara once again and eventually persuaded him to hand over Lord Shiva to her. He did this without much resistance.

The sages seem to delight in such pranks and unreasonable behaviour. This is because they want to test the mental strength of the person who has undertaken a vow. Of course it also provides an added zest to the story.

Just at that time an old Brahmin appeared who begged Parvati for food. He wanted to be fed with all sorts of delicious food so that his belly would become huge. He also wanted to be clothed in silks and satins and adorned with ornaments and placed on a golden throne. Parvati was preparing to give him everything he asked for but before she could do this, the Brahmin disappeared from view. Simultaneously she heard a heavenly voice advising her to return to her house and look on her bed. Hearing this, she rushed to her room and found a divinely beautiful baby boy lying on her bed and kicking his hands and feet in the air. The voice assured her that her son was Krishna himself. The Lord had taken the form of her son due to the successful accomplishment of her vow. The whole of Kailasa now resounded with music and chanting of hymns and the sound of divine musical instruments.

There is another interesting version of this story. One night when Parvati was resting, Lord Vishnu appeared in the guise of an old and emaciated priest. He begged for food. After having fed him to his hearts content, she asked him what else he desired. He said that he would like to become her son. Immediately he became a small infant lying on Parvati's bed and kicking his feet and hands merrily in the air as small babies do. Shiva and Parvati were delighted at getting Vishnu as their son. They invited all the gods and goddesses to come and bless their son. Vishnu gave him knowledge, Brahma, fame and adulation, Dharma, righteousness and mercy and Shiva, generosity, intelligence, peace and self-control. Lakshmi promised to dwell in all the places where he was worshipped and Saraswati gave him power of speech, memory and eloquence, while Savitri gave all wisdom.

Shani or Saturn was amongst the deities who had come to Kailasa. He kept his eyes steadfastly fixed to the ground and Parvati asked him the reason for his not looking at her lovely child.

Saturn said, "I was an ardent devotee of Lord Krishna and was not interested in a marital life but my father got me married to the daughter of Chitrarata, one of the celestials. One day she approached me when I was meditating. I was totally oblivious of her presence. She became furious at this slight and cursed me that if I looked at anyone his head would be severed. Since then I have avoided looking directly at anyone."

Parvati felt sorry for him and told him to gaze on her son if he so wished. Shani was reluctant and called Dharma to witness the fact that he had been given permission to gaze at the infant. With great unwillingness he took a peep at the baby. Immediately the child's head was severed from his body and flew to Goloka, or the abode of Krishna where it was re-united with the Lord from whom it had come.

Parvati was grief-stricken and taking the headless trunk of the baby in her arms, she sank to the ground and wept aloud. All the gods except Vishnu followed her example and started weeping. Vishnu mounted on his vehicle, Garuda and flew to the river Pushpabhadra where he found an elephant sleeping with his head turned to the north (which is condoned in the scriptures). He cut off his head with his discus and flew back to Kailasa and clapped this head on to the body of the baby and resuscitated it. The parents were delighted and made gifts to all the Brahmins.

Vishnu took the divine child in his lap and adorned it with garlands and ornaments and offered ceremonial worship to him and gave him eight names – Vighnesa, Ganesha, Heramba, Gajanana, Lambodara, Ekadanta, Soorpakarna and Vinayaka.

He declared, "Since you have been worshipped by me first, you will be offered the first worship by everyone before commencing any other ritual."

Parvati now turned to Shani who was standing with his head cast down. She decided that for his own good it would be better if he remained disembodied so that his gaze could no longer harm anyone. Out of her compassion she pronounced this curse on him that he would become a disembodied spirit in future.

Destruction is easier than construction and wicked people are very quick in destroying the wonderful creations of others, either physically or with their tongues. Shani or Saturn represents the fiercely critical intellect by whose very look an artistic creation can be beheaded. But the Lord will always be there to bless the sincere efforts of his devotee and thus Lord Vishnu saved the day.

Another account of Ganesha's origin is given in the *Matsya Purana*. When Parvati was bathing, she took the oil and powders like turmeric, *sandal* paste and pure mud which she used for her bath together with the bits of skin which flaked off her body and formed them into the figure of a boy to which she gave life since she was the Divine Mother who could give life to anything. In this story she made the baby with an elephant's head since she had seen this mystic figure in the halls of the gods at one time and had imprinted it in her memory.

Parvati stands for primeval nature or *Mula Prakriti* latent with infinite creative potency. From matter (from the dust and skin which she scrapes off her own body) life emerges and evolves, giving rise to the human being in whom consciousness eventually assumes the character of the human mind with all its wonderful faculties.

The *Padma Purana* gives a similar version of the story. One day while in a state of bliss after having been in the company of her Lord, Parvati decided to take a bath. She anointed her body with fragrant oils and powders. She then scrubbed off the dough with her hands and fashioned a baby with an elephant's head. She took the figure in her arms and lowered it into the waters of the Ganga. The moment it was immersed the figure came alive and grew big and strong. Parvati was delighted and held out her arms to him and cried, "My son". Ganga who was Lord Shiva's second consort also held out her arms and called him her son. The gods and *rishi*s arrived to pay obeisance to this new deity. They addressed him as "Gangeya", son of Ganga. Brahma gave him the name "Ganapati", and told him that he would be the chief of Shiva's *gana*s.

Parvati is the embodiment of the universal *Prakriti* or the creative aspect of the Supreme. She has the three *parvas* or aspects of creation, which are *jnana Shakti*, or the power of knowledge, *iccha Shakti* or the power of will and desire and *kriya Shakti* or the power of action. These three are imperative before any type of creation can take place. However even though she possesses all three, she is powerless to create without the support of the Supreme

Consciousness or *chit Shakti*, embodied by Shiva. Hence she is married to him. She creates her son out of her own fragrance. The head of the elephant demonstrates his unlimited power and wisdom. Ganga represents dynamic, divine knowledge that is ever flowing. Parvati dips her creation in Ganga to show that the image of the Lord enshrined in our hearts should be enlivened by soaking it in the dynamic flow of knowledge. Only then will it carry us to self-realization.

The *Shiva Purana* gives another version. Once it happened that when Parvati was bathing she asked Nandi, Shiva's chief *gana* to guard the door and not to let anyone enter. But Shiva himself came to the door and Nandi was powerless to stop him. Parvati was not happy at this untimely intrusion. She had two maids called Jaya and Vijaya and one day they also brought similar complaints to her. They said that they had no one to protect them while Shiva had so many *gana*s. So Parvati decided to create a person to guard her. The next time she took a bath she anointed herself with many divine unguents and turmeric and sandal paste and some fine mud. She scraped this off her body and fashioned a beautiful child out of it and enlivened it with her breath. The child was beautiful to behold and he was told to guard his mother's inner apartments from all intruders.

Once it happened that Shiva himself came to visit Parvati and Ganesha obstructed him as he had been told to do. He did not realize that Shiva was his father since he had never seen him before. Shiva peremptorily ordered the upstart to move and allow him to enter but the boy refused and defended the door with his stick. When Shiva asked him who he was, he replied that he was Parvati's son and had been told to guard the door at all cost. Shiva then declared that if this was the case, he was his father and should obey him. Ganesha refused and blocked his way. Incensed by this Shiva returned and told his *gana*s to go and shoo the minion off. The *gana*s came and did their best but were fended off by the boy. They returned and reported the matter to Shiva. At this Shiva himself came and in the battle that followed he cut off the boy's head with his trident.

In this legend, the mind is the guard, which stands between Parvati, the creative energy and Shiva, the Pure Consciousness. The conditioned human mind has a tendency to resist its own spiritual evolution and hence in the story, Ganesha obstructs Shiva from entering the precincts of *Prakriti* or Parvati. The union between the two would result in total freedom for the human being but we continue to resist this.

When Parvati arrived she found the headless torso of her beautiful son. She wept and upbraided Shiva. She threatened to destroy the whole world if her son was not restored to her. Shiva was intensely sorry for his act and tried his best to pacify her.

"My son has been killed," she cried, "and I shall never forgive you, unless he is revived."

Shiva immediately sent his *gana*s to cut off the head of the first creature they found who was sleeping with his head turned to the north and bring it to him. As it happened the first creature they found in this position was an elephant. They cut off the head and brought it to Shiva who fixed it on the headless body. The priest chanted *mantra*s for the resuscitation of the body and sprinkled Ganga water on it and immediately the body rose up. The torso was that of the original Vinayaka but the head was that of an elephant. Parvati was happy to see her son alive even though with the head of an elephant.

Once, long ago she had gone to the art gallery of the gods. She had been entranced when she saw the glorious figure of ॐ. It was at that moment that the figure of Vinayaka came into her mind and she being the mother goddess, naturally the figure came to be created. When his trunk is turned to the right, Ganesha's figure is a dynamic, anthropomorphic representation of the *mantra* ॐ, which is the symbol of the Supreme Brahman. Parvati was delighted to see how closely his figure tallied with her conception of ॐ. She took him on her lap and christened him Vinayaka – the one who is born without a sire – *vi-nayaka*. *Nayaka* is master or husband and *vi* means without. The word *vi* also stands for light, so the name also means "one who is the Lord of light". He was born on the fourth day of the bright fortnight of the month of *Bhadra* (August/September). Hence this day is celebrated by all as his birthday. Shiva declared that the fourth day of every lunar fortnight would also be special for Ganesha.

Parvati is *Shakti* or the generative force of the Supreme as personified by Shiva. It is only *Shakti* who creates. Ganesha's origin is from the dirt and other material things scraped off her body. Thus he represents the consciousness that evolves from matter and expands to its highest state of spiritual freedom. In the form of Ganesha we find the symbol of the emergence of life from earth and the unfoldment of consciousness from matter. He represents the initiating spiritual power that underlies everything. Hence he has to be worshipped first.

The annihilation of the obstinate and belligerent boy by Shiva is for transforming him into a calm and reasonable being. Since Shiva is the Lord of yoga, the fixing of the elephant head on the trunk of the boy is symbolic of his transformation into an evolved, intelligent being. The north facing head denotes the northern path that is described in the scriptures as the path leading to salvation. As has been said before, we can understand the inner meanings of all mythological stories only if we are able to rise above our mental conditioning and pre-conceived notions.

Although Vinayaka was created without his help, Shiva took great pride in him and accepted him as his elder son. It should be noted that his second son Kartikeya, had a father alone and Parvati had nothing to do with him even though she accepted him as her own.

Ambikahridayaanadam,
Mathrubhi paripaalitam,
Bhaktapriyam madonmattham,
Vandeham Gananaayakam.

"I bow to Lord Ganesha,
Who is the delight of his mother, Ambika,
And who in turn looks after her,
Who is intoxicated with love for his devotees."

— *Sri Ganashtakam*

ॐ *Gam Ganapataye Namaha!*

"I bow to Lord Ganesha, the destroyer of all afflictions,
Who is the Supreme Brahman according to Vedanta,
Who is known as the foremost being or the root cause of the creation of
this universe."

— *Sri Ganapati Stotram*

CHAPTER SIX

VIKATA

Wives of Ganesha

Aum Sri Ganeshaaya Namaha!
Aum Namah Sri Aadya,
Veda pradipaadya,
Jaya Jaya swasamvedya,
Atmarupa

Aum, Salutations to the auspicious first cause,
Who is the very theme of the Vedas.
Glory to him who is the Supreme Truth,
In supreme awareness of himself.

There are a number of interesting stories about Ganesha's marital status that are found in various Puranas. In his highest aspect Ganesha is said to be a celibate. But in another aspect he is found to have two wives. The *Shiva Purana* gives an interesting version of his marriage. Kartikeya was born after Ganesha. One day when the boys had attained marriageable age the parents were discussing their marriage. When they heard this, both of them said, "I want to marry first." Parvati was in a dilemma and said, "All right we will keep a condition. Both of you should go round the world and the one who returns first will get married first." As soon as he heard this, Kartikeya mounted his vehicle – the peacock and started his journey round the world. Ganesha was in a fix. He was decidedly at a disadvantage where races were concerned. His brother was slim and had a peacock as his vehicle while he had a stout and cumbersome body and a tiny mouse as his mount. But Ganesha as we have seen is the embodiment of the super intellect. He thought for a while and then brought two cushioned seats and made his parents sit on them. Then he went round them seven times and came and stood before them with folded palms.

"I've gone round the world seven times not just once," he said, "So you may arrange my marriage."

Shiva and Parvati laughed and asked him to explain himself.

Ganesha smiled and said, "The scriptures say that worshipping one's parents and circumambulating them is tantamount to going round the world. I have just done this so if you believe in the scriptures, you should judge me to be the first?"

Ganesha shows us how we can use our intellect and convert our weaknesses into our strength. True wisdom lies in the ability to change every circumstance and make it favourable to us. All circumstances are given to us by God to prove ourselves and it's best to learn to handle them correctly and not avoid them.

Shiva and Parvati were delighted at their precocious son's intelligence and arranged for him to be married to the two beautiful daughters of the Prajapati, Viswarupa. The daughters were called Siddhi – supernormal powers – and Buddhi or the discriminative intelligence. Sometimes the name Riddhi – prosperity or affluence, is given in the place of Buddhi. Ganesha represents the enlightened person and such a person is wedded to Buddhi or the discriminative intellect and also acquires Siddhi or supernormal power as well as affluence. Esoterically speaking the evolved person will be blessed by having both these as his consorts. Having attained the highest state of cosmic consciousness, the man of realization will lack for nothing.

Both his wives had offspring. Buddhi's child was called Kshema or well being and prosperity and Siddhi's child was Labha or gain. The realized soul lacks for nothing. He or she gets both material prosperity and a higher state of consciousness.

The Puranic stories may appear to be the flights of fancy of the ancient sages but they conceal many subjective truths. They are like abstract paintings that seem weird to the casual gaze since they have broken away from the common vision and deflect the intellect from its ordinary grooves but these paintings also enables the intellect to reach for the extraordinary. The *rishi*s intended these stories to help the ordinary man to transcend the limitations of conditioned thinking. A mathematical equation may appear meaningless to most people but to the initiate it reveals some deep meaning.

Another story in the *Shiva Purana* tells us how Ganesha got the *modakam* or sweet ball, which he always carries in his hand. Once, the gods went to Kailasa to pay their respects to Shiva and Parvati. They took the sweet known as *modakam* with them and presented it to Parvati. Both the children, Ganesha and Kartikeya demanded to have it so Parvati told them to listen to the story first.

"This is not an ordinary sweet. It is known as a *modakam* and it is prepared with rare ingredients and dipped in nectar. One can gain immortality just by smelling this sweet and one who eats it will become greater than the gods. Therefore the one who can prove himself to be superior to the other will get this sweet. Let me see which of you will be able to go round the world first?"

Kartikeya as usual was a simple soul and took off on his peacock and dipped himself in all the sacred rivers and waters of the world and worshipped all the gods and goddesses and returned to Kailasa within an hour. However, Ganesha the intelligent one had already gone round his parents three times with all humility and reverence and been presented with the *modakam*. The lesson to be learnt is that one who stays with his parents and worships them and looks after their welfare has acquired sixteen times the amount of merit of the one who goes all over the world worshipping various gods and dipping in holy rivers. Our debt to our parents has to be paid first before we can acquire any merit by doing other noble actions.

One day it is said that baby Ganesha was playing with a cat in Kailasa. He pulled its tail and rolled it on the ground before letting it go. It started mewing piteously. After some time he tired of this game and ran to his mother and begged to be put on her lap. He was concerned to see that she was smeared with dirt and looked as if she was in pain. He had never seen her in this condition before and was deeply troubled and asked her what had happened.

She looked at him reproachfully and said, "You are the one who did this to me."

Ganesha was amazed and protested that he had done no such thing.

She told him reprovingly, "Ganesha didn't you pull my tail and roll me in the dirt?"

Ganesha immediately understood what she meant and the lesson she wanted to convey. "O Mother!" He said, "I now understand that all forms are yours and I should never harm anyone if I don't want to hurt you."

Puranic stories bring the divine to the level of the human understanding and enable us to elevate our emotions and reach a sublime state.

Another sweet story is told about how Ganesha effected a reconciliation between his parents when they were having a quarrel and refused to talk to each other. Ganesha begged them to kiss his cheeks one on either side. As they kissed him, he withdrew suddenly and thus they ended up by kissing each other.

Kubera was the king of the Yakshas who were the guardians of wealth. He was inordinately proud of his riches and thought that there was nothing that he couldn't accomplish. Once he went to Kailasa to have *darshan* of the Lord. Wanting to show off his wealth he invited Shiva to his city of Alakapuri for lunch. Shiva declined the offer since he said a yogi had no need to attend social functions. He told Kubera to take his son Ganesha instead but warned him of his voracious appetite. Kubera gave a proud smile and promised to feed him to his heart's content.

Ganesha was only a small boy at this time and he caught Kubera's hand and was whisked off to his city in his aerial vehicle called the Pushpaka. Kubera gave him a ceremonial bath and dressed him in costly apparel and adorned him with golden necklaces. Then they sat down to a sumptuous feast. One by one the items started arriving and one by one Ganesha polished off whatever was given to him without the slightest difficulty. The more he ate the more his appetite seemed to grow so that he started to eat faster. Kubera had a retinue of servants but even they found it difficult to see that Ganesha's plate remained full. Anything that was put into it vanished in a trice since Ganesha immediately stuffed the whole thing into his mouth. Very soon Ganesha started to show signs of impatience at the slow rate at which food was being served despite the fact that there was a line of servers putting food every minute into his plate. He started grabbing the food straight from the containers before the servers could serve him. Then he started crunching up the dishes. Everyone was confounded to see the voracious appetite of such a small boy.

Before they could stop him, he marched to the kitchen grumbling all the while about the poor reception that was being given to him. In the kitchen he polished off all the cooked food and then turned his attention to the vegetables and grain that had been stored there. Everything vanished into the cauldron of his stomach. The cooks and servants were horrified to see this and ran to the hall to complain to Kubera. In the meantime Ganesha was calmly munching his way through the furniture and hangings. He then went to the garden and uprooted trees and flowers and ate them all. Next he turned his attention to Kubera's apartments. His pride totally humbled, Kubera fell at his feet and begged him not to destroy his palace.

"You promised to appease my hunger," Ganesha exclaimed, "and I'm still hungry. If you don't keep your promise I'll eat you up!"

The terrified Kubera ran to Kailasa with Ganesha hot on his heels, and begged Shiva to save him.

Shiva said, "I warned you of his voracious appetite but you wouldn't listen. All you wanted was to show off your enormous wealth but remember that the Divine will not be satisfied by wealth alone. Only devotion and surrender can conquer God!"

Kubera is an example of the human being who loves to show off his wealth in ostentatious feasts and gifts to those who are already satiated with wealth. He thought that by feeding Shiva's son, he would gain great repute as a most wealthy and liberal man.

Shiva took pity on Kubera and gave him a fistful of roasted rice and told him to offer it to Ganesha to appease his hunger. Ganesha ate the rice and declared himself to be replete.

Here Ganesha symbolises the power of all-consuming Time. The human being expends his entire energy in the accumulation of wealth by which he hopes to get everlasting security. But in the feast of life, Time is his chief guest and eventually consumes everything including his own body.

Roasted rice has a symbolic meaning. Like our desires, grain will sprout if left to itself and given a conducive environment, but if it is husked and roasted it can never sprout. So also if our desires are roasted in the fire of devotion to the Lord they will not sprout and our ego will be brought under control. This was a lesson for the proud Kubera.

Another story tells about the time when Ganesha outwitted the demon king, Ravana. After doing a lot of *tapasya*, Shiva had given Ravana a very powerful *linga* of himself. Shiva told him never to put the *linga* on the ground for it would become stabilized at that spot. Ravana was in a great hurry to take it off to his island kingdom of Sri Lanka. The *rakshasas* have the power to fly and he held the *linga* carefully in his hands and was skimming across the continent when he reached a spot known as Gokarna in the south of India. At that time Ravana had an urgent need to answer the call of Nature and he came down to the earth. He was in a fix and did not know what to do with the *lingam* since he was not supposed to put it down on the ground. At that time he saw a little Brahmin boy loitering around and ordered him to hold the *lingam* while he went into the bushes. The boy was none other than Ganesha who did not like the idea of the demon carrying off such a precious article, which he would no doubt put to his own nefarious use. When Ravana came back, he found to his dismay that the child had put the *lingam* down on the ground and it had become rooted to the spot. This is the story of the famous shrine of Shiva in Gokarna. Of the boy there was no sign.

The river Kaveri is one of the holy rivers of South India. The sage Agastya is said to have contained the river in his water pot (*kamandalu*) and taken her to his *ashrama*. He quite forgot that the river was given to him for the benefit of the people of South India and kept the pot beside him while he did *tapasya*. At one time there was a big drought in South India and a terrible famine swept across the land. Indra, the king of the gods invoked Ganesha's aid. He took on the form of a crow and flew into the impenetrable forest of the Sahya Mountains where the sage was immersed in deep meditation. The crow went and sat on top of the *kamandalu* and tilted it. The river Kaveri joyfully came gushing out and inundated the plains of the south, thus bringing relief to the thirsty population.

The *Bhargava Purana* gives another story, which is meant to point out the essential oneness between the gods. Once Parvati was celebrating the birthday of Ganesha. At that time, Vishwadeva, who was a great devotee of Vishnu, arrived at the spot. Parvati immediately invited him to take part in the feast. Vishwadeva politely declined since he said he was in the habit of taking food only after getting a vision of Lord Vishnu. When he turned his gaze on Ganesha, he found that he had transformed himself to the figure of Vishnu complete with conch, discus, mace, and lotus and garlanded with the *vanamala*.

This story points out that all spiritual seekers, no matter which form they worship will eventually reach the same goal. The Hindu religion teaches us to behold the One as the many and the many as the One. Each path has its own special characteristic and is chosen by the aspirant according to his psychological make up. Hinduism gives full freedom of choice and enquiry to its votaries. Each one is free to choose his or her own path. There can never be a conflict between unity and diversity because diversity is only the expression of unity.

Yakshakinnara gandharvam,
Siddhavidyadaroragai,
Sthuyamaanam cha varadam,
Vandeham Gananaayakam

"I bow to Lord Ganesha, the giver of boons,
Who is extolled by the Yakshas and Kinnaras,
Siddhas and Vidyadaras."

— *Sri Ganashtakam*

ॐ *Gam Ganapataye Namaha!*

"May Lord Ganapati, with a beautiful elephant face,
Who is the repository of all wisdom and a mine of all virtues, Be gracious unto me.
Success in every mission is ensured just by remembering him."

— Tulsidas

ॐ

Vighnarajaya Namaha!

CHAPTER SEVEN

VIGHNARAJA

Stories of Ganesha

Twam Brahma, twam Vishnur,
Twam Rudrastwam Indrastwam Agnistwam,
Vayurstwam Suryastwam Chandrabhastwam,
Brahma Bhur bhuva swarom!

You are the trinity, Brahma, Vishnu and Shiva.
You are Indra, Agni and Vayu.
You are the sun and the moon.
You are the Brahman.
You are the three worlds,
You are the sound of Aum.

Once when Brahma and Shiva were sitting in Kailasa, the celestial sage Narada came there and offered a divine fruit to Lord Shiva. Both Ganesha and Kartikeya clamoured to have it. Shiva asked Brahma to choose the one to whom he should give it. Brahma said that since Kartikeya was younger, he should be given the fruit. Ganesha was quite angry with this.

Very soon Brahma found that he was beset with obstacles every time he wanted to start any work of creation. He was wondering why such unpleasant things were happening to him when Ganesha, who had a good sense of humour, assumed a terrible form and suddenly appeared in front of him. Even Brahma, the grandsire was frightened out of his wits to see this horrific shape and jumped back aghast. The Moon who was watching the scene with great interest burst into laughter at the sight of a small boy frightening the creator of the world!

Ganesha now turned his wrath on the Moon and cursed him that he would become ugly and cause unhappiness to all who looked at him. The Moon

ॐ

immediately lost all his grace and charm. He implored Ganesha to retract the curse. Ganesha modified his curse and told him that only those who looked at him on the fourth day of the bright fortnight of the month of *Bhadra* – August/September, would become wretched and acquire ill repute and on other days he would continue to fascinate people as he had always done. This was the day on which Ganesha was born and is known as Ganesha Chaturthi and is one of the most famous festivals connected with him.

There is another version of the same story. Once Ganesha had eaten a large number of *modakams* and decided to take a round in the forest. However he felt lazy to walk and called his tiny mouse to carry him. As they were merrily proceeding along the forest, the snake Vasuki crossed their path. The mouse was frightened and lost his balance and Ganesha was thrown to the ground. His stomach burst open and the *modakams* rolled to the ground. Ganesha was not at all happy about losing his favourite food and quickly stuffed them all back into his stomach. To prevent them from falling again he caught hold of the snake Vasuki and tied him across his belly like a belt! Seeing this comical sight, the Moon rolled with laughter. Ganesha cursed him that anyone who saw him on that day would be subject to unjust scandals. This happened to be the fourth day of the bright fortnight of the month of *Bhadra*.

The Puranas very kindly give an antidote for those who happen to see the moon accidentally on that day. They say that the effect will be nullified by reciting the scandalous story of the false charges that were levelled at Lord Krishna over the gem called the Syamantaka.

This story as all others has a symbolic meaning to it. The moon depicts the mind and Ganesha is the symbol of the man seeking spiritual perfection. On this path it is easy to slip and fall but one has to get up and proceed without bothering about the opinion of the world. Scoffers and scandal mongerers are always ready to laugh when anyone falls. Their superficial minds only have the capacity to reason in the normal channels and they are ever ready to mock at spiritual seekers since they have no idea what prompts such people to take up this path. The true spiritual seeker should push forward undaunted by the world's opinion.

Ganesha's encounter with Parashurama, the sixth incarnation of Lord Vishnu, is given in the *Brahmavaivarta Purana*. Parashurama had done *tapasya* in the

देवातूंचिगणेश॥ सकव्ळाय॑मतिप्रकाश॥
ळणनिवृतिदास॥ अवधारिज्ञोढी॥श॥

Ganesha (from an Illus. Manuscript of the *Jnaneshvari*).

Himalayas and propitiated Lord Shiva who presented him with an axe or *parashu*, which had divine powers. One day Parashurama went to Kailasa to pay his respects to Lord Shiva. Both Kartikeya and Ganesha were guarding the gate. When he tried to enter, Ganesha stopped him and said that his father was resting and he would have to wait outside while he went inside and asked his father's permission to let him in. Parashurama was an irate man and said that since he was Shiva's favourite disciple there was no need for Ganesha to announce his arrival.

Ganesha as can be expected did not yield and soon the argument went from words to blows. Parashurama took his axe and threw it at Ganesha. Ganesha knew that it was his father's axe and did nothing to avoid it. Fortunately it did not damage his face but chopped off his right tusk, which fell on the earth with a tremendous thud. Everyone came running to find out the cause of this racket. They found Ganesha lying unconscious on the ground and Parashurama standing with his head hanging down in shame. Parvati took her darling son in her arms and revived him. She turned her wrath on Parashurama and said angrily:

"Do you know the strength of my son? He could have crushed you to powder in a trice, yet he desisted from doing so since you had flung his father's weapon at him. He showed great patience and devotion in the face of your insufferable anger and pride."

She was about to curse him, when Lord Krishna came and pacified her. Parashurama went and bathed in the Ganga to cool himself and then worshipped all three deities separately – Shiva, Parvati and Ganesha – and thus managed to get their blessings instead of their curses.

The *Brahmavaivarta Purana* tells the story of how Tulasi was cursed by Ganesha. Tulasi was the daughter of Dharmaraja, the god of righteousness. She was an incarnation of Lakshmi and thus a great devotee of Narayana. Even as a young girl she had gone to the Himalayas to do *tapasya* in order to propitiate Narayana. Once when she was taking a walk she came upon a lovely *ashrama* situated on the banks of the Ganga. There she saw an ascetic in the prime of his youth, clad in yellow silk sitting in deep meditation. She was captivated by his good looks and entreated him to marry her. The youth was actually Ganesha and he told her that he was least interested in marriage. Tulasi was

unhappy at this repudiation and cursed him that he would definitely marry not
one but two wives. Ganesha in return cursed her that she would marry an
asura and later on she would be born as a plant.

When Tulasi realized who Ganesha was, she fell at his feet and begged
him to retract the curse. He relented and told her, "You will be born as the
holy *tulasi* plant which will contain the essence of all fragrances. You will be
especially pleasing to Lord Narayana. No *puja* of his or of Krishna's will be
complete without an offering of your leaves. All the holy rivers of this land
will be found at your roots and all the gods in your stem. However, I personally
will not accept you in my *puja*!"

Hence it is that *tulasi* leaves are never offered to Ganesha except on Ganesha
Chaturthi day. Tulasi had been very repentant and begged him to allow her
to worship him. He had relented and agreed that her leaves could be used
for his worship on Chaturthi day.

The *Mahabharata* gives the story of how Ganesha became Vyasa's scribe.
Veda Vyasa as we have seen was the compiler of the Vedas and the author
 of all the Puranas. He had conceived the outlay of the magnificent epic known
as the *Mahabharata*, which is the largest manuscript ever composed in the world.
He wanted to put it down in writing so that others could study it. At that
time Brahma came to his *ashrama*. After having welcomed him with all due
honours, Vyasa posed his question to him.

"O Grandsire!" he said, "I have conceived of a wonderful story in my
mind which carries the import of the Vedas and the Upanishads and will cover
all aspects of *dharma* in this world. However I haven't been able to find someone
who is capable of taking it down while I dictate."

Brahma was very pleased to hear about such a book and told him to meditate
on Ganesha. Vyasa sat and meditated on Ganesha and very soon he appeared
before him. Vyasa prostrated to him and begged him to be his scribe.

Ganesha agreed but on one condition. "You should not allow my pen
to stop writing even for a minute. I will keep writing as long as you keep
talking. Once you stop I will also stop and will not continue."

Vyasa thought for a while and put a counter condition. "I agree to your
terms provided you agree to my proviso. You can keep writing so long as

you understand what you are writing but you should stop when you do not understand what I have said."

Ganesha agreed and so the saint and the Lord sat together in a cave, which still exists to the north of the temple of Badrinarayana in the Himalayas. This cave is known as Vyasa Gupha or the cave of Vyasa. Another cave which is situated close by is known as Ganesha Gupha or the cave of Ganesha. The story goes that Ganesha broke one of his tusks and used it as a stylus but this story is not found in the *Mahabharata*.

Vyasa meditated on Lord Narayana, the friend of humanity and on Saraswati, the goddess of knowledge and then proceeded to dictate the book. Sometimes Vyasa found that Ganesha was too swift for him. Immediately he would compose a few abstruse stanzas, which would make Ganesha stop and nibble his stylus while he pondered on the meaning of the verse. This would give enough time for Vyasa to think of more verses. Thus did Vyasa write the *Mahabharata* with Ganesha as his scribe.

The implication of the story is that the book is not one to be read casually without understanding the meaning. Every stanza is pregnant with a deep significance and should be carefully studied and assimilated. If Ganesha, the mighty intellect himself could not grasp some of the ideas immediately, how much longer would it take us to understand it?

Another interesting fact is that Ganesha must have been the first student of the *Bhagavad Gita*, which comes in the middle of the *Mahabharata*. So the *Bhagavad Gita* as well as the whole of the *Mahabharata* must have had the full approval of Lord Ganesha.

The three sons of the demon, Taraka once propitiated Brahma by their severe penance and asked him to make three cities for them. Mayan, the architect of the demons created three wonderful cities for them, in gold, silver and iron. The demons were able to fly around in these cities since they could be airborne. They soon became very powerful and started to harass the gods who as usual went and begged Vishnu to help them. The gods came together and hatched a plan to kill the demons of the three cities. Unfortunately Brahma had given them a boon that they could be killed only when all three cities came in a perfect line while flying around. After a lot of manipulation, Vishnu managed to get them in a line. Shiva was allotted the task of shooting the fatal arrow. However, each time Shiva tried to fix the arrow to his bow, he found that some unexpected hitch would thwart him. The gods appealed to Ganesha to help them and Ganesha admitted that he was the one who was creating obstacles.

"You gave your word to my mother that I should be propitiated before starting any undertaking and now you seem to have forgotten this promise. Nobody, not even my father thought of worshipping me before starting on this venture. How do you expect to succeed?"

The gods realized their mistake and immediately worshipped Ganesha who cleared all the obstacles so that they were able to defeat the demons easily.

This story is meant to show that no human endeavour can succeed without divine aid. We tend to forget the fact that without the help of God we are totally helpless. All human striving would be in vain if it is done without invoking the divine spirit within us. However much we struggle we will not be able to succeed. In this story, Shiva himself plays the part of the bewildered intellect that thinks it is in control of everything and has no need of divine aid.

In another explanation, Shiva represents the Supreme Reality. The three demons are the three *gunas* or qualities of nature that bind the human being to the body. In fact the human body is the fortress of these three demons. These three *gunas* are known as *sattva, rajas* and *tamas. Sattva* has a golden city, *rajas* has a silver one and *tamas* an iron one. The one who wants liberation has to overcome all the three *gunas* or conditioning modes of nature. Shiva – the Supreme Spirit has to be invoked to slay the three demons.

Such legends remind us that human life is not to be wasted in material attainment but it is the field for our expansion to the highest state.

Once it is said that Ganesha, with the permission of his father set forth to Kashi or Varanasi. He disguised himself as an astrologer. Many people flocked to him for he had a wide knowledge of the subject. The queen of Kashi now requested her husband, Devadasa to be allowed to see this astrologer. Both of them went to the astrologer who told them that a Brahmin priest would come to them within eighteen days and they should abide by what he said. Having said this much Ganesha left Kashi and roamed around. Since he did not return to Kailasa, Shiva became a bit worried and requested Vishnu to go to Kashi and search for him. Vishnu, accompanied by Lakshmi went to

Kashi and went to see the king on the eighteenth day as prophesied by Ganesha. Devadasa welcomed the Brahmin, who was none other than Vishnu in disguise and begged him to give some advice. Vishnu told him that though he had all the qualities of a just king, he lacked one thing and that was that he had not invited Lord Shiva to take up his abode in his capital city. Devadasa was most penitent and built a magnificent temple to Shiva and spent the rest of his life in meditation and prayers to Shiva. Thus thanks to Ganesha, Kashi became the abode of Shiva and was blessed by him.

Once there was a demon called Bhanda who lived in Bhuvaneshwar. He approached the king and asked him for assistance in building a temple for Ganesha.

"Give me a hundred thousand gold coins and I shall build a magnificent temple to Ganesha. The spire will aspire to reach the heavens. On its completion I shall invite a hundred thousand Brahmins and lay the table for them with leaf plates and glasses of water."

The simple king handed over the required amount and the demon spent a very small part of the money and built a modest temple on a hill. He invited hundred thousand poor Brahmins but when they came he gave them water and then drove them away. The king was naturally incensed at this behaviour and called him to task.

The cheeky demon retorted, "I only promised that the temple spire would aspire to reach heaven but did not say anything about the size of the temple. I said I would invite a hundred thousand Brahmins and lay the table for them with leaves and give them water. I certainly did not say anything about feeding them! I have fulfilled both these promises!"

There was nothing that the poor king could do but to accept the fact that he had been neatly tricked by the clever demon.

The goddess eventually killed Bhanda in her incarnation as Lalitha. Even she had to invoke Ganesha's aid to kill him.

The image of Ganesha that was installed at this spot eventually came to be known as Bhanda Ganesha. This image was subsequently removed to the Jagannath temple at Puri where it still exists in the inner quadrangle.

There is an interesting story about the descent of the Ganga to the earth that is connected with Ganesha.

After Bhagiratha's *tapasya*, Ganga agreed to come to the earth but since the earth would not be able to endure her might, Shiva was requested to catch her in his locks. This he did without any problem and kept her there much to Parvati's annoyance. She could not bear the thought of his having a secret love tucked away in his locks that she could not even see. She begged Shiva to bring Ganga out into the open but he refused. She decided to consult her two sons, Ganesha and Kartikeya and begged them to help her.

They got together and thought of a master plan by which their father would agree to release Ganga. At that time Indra the god of rains let loose his entire stock of water so it kept raining for many years. All places except the *ashrama* of sage Gautama were devastated. Everyone rushed to his *ashrama* where he welcomed them and gave them food and shelter and kept them safe for a long time.

Ganesha and Kartikeya knew that if there was anyone who could influence their father it was the sage, Gautama. Ganesha requested Jaya, his mother's maid to transform herself into a cow and go to Gautama's *ashrama*. She was to pretend to be lame and emaciated. When the sages who were living in the *ashrama* saw this pitiable sight they decided to leave. Gautama begged them to remain but they said that they could not continue to stay in a place that was obviously having negative vibrations since one of the cows was in such a pathetic condition. Gautama promised to undertake any penance they decided to rectify this shortcoming in his *ashrama*.

In the meantime Ganesha, disguised as a Brahmin was sitting under the shade of a tree. The sages requested Gautama to approach him since he looked very wise. Gautama humbly approached the sage and asked him what he should do. Ganesha said that the only thing that would purify the place would be the water of the sacred Ganga. If she washed the feet of the dying cow all impurities would vanish. Gautama did severe *tapasya* to Lord Shiva and begged him to release the waters of the Ganga so that his *ashrama* would become pure and free of negativity.

Pleased with his worship, Shiva loosened his locks and allowed Ganga to come tumbling out much to Parvati's delight. Here again it was Ganesha's sagacity that enabled him to fulfil his mother's wish.

The late 11th century showed the rise of many great Shiva *bhaktas* known as Nayanmars who displayed an amazing ability to sacrifice themselves for the attainment of their personal deity. In the spiritual history of the world it would be difficult to find such matchless devotion to God as evinced by these sixty-three saints. Of these the greatest were four in number and were known as Appar, Sambandar, Sundarar and Manikkavachakar. The story of saint Auvaiyar Ma who was a great devotee of Lord Ganesha took place during this period.

She was abandoned by her parents at birth and adopted by a band of minstrels. She was very beautiful and had many suitors. Unlike normal girls who would have delighted in their beauty and the fact that they had suiters, she was desperately unhappy. She had no desire to wed any of them and cursed her beauty, which made her a cynosure in the eyes of all men. She beseeched Ganesha to take away her youth and beauty so that she could spend her life in his worship. Soon her skin wrinkled, her hair became grey, her brilliant eyes were dulled, her limbs stiffened and her breast sagged. She was overcome with joy and left her home and wandered far and wide in the kingdoms of Chola, Pandya and Chera. Her life was simple and dedicated to the worship of her favourite deity. She composed many poetic works. She was a contemporary of the noble Shiva *bhaktas,* Sundarar and Cheraman Perumal. Once when she was doing her *puja* she saw a vision of Sundarar and his friend the king being taken to Kailasa in a divine vehicle. She also wanted to join her spiritual friends and tried to rush through her rituals. At this Ganesha appeared before her and told her to finish her *puja* calmly as she had always done and he would fulfil her desire. At the end of her worship, she went into a trance as she normally did and composed one of her greatest hymns in praise of Ganesha called *Vinayaka Ahval.* As she finished it Ganesha appeared and lifted her in his trunk and wafted her off so that she reached Kailasa before her two friends arrived. Cheraman Perulmal asked her how she had reached before them and this is what she sang.

O king is there anything unattainable
By one who intensely concentrates
On the fragrant feet of the son of Ummaiyal (Ganesha),
Of sweet and comely speech?

"The thunderous thud of the swift elephant,
And that of the agile horse must give place,
To that of the rider of this old dame,
Who is none other than the mighty Mahaganapati."

ॐ *Gam Ganapataye Namaha!*

"May that kind hearted Lord who is capable of burning all the sins of the
Age of Kali,
Be gracious unto me.
By his grace the mute become eloquent and the lame climb mountains."

— Tulsidas

"I worship the son of Shankara in the morning to attain his grace. He is the
head of ganas and has a beautiful elephant face. He grants security to his devotees
and is like the forest fire which destroys the jungle of our problems. His divine
fire burns our ignorance and lights up the spark of knowledge in us."

ॐ
Vinayakaaya Namaha!

CHAPTER EIGHT

VINAYAKA

Forms of Ganesha

ॐ *Srim Hreem kleem,*
Ganeshwaraya Brahmaswarupaaya, charave,
Sarvam Siddhi pradeshaya,
Vighneshaya namo Namaha!

Salutations to Vighnesha,
Who is of the form of the Brahman,
Who is giver of all perfections.

Ganesha has many appellations that show that he is the remover of obstacles – Vigneshwara, Vignanayaka, Vignaraaja, etc. "Vighna" means obstacle. He is the God of wisdom, prudence and policy, all of which are essential for the one who wants to overcome the different types of obstacles that beset us in life. He is a product of both worldly astuteness and heavenly calm. He is the favourite of his mother Parvati, the goddess of the finite universe and the beloved son of Shiva, the all-pervading Supreme Consciousness.

In North India Ganesha is considered to be the second son of Shiva and Parvati but in South India he is said to be the eldest.

There are many stories connected with him in the *Upa Puranas* or subsidiary Puranas. In these Puranas, Ganesha is taken as an already existing Supreme deity who is invoked by a host of gods including Shiva, Parvati, Brahma and others for redeeming the world from *asuric* forces. The two Puranas, which describe in detail all the manifestations of Ganesha, are the *Ganesha Purana* and the *Mudgala Purana*.

Once a king called Abhinandana was performing a great *yajna*, in which he did not reserve a share of the offering for Indra, king of gods. Enraged by this, Indra called Kaala or the personification of Time and ordered him to destroy the *yajna* or sacrifice. Kaala knew that good deeds were always productive of good results and if he wanted to harm anyone he would have to first stop the person from performing holy deeds like *yajnas*. He assumed the form of a demon called Vighnasura. He killed Abhinandana and then started persecuting the holy people who were involved in pious acts. The sages sought the protection of Brahma. He told them to approach Ganesha since no one else had the power to destroy Kaala, the power of Time. Ganesha subdued Vighnasura who grovelled for mercy. Ganesha then made him subservient to him and assumed the title of Vighnaraja or Vighneshwara. He told Vighna that he could go and place obstacles in the way of anyone who performed a ritual without having first invoked Ganesha. This story has been related in the Vinayaka *Mahatmya* and the *Skanda* and *Mudgala Puranas*.

The *Ganesha Purana* describes four incarnations of Lord Ganesha in different forms, which took place in four separate *yugas* or epochs, in order to destroy the demonic forces and establish the equilibrium of the universe.

In the first epoch known as Krita he was incarnated as Mahotkata. His complexion was brilliant and he had ten hands and was mounted on a lion. In the *Treta Yuga* he was incarnated as Mayuresha mounted on a peacock. He had six hands and a fair complexion. In the *Dwapara Yuga* he incarnated as Gajaanana. He was crimson coloured and had four hands and was mounted on a mouse. His incarnation in this age of Kali is known as Dhoomraketu. He is smoky in colour and has two hands and is mounted on a horse. These incarnations were taken to annihilate certain types of *asuras*.

Once upon a time in the epoch known as *Krita*, there lived a *rishi* called Rudraketu and his wife Sharada. They lived on the banks of the river Ganga. They had two sons called Devantaka and Narantaka. They were strong and handsome and they decided to propitiate Lord Shiva and gain some boons from him. When Shiva appeared they requested that no one would be able to kill them whether god, angel, human, demon or animal. Shiva is known for being easily propitiated and he gave them the boon and thus turned them into veritable monsters. Narantaka assumed sovereignty over the nether worlds and over humans and Devantaka conquered the heavens and chased the gods off to the nether world. The unhappy gods did not know what to do and begged Shiva to help them. He said, "So be it".

Aditi is known to be the mother of the gods like Indra, Varuna, Vayu and so on. Once she approached her husband and begged him to instruct her in a vow by which the Supreme himself would come as her son so that she could have the honour of serving him. The sage then initiated her into the esoteric secret of meditation on Lord Vinayaka. She completed her vow successfully and Ganesha descended to the world as the son of Aditi and Kasyapa. They named him Mahotkata, or the strong one, since he was a really big and bonny baby. All the *rishi*s came to the *ashrama* to bless the baby. Some of the *asuras* also came disguised as human beings in order to kill the baby about whom they had heard. But the baby killed them all secretly when they went near him.

One day the king of Kashi went to the *ashrama* and requested Kasyapa to come and do the nuptial ceremony of his son. The sage was already engaged in a year-long vow and sent his son Mahotkata instead. On their way to Kashi while they passed through a forest, they found all the quarters blazing with a brilliant light. Mahotkata jumped out of the chariot and rushed to the light. The fierce demon called Dhumraksha had practised severe austerities and propitiated Surya, the sun god who had just come down and was in the act of giving a terrible weapon of destruction to the *asura*, which would make him invincible. The forest was lit up with the brilliance of this weapon, which would prove fatal to the world if given into the wrong hands. Mahotkata rushed to the spot and grabbed the weapon before the *asura* could get hold of it and threw it on the demon himself and killed him instantly. The king was amazed at this sight but refrained from asking too many questions.

They proceeded on their journey and reached the capital in good time and found that there were a few more weeks to go before the wedding took place. Mahotkata engaged himself in wrestling bouts and other sports in order to pass the time, much to the delight of the citizens.

The two demon brothers soon heard about this boy who seemed to have super-human skills. Narantaka decided to attack and kill the boy straightaway. Both the king and citizens were terrified but Mahotkata encouraged them to accompany him and routed the *asura* army and killed Narantaka.

Devantaka heard of the death of his brother and sent eight of his invincible generals to destroy the king's army. Mahotkata invoked the eight goddesses called Anima, Mahima, Garima, Laghima, Isitwa, Praapti and Praakasya who routed the demonic army with ease. These eight goddesses are the personifications of the great *siddhis* or supernormal powers that are at the beck and call of Lord Ganesha. Mahotkata now assumed his form as Ganesha and confronted Devantaka who had resorted to black magic rites. Devantaka grabbed hold of Ganesha's tusks. Ganesha threw him off but his hold was so strong that a piece of his tusk broke off. Ganesha now thrust the other tusk into the *asura's* body and killed him.

Narantaka and Devantaka stand for the divided mind of man that has both good and bad qualities. Narantaka is the one who rules the lower world of feelings, emotions, likes, dislikes and so on. *Nara* stands for "man". *Deva* means "god". The story is meant to show that the intellect can transcend these human qualities and rise to its divine status where virtues like nobility, unselfishness and courage predominate. Devantaka is the ruler of this realm. The Lord takes on an incarnation to enable people to rise above both these qualities and attain the highest state of the Supreme, which is above all the *gunas*.

The king and citizens were overjoyed. Ganesha resumed his form as Mahotkata and returned to his parents, Kasyapa and Aditi. He told them that the purpose of his incarnation was fulfilled and he had to return to his divine abode. The parents were filled with sorrow but he consoled them and promised that he would be present wherever the Divine Mother – Parvati was worshipped. With this promise he left the world.

In the second epoch known as Treta, there was a king called Chakrapani who ruled over the kingdom of Mithila. The king was very sad that he had no son to inherit the kingdom. The great sage Shaunaka initiated him into the esoteric secret of the worship of Surya, the sun god and told him and the queen to undertake a vow for a year. Very soon the queen became pregnant but during the first few months of her pregnancy she had severe pains and physical troubles. At last she could bear it no longer. She dared not tell her husband since she knew how much he longed to have a child. So she went secretly to the sea with her attendant and aborted the foetus into the water.

The sea god, Varuna nurtured the foetus and soon it turned into a muscular boy with a brilliant face and three eyes. The whole earth trembled when the monstrous child opened its mouth and howled. Varuna took the boy to the king and told him that it was his son.

The king was overjoyed and named the boy, Sindhu since he was born in the sea. After completing his studies the boy did severe *tapasya* and propitiated the sun god and procured from him a most powerful weapon of destruction. The king handed over his empire to his son and retired to the forest with his wife. Sindhu soon defeated all the kings of the earth and even extended his domain to the nether world and the heavens. He invoked Lord Vishnu and begged him to come and stay in his capital.

Hearing this Lord Shiva accompanied by Parvati and the *gana*s decided to go and settle in another place. As usual Shiva went into deep meditation. When he came out of it, Parvati asked him, "On whom are you meditating?"

He replied, "On the One who supports the entire universe."

Parvati begged to be initiated into the *mantra* for such a one and Shiva gave her the *bija mantra* for Ganesha – *gam*. She went to a lonely place on the hill and performed severe penance for twelve years. Ganesha appeared before her and asked her what she wanted.

She said, "I want you as my son so that I can serve you."

"So be it," he said and vanished from sight.

In due course on the fourth day of the bright half of the month of Bhadra, August/September, Lord Ganesha manifested himself before Parvati in all his glory. After giving her his divine vision he changed into a normal child. All the sages and gods arrived to bless the child and Shiva named him "Gunesha", which means the repository of all the *gunas* or noble qualities.

Once while he was playing with the other children in a mango grove, he came across a woman on top of a tree, who was guarding a big egg. The children were pelting mango seeds at each other and one of the seeds happened to fall on her. She was furious and jumped down and chased off the children. Gunesha climbed the tree and took the egg in his hands. It cracked open and out came a huge bird, which looked like a peacock. It hopped to the earth and started foraging for food. In fact it chased the boys and was all set to devour them. Gunesha jumped on the bird and brought it under his control. The woman returned and fell at his feet and said, "I am Vinata, wife of sage Kasyapa, mother of all birds. My husband has told me that the person who breaks this egg would become its master. I have been waiting here for years for this to happen. My other sons like Jatayu, Sampaati and Shyana are being held captive by powerful serpents in their kingdom. I would be grateful if you would kindly release them."

Gunesha agreed to this and mounted on his new vehicle, the peacock, he returned to his parents. He was re-named Mayuresha by the *rishi*s. *Mayura* means "peacock". He proceeded to the kingdom of the serpents and released the birds that had been kept captive there.

He then overcame a number of demons that had become powerful under the reign of the demon king, Sindhu. Seeing the wonderful powers of Mayuresha, Brahma offered his two daughters, Siddhi and Buddhi to him in marriage. He said he would marry them only after fulfilling his mission on earth.

Shiva and Parvati now decided to return to Kailasa. On the way they were attacked by the demonic hoards of Sindhu who was getting apprehensive about Mayuresha's feats. He sent his powerful sons Dharma and Adharma to defeat him. They were both killed and Sindhu himself entered the fray. Mayuresha killed him without more ado. With the annihilation of the demon, the cosmic balance was restored. It was only now that Mayuresha agreed to marry Siddhi and Buddhi.

It was time for Mayuresha to return to his celestial abode. Parvati asked him when he would appear before her again. He promised to return in the third epoch of *Dwapara* in order to kill the demon Sindur.

His younger brother, Kartikeya, begged him to take him with him. "Don't leave me alone," he cried.

Mayuresha said, "I am the inner consciousness in all beings so I am ever in your heart. I will never leave you." To comfort him, Mayuresha presented his peacock to Kartikeya and ascended to his imperishable abode.

Mounjikrishnajinadharam,
Nagayájnopavithinam,
Balenduvilasatmoulim,
Vandeham Gananaanaayakam.

"I bow to Lord Ganesha
Who is clad in deer skin,
Has a serpent as his sacred thread,
And wears the crescent moon on his forehead."

— *Sri Ganashtakam*

ॐ *Gam Ganapataye Namaha!*

"To him, whom the great sages disclose as the supreme single-syllabled sound – Aum, stainless, unconditioned, transcending the qualities, blissful, formless, the transcendent, beyond all beginnings, the very essence of the sacred texts, to that Primeval One I offer my adoration."

— Adi Shankaracharya

"Early in the morning I worship Lord Ganesha who is adored by all the gods including Indra. His cheeks are anointed with vermilion and he is the sole refuge for those who are helpless. His rod destroys all obstacles."

"I bow to the playful son of Shiva and Parvati in order to get his blessings. He has a pot belly and his sacred thread is a serpent. He grants all the desires of his devotees and is adored even by the four-faced Brahma."

CHAPTER NINE

DHUMRAKETU

Incarnations in other Epochs

Twam gunatrayatheeta,
Twam dehatryaatheeta,,
Twam avasthaatrayaatheeta,
Twam kaalatrayaatheeta!

O Lord! You are beyond the three gunas (sattva, rajas, tamas)
You are above the three bodies (causal, subtle and gross)
You are beyond the three states of consciousness (waking, dreaming
and deep sleep)
You are beyond the three periods of time (past, presnt and future)."

Now we come to the incarnation of Ganesha, which took place in the
epoch known as *Dwapara.* Once it is said that Shiva paid a visit to Brahma
who happened to be sleeping. He woke up and yawned and out of his open
mouth appeared a big, handsome boy. Very soon this form reached enormous
proportions. He raised his fists into the air and roared. The sound was enough
to churn the oceans and rend the clouds. Brahma was wonderstruck at this
apparition and asked him.

"Who are you and what do you want?"

The being replied, "Why do you ask me this question? I am your son since
I have emerged from your mouth. Give me a name and allot some duties
to me."

Brahma was delighted with his new son and said, "Since you have a pink
complexion I shall call you 'Sindur' and give you power over the three worlds.
You need not fear anyone and you are free to go wherever you like and choose

a place for your abode." He also gave him a boon that if he touched anyone in anger, the person would fall apart in his hands.

Sindur was very pleased with these boons and roamed about the three worlds spreading terror wherever he went. Soon he wanted to try out the success of the boon given to him by his doting father. He decided to try it out on Brahma himself and returned to his parental home. Brahma was shocked at his ingratitude and audacity and took to his heels without waiting to reason with him since he knew *asuras* to be unreasonable creatures. He reached Vaikunta, the abode of Vishnu and begged him to save him.

Vishnu stopped Sindur and said, "Calm down and remember he is your father and leave him alone."

Sindur promptly turned to Vishnu and said, "Well then you can fight with me since I'm itching for a good fight."

Vishnu very tactfully said, "Look I'm not the fighting type. You would be able to defeat me very easily. But there is someone called Shiva in Kailasa who would be worthy of your mettle so why don't you approach him!"

Sindur made a beeline to Kailasa but when he saw Lord Shiva, with matted hair, clad in a tiger skin and immersed in deep meditation, he thought he was an ordinary mendicant and not a worthy opponent. Just then he saw Parvati and decided that she was a fitting mate for him. The *gana*s tried to stop him as he carried her away but they were no match for Sindur. Parvati invoked Mayuresha, who appeared instantly and vanquished the demon and sent him, hurtling to the nether regions. He then assured Parvati that he would be born as her son as he had promised her in another age and kill Sindur.

Sindur like all *asuras,* is the personification of brute force and blunt intellect. He collected his demonic hoard and started harassing all the worlds. All noble people fled to the mountains and caves. The gods begged Lord Ganesha to take another incarnation and save them from this new threat.

Parvati became pregnant and she told Shiva that she would like to go to the plains and get her child. Shiva took her to a beautiful lake surrounded by woods and the celestial couple decided to live there. Very soon she delivered a beautiful, bonny boy. As soon as he was born, he showed her his resplendent divine form. She requested him to become an infant once again so that she could cuddle and hug him. But the child transformed himself into a strange specimen. It had a bulging head, small eyes, ears like winnows, and nose like the trunk of an elephant. It was pot-bellied and had four arms, short legs and a red complexion. Parvati felt very sad to see this form and was wondering how she could show the infant to the people who had come to see him. While she was wondering thus, Shiva came and consoled her, "Don't you remember the promise made by Mayuresha that he would be born to you in an elephant-headed form in order to kill the demon Sindur?"

The child turned to Parvati and said, "What my father said is true. My name is Gajanana and I have come to kill Sindur as I promised you. But now you have to transport me to the labour room of queen Pushpika in the city of Mahishmati. She has just given birth but a demoness has stolen the baby. Before the queen regains consciousness place me by her side for I have promised her that I would be born as her son."

Lord Shiva summoned Nandi and told him to take the child and place him beside the unconscious queen. When the queen woke up and saw the strange misshapen figure of her son she was aghast, as were all the people who came to see the child. The astrologer predicted that the child would cause the destruction of their dynasty. So the people took the baby to a deep forest and abandoned it there.

The sage Parashara had his *ashrama* in that forest. He saw the baby and recognized the signs of divinity in him and took it home to his wife. They brought up the child with great love. Seeing this Shiva and Parvati were happy and returned to Kailasa.

The *rishi* now imparted all his knowledge to his son. When he was nine years old a monstrous mouse appeared in the forest and started to destroy everything. Even the bigger animals were frightened of him since he was so huge. The sage did not know what to do but as soon as the mouse saw Gajanana, it disappeared into a burrow. Gajanana threw a noose into the hole and captured the mouse and dragged it out. He then mounted the mouse and made it his vehicle.

The mouse now narrated his tale. "I was once a Gandharva (celestial singer). Once when I was coming out of Indra's audience hall I stepped on the sage, Vamana who has a very short stature. He cursed me to be born as a mouse. When I appealed to him to mitigate the curse, he told me not to worry and that I would meet Lord Gajanana in sage Parashara's *ashrama* and would become his vehicle and thus be worshipped by everyone."

Gajanana now took leave of his foster parents and set out to fulfil his mission. He armed himself with a goad used by elephant trainers to subdue their elephants, a noose, an axe and a lotus flower in his four hands. Riding on his mouse, he went to Sindur's citadel and challenged him to fight. In the fight that followed Gajanana strangled the demon with his powerful hands. The gods and sages sang his praises. The king and queen of Mahismati who had abandoned him due to his ugliness now repented and fell at his feet and asked him to pardon them. Gajanana gave them a discourse, which is known as the "Ganesha Gita" and contains the essence of *Samkhya Yoga*. After thus instructing them, he returned to his celestial abode.

The epoch in which we are now living is known as the *Kali Yuga*. In this age Lord Ganesha is supposed to incarnate himself as Dhumraketu (the comet), riding on a horse. This is very similar to the incarnation of Lord Vishnu as Kalki, who is also mounted on a horse. He is supposed to come in this very epoch. The age of *Kali* is a decadent one in which terror and violence are the order of the day as we are seeing now. The Lord is supposed to come and rescue the earth from total annihilation.

These *yugas* or epochs are not merely cosmic events but also denote the upheavals that take place on the individual level. The three *gunas* called *sattva, rajas* and *tamas* are always present in creation. These are the basic strands or qualities of Nature by whose combinations and permutations, numerous differences are created both in the universe and in individuals. *Rajas* is the quality of kinesis or action, *tamas* is its opposite of inertia or laziness and *sattva* is the quality of balance and equilibrium. In the Krita Yuga, *sattva* is in preponderance and the minds of people are calm and peaceful and inclined towards spiritual activities. In Treta Yuga, *sattva* is mixed with some *rajas* so people become more active but since there is a strong vein of *sattva* in them their activities are based on *dharma* and righteousness. Hence we find the incarnation of Sri Rama in Treta Yuga, who was the very soul of *dharma* even though he was very active. When *sattva* is mixed with both *rajas* and *tamas* we find that actions are less *dharmic* and there is pride, hypocrisy and greed. This is what happens in the age of *Dwapara*. In this age of *Kali* there is very little of *sattva* and more of *rajas* and *tamas*. Hence we find indolence, fear and delusion, cunning and cruelty. Noble people are rare in this age, whereas cruel, greedy and selfish people are found in plenty. Both on the national and international level as well as on the individual level we pass through these epochs. Of course human nature being an admixture of all these three *gunas*, a certain amount of ups and downs is common in the life of all epochs but when they reach devastating heights and degrading depths, the Supreme Lord is forced to take a hand and manifest himself to restore the balance. This takes place in every age.

Sindur is the typical example of an *asura*. *Asuras* are prepared to do hard work and persevere without respite in the field of worldly achievements. Since he was an *asura* Sindur was filled with equal portions of *rajas* and *tamas*. The normal pattern that we find in life is that material glory fosters arrogance, which in turn brings about its own downfall.

The various *asuras* that form the army of these demons represent the demonic forces created in our mind by our *rajasic* and *tamasic* tendencies.

The stories of the Lord's incarnations are meant to be studied so that we can relate to their esoteric secrets and try to change our own natures according to the examples given.

Chitraratna vichitrangam,
Chitramalavibhushitam,
Chitrarupadharam devam,
Vandeham Gananayakam

"I bow to Lord Ganesha,
Who is adorned with many splendoured jewels,
Who wears garlands with multi-coloured flowers,
Who takes on multifarious forms."

— *Sri Ganashtakam*

ॐ *Gam Ganapataye Namaha!*

ॐ

Ganadyakshaaya Namaha!

CHAPTER TEN

GANADYAKSHA

The Eight Passions

Twam Mulaadharasthitosi nityam,
Twam shaktitrayaatmakam,
Twaam yogino dhyayanti nityam!

All three great powers are invested in you (creation, maintenance, destruction)
You have a permanent abode in the Muladhara Chakra.
Yogis constantly meditate on you.

The eight negative emotions are *kaama, krodha, lobha, moha, mada, matsarya, mamta* ॐ
and *abhimaana*. Each of these have been personified in the poetic manner that
is peculiar to the Puranas in order to make us aware of them and also to
teach us how important it is to seek divine aid to subdue them.

The *Mudgala Purana* enumerates eight important incarnations of Lord
Ganesha. Each of these incarnations was taken to kill a particular demon. But
we find these eight *asuras* are actually the eight human passions that wreck our
spiritual life. As Ekadanta, he vanquished *mada* or arrogance, as Vakrathunda,
he subdued *matsara* or jealousy, as Mahodara he vanquished *moha* or illusion
and infatuation, as Gajanana he subdued *lobha* or greed, as Lambodara he killed
krodha or anger, as Vikata he killed *kama* or lust, as Vignaraaja he vanquished
mamta or ego, and as Dhumravarna he vanquished *abhimaana* or pride. Each
of these has a story connected to it.

In these incarnations we find that he does not totally annihilate these *asuras*
but merely brings them to heel. This is because most of these emotions have
a positive as well as a negative side to them. The positive side can actually
help us in our spiritual progress. The mind can never be totally emptied of

all these human passions. All we can do is to shine the light of our awareness on them and thus bring them into our conscious mind. This is the only way to bring them under our control. For example, *kama* or lust for material things can be turned into love or desire for God.

Once a demon called Matsara (jealousy) was born out of the Indra's pride. He performed penance to Shiva and got the boon of fearlessness from him. He was made the king of the *asuras* and defeated the gods and chased them out of heaven. They went to Kailasa and prayed to Shiva to protect them. On hearing this Matsara had the audacity to go to Kailasa and challenge Shiva. Vishnu advised the gods to pray to Ganesha in the form of Vakratunda and gave them the esoteric *mantra – gam*. All the gods including Shiva worshipped Vakratunda who promised to help them. When Matsara saw Vakratunda he was so terrified that he sought refuge at his feet. The Lord forgave him and kept him under his control and gave back their lost kingdom to the gods.

It was the famous sage Chyavana who created Madasura (arrogance). His wife's name was Salasa (indolence), a fitting mate for arrogance! Sukracharya, the preceptor of the *asuras* was Chyavana's brother so he sent Madasura to him for instruction. At the end of his period of learning, Madasura told his *guru* that he wanted to become the ruler of the whole universe. Shukracharya initiated him into the Devi *mantra – hreem*. After doing *tapasya* for thousands of years the goddess appeared and granted his wish. This was the signal for him to rampage across the whole universe and bring the gods and humans under his control. The worried gods approached the sage, Sanat Kumara and asked his advice. He told them to seek the protection of Lord Ganesha as Ekadanta.

The gods meditated on Ekadanta for many years until he appeared and assured them that he would bring the *asura* to heel. The celestial sage Narada, who is noted for his tactics in instigating the Lord to make a fast appearance, approached Madasura and urged him to take up arms against Ekadanta before he slew him. Nothing loathe the demon marched to the battlefield filled with rage but the moment he saw the fearful form of Ekadanta, he became as meek as a puppy dog and grovelled at the feet of the Lord.

Ekadanta spared his life and told him, "Never enter the heart of one who has surrendered to me and is worshipping me with the correct attitude. However you may torment those who do actions with selfish desires."

Tarakasura was a terrible demon that had a boon that only the son of Shiva could kill him, so the gods went to Kailasa and begged Parvati to help them. She took on the form of a tribal woman and wandered around the place where Shiva was sitting in deep meditation. She scattered intoxicating flowers and luscious fruits around him. At last he opened his eyes and looked piercingly at the woman who had dared to disturb him. She vanished and in her place there appeared a powerful male form.

This was the demon called Mohasura (infatuation). Before Shiva could annihilate him, Sukracharya, the preceptor of the demons whisked him away and initiated him into the *mantra* of the sun god. After practising severe austerities, the sun god appeared and gave him the boons of fearlessness and invincibility. Immediately Mohasura defeated the gods and humans and assumed control over heaven and earth. The gods went to the sun god and begged him to help them. He gave them the method of invoking Ganesha in his form as Mahodara. Pleased with their penance, Lord Mahodara appeared and granted them freedom from *Moha* (infatuation). He then proceeded to the capital city of the *asura* who surrendered to him without a murmur.

Once, Kubera, the king of the *yakshas* who were the guardians of wealth, visited Kailasa. Parvati was so beautiful that Kubera could not take his eyes off her. Parvati was quite angry and Kubera became very frightened. Out of his fear the demon known as Lobhasura (greed) manifested. He descended to the world of the *asuras*, where their preceptor Sukracharya initiated him into the five-syllabled *mantra* of Lord Shiva. The *asura* performed severe penance until Shiva manifested before him and gave him the boon of fearlessness. Lobha, true to his race now ran around all the worlds and conquered everyone. Greed always has an easy victory wherever he goes! He even had the audacity to send a declaration to Shiva to quit Kailasa since he wanted to rule over it. (Greed has no limits!) Shiva laughingly agreed and left Kailasa. The gods now approached the sage Raibhya who told them to pray to Ganesha in the form of Gajanana. He promised to help them and sent Lord Vishnu to the demon to persuade him to surrender himself to Gajanana. Vishnu who is noted for his diplomacy, managed to convince Lobhasura who surrendered without further ado.

Thus we see that the negative emotions can only be vanquished with the help of the divine. Ganesha is one who is ever ready to help the devotees who ask him to help them overcome their lower emotions.

"Praise to thee O Ganesha! Thou art manifestly the Truth.

Thou art undoubtedly the Creator, the Preserver and the Destroyer, the Supreme Brahman, the eternal Spirit.

By thee was this universe manifested.

Thou art Brahma, Vishnu and Rudra.

Thou are earth, water, fire, air and ether.

We acknowledge thy divinity O Ekadanta!

Protect me while speaking, listening, giving, possessing, teaching and learning at all times and everywhere.

He who continually meditates on thy divine form,

Conceiving it to be with one tusk, four hands, of red hue, with a large belly,

Anointed with red perfumes, arrayed in red garments, worshipped with red flowers,

With a mouse as thy banner and vehicle,

Such a one becomes the most excellent of *yogis*.

Praise to thee O Ganapati,

Thou art abounding in compassion, the cause of this universe,

Imperishable, unproduced and unaffected by creation."

— *Ganapati Upanishad*

ॐ *Gam Ganapataye Namaha!*

"The devotee should first bow to the great god, Ganesha, the son of Parvati and chant the twelve names of the Lord, dwelling in the heart of his devotees, in order to get good health, long life and material benefits."

CHAPTER ELEVEN

PHALACHANDRA

Conquest of the Passions

Pranamya shirasa devam Gouriputram Vinayakam,
Bhaktaavaasam Smarennityam,
Ayur kaamarthasiddhaye

Bow to Lord Ganesha, the son of Gauri (Parvati),
Think constantly of Him who dwells in the heart of his devotees,
And you will get good health, long life and the fulfilment of all desires.

During the time of the churning of the milky ocean, the pot of nectar was
stolen by the demons. In order to retrieve the nectar, Vishnu took on the form
of Mohini – the enchantress. Vishnu's *maya* is so powerful that even though
he was the one who had destroyed Cupid, Shiva fell for Mohini's charms.
Vishnu immediately gave up his female form and assumed his own form. Shiva
became very disappointed. Out of the furrows on his brow was born the
demon known as Krodha (anger). He invoked the power of the sun and became
invincible. He married and begot two daughters known as Harsha (happiness)
and Shoka (sorrow).

The gods at last invoked the grace of Lord Ganesha who came in the
form of Lambodara and subdued Krodha.

Ganesha is noted for his wisdom and calm disposition. Nothing disturbs
the even tenour of his mind. His passions are totally under control. Hence he
is the one who we have to approach to curb our negative passions, especially
anger.

Once there was a demon called Kamasura. He was the embodiment of
lust. He was born of Lord Vishnu's seed. He performed severe austerities to

Lord Shiva and propitiated him. He became the supreme ruler of the three worlds. He married a woman called Trishna (thirst). The gods approached *rishi* Mudgala and begged him to tell them how to subdue this demon. He advised them to meditate on the *mantra*, "ॐ" at a place called Mayuresha. Pleased with their devotion, Lord Ganesha took the *avatara* known as Vikata and brought the demon to heel.

One day Parvati was in a playful mood. She burst into a peal of laughter at the jokes of her friends. A handsome male form was born of her laughter. He prostrated to his mother and asked her to order him to serve her. She was surprised to see him and asked him to explain how he had appeared there. He said he was born of her laughter. She named him "Mama" which means, "my" and comes from the ego.

The word "I" as it is commonly used is actually the illusory self. It is not the real Self that is identical with the Supreme Self. This illusory self becomes the basis of all our misinterpretations of reality. Our attachments to the words "me" and "mine" actually constitute the whole world of *maya*. That is why Hindu philosophy says *ahamtwa* or "I-ness" and *mamatwa* or "mine-ness" is the root cause of the human problem. These words are fraught with a deep sense of isolation. They cut you off from the rest of creation and confine you within an illusory world that belongs to you alone and has to be guarded at all costs from intrusion by others. This is true both on the individual level as well as the international level. Just as "my" body and "my" things have to be protected from others so also "my" country and my "nation" are sacrosanct and no other nation may cross my border without sanction. Objects, which are connected with "me", have great value in my mind even if they are actually worthless. In themselves these objects have no intrinsic value. Their value arises only from the fact that they belong to "me". As is the case of all puranic stories, these negative traits are depicted in the personality of an *asura* who can be subdued only with the grace of God. This becomes very obvious to us when we analyse the structure of the ego and the million ways in which it can trap us into believing that "I" am the greatest and that everything that belongs to "me" is also intrinsically precious.

The person created by Parvati retired to the forest to meditate on Lord Ganesha. On the way he met the fierce demon called Sambara who lured him away from this desire and initiated him into the *asuric* cult. Thus, Mama who had an angelic disposition now became the *asura* known as Mamasura. He married a woman called Mohini from the *asuric* clan and in due course became the ruler of the three worlds. This again is the basis of a great truth. When the ego by some chance decides that it should have recourse to God alone, it happens that it is tempted by the woman "Mohini" in the form of so many alluring objects which it can possess and which it eventually gets possessed by. The gods as usual propitiated Lord Ganesha in order to curb the arrogance of this *asura*. Ganesha incarnated as Vighnaraja and subdued Mamasura and once more established the reign of peace and righteousness.

Brahma had bestowed on Surya, the sun god, the name Karma Raja or the Lord of all activities. After some time it occurred to Surya that now he was literally the Lord of the three worlds since all the worlds are governed by *karma*. As this thought came into his mind, he sneezed and out of his sneeze was born the demon that came to be known as "Aham" which means "I" and is the first emergence of the ego.

He meditated on Lord Ganesha who appeared before him in the form of Dhumravarna and blessed him. He became the ruler of the three worlds. He married a woman called Mamta, which means "mineness". As we have seen this is the beginning of the human bondage. One of the most ludicrous aspects of this sense of possession is the possession of land. If god laughs loudly, it must be when he hears a man say, "This land is mine". This is most obvious yet people fight and quarrel and kill for the sake of "their land". This happens both on the individual field as well as on an international field. If and when we get tired of the demonic rule of these two *asuras* "Aham" and "Mamta", we can approach Ganesha and he will rescue us from their tyrannical hold. When the gods tired of this demonic rule they begged Ganesha to help them. The Lord came in the form of Dhumravarna and subdued him.

As we can see all the demons mentioned in these stories as well as their wives and children are allegorical representations of the worst types of negative traits found in the human mind. They form the citadel of the ego and are the basis of our bondage to the body. These stories show how they can be subdued with the help of Lord Ganesha. It is interesting to note that in all these stories, the Lord does not kill the demon but merely subdues him. This is because these traits are the ones that initially help us to establish our identity in this world. Without these traits we would have no personality and would consequently be very dull. But when these traits get out of control they turn into demons and ruin our lives.

When these traits make us forget the "Person" underlying the "personality", we are in trouble. The cause of all suffering in the human being is the fact that we have allowed the "Person" to be obliterated by the "personality". This is a universal dysfunction and the very basis of the human predicament. We have totally forgotten the "Person" and completely identified with the "personality". This is like a man who has forgotton his own abode and chooses to wander about in the market place engrossed in the many enticing objects he finds there. Deep down within him there is a gnawing pain, which he attributes to the fact that he doesn't have enough objects. So he continues to buy more and more objects but never succeeds in eradicating the pain, which is caused by the fact that he has forgotten his real home. Until we return to our true abode we can never know the meaning of peace of happiness.

Mushikothamamaaruhya,
Devasuramhohavea,
Yodhukaamam mahaveeryam,
Vandeham Gananaayakam

"I bow to Lord Ganesha,
Who is filled with infinite powers,
Who loves to fight,
Who is seated on his vehicle, the rat,
And takes part in the battles between the gods and the demons."

— *Sri Ganaashtakam*

ॐ *Gam Ganapathaye Namaha!*

ॐ

Gajananaaya Namaha!

CHAPTER TWELVE

GAJANANA

Eight Temples

Namo vraatapathaye,
Namo Ganapathaye,
Nama pramathapathaye,
Namasthesthu lambodaraaya, Ekadantaaya,
Vighnanaashine, Shivasuthaya,
Sri varadamurthaye Namaha!

My salutations to Vrataapati, to Ganapati,
My salutations to Pramathapati,
My salutations to Lambodara, Ekadanta, Vighnanashin, the son of Shiva,
Salutations again and again to Varadamurti.

Ganesha is the most revered deity in Maharashtra. There are eight very important temples here that are exclusively for him and are most sacred to all his devotees. These eight temples are known as the Ashtavinayakas or the eight Vinayakas. His image is said to have sprung up of its own accord (*swayambhu*) at these places.

The idols in all these temples are not very elaborately carved. His face is shown only in a broad outline and is heavily smeared with vermillion powder which has been applied over and over again through the centuries so as to form a thick coating, thus hiding the details of the idol beneath.

The eight icons are located in scenic spots scattered over three districts of West Maharashtra. In olden days it took at least eight days to visit all of them but today one can complete the pilgrimage in three days. To wipe out our *karmas* of a past life we are asked to walk or go by 3rd class compartment to each of these temples in succession. Such penances are capable of condensing into a short period of time, those *karmas* which would normally take many births to work out.

The first of these eight temples are the Morgaon temple dedicated to Sri Mayureshwara. It is sixty-four kilometres from Pune and is on the banks of the river Karha. The village has a lot of peacocks, hence its name. "Mor" in Hindi means peacock. The idol is seated with the trunk turned to the left. He has diamonds for his eyes. Due to the thick application of vermillion the original idol is hardly to be seen. However once in about hundred years the coating comes off and the original idol is revealed. The last time this happened was in the year 1882. There is a Nandi or bull of Shiva here which is facing the idol of Ganesha. The story goes that while this Nandi was being transported to a Shiva temple, the cart which was carrying it, broke down in front of the Ganesha temple and the idol refused to budge despite all efforts to dislodge it. It was therefore installed there.

The legend concerning this temple is very interesting. Once upon a time there was a city called Gandaki ruled by a king called Chakrapani. He had no children so he worshipped the sun god and got a son called Sindhu. The boy also worshipped the sun and was blessed with immortality. He conquered all the kings of the earth and then turned his attention to the heavens. He overcame Indra and Vishnu and started to proceed towards Kailasa. The gods prayed to Ganesha to stop his progress. Ganesha incarnated himself as the son of Parvati and fought with Sindhu. He cut his body into three pieces. The head fell near Morgaon and the temple to Ganesha was constructed at that spot. Lord Ganesha was riding on a peacock during the battle and came to be known as Mayureshwara ("mayura" means peacock in Sanskrit).

The next temple is the Sri Siddhivinayaka temple of Siddhatek. *Siddhi* means "spiritual perfection" so this place is one which can give us spiritual excellence. It is a hundred and one kilometres from Pune and is on the banks of the river Bhima. The idol is seated facing north with its trunk curled to the right.

Many sages are supposed to have worshipped Lord Ganesha here and attained *siddhi*. The sanctum sanctorum is said to have been built by Queen Ahalyabai Holkar.

An interesting story is connected with this temple. The Creator, Brahma is always seated on the lotus that comes from the navel of Lord Vishnu. Once it happened that two demons called Madhu and Kaitabha emerged from a pellet of wax and a drop of honey that fell from Vishnu's ears. They challenged Brahma to fight. He begged Vishnu to help him. The demons proved to be too powerful for even Vishnu so he started to worship Lord Ganesha using the *mantra – Aum Sri Ganeshaya Namaha*! Ganesha gave him the power to kill the demons. The place where Vishnu attained *siddhi* came to be known as Siddhatek and Lord Ganesha was given the name Siddhi Vinayaka.

The third temple in this list is the one to Sri Balleshwar in the place called Pali, which is a hundred and ten kilometres from Pune. The idol is about three feet high and is facing east. There is another small idol of Ganesha at the back of this temple known as Dhundi Vinayaka that is supposed to be the original idol and is said to be *swayambhu*. Everyday the first *puja* is performed here before it is done to the main idol.

There is an interesting story connected with this temple. Once there was a grocer called Kalyan who lived with his wife and son Ballal. The boy was always engrossed in worshipping Ganesha. Very soon his friends were inspired to follow his example. This worried the villagers who felt that their children were neglecting their duties. They complained to the grocer who became very angry. He went to the forest where he found his son in deep meditation. When they saw the approach of the irate father, his friends ran away. The father smashed the idol of Ganesha in front of his son and thrashed the boy without mercy. He tied him to a tree and left him to be eaten by wild animals. However it was inconceivable that Lord Ganesha would let his devotee suffer. He took the form of a Brahmin and freed Ballal and healed his wounds.

Ballal recognised him to be none other that his favourite deity and became quite ecstatic. The Lord asked him to choose a boon. Ballal requested him to remain forever in that forest. The Brahmin disappeared and in his place there appeared a big black rock with the form of Ganesha carved on it. The deity came to be known as Sri Balleshwar Vinayaka after his great devotee.

The story about the fourth temple is also interesting. Once in the country of Vidharba there was a king called Bhima who was very brave. With the blessings of Lord Ganesha he got a son who was equally devoted to Ganesha.

He was called Rukmangada. Once while hunting he felt very thirsty and went to the *ashrama* of the sage, Vachkni. The *rishi's* wife became infatuated with him and solicited him. When the king repulsed her she cursed him that he would become a leper. The dejected prince performed austerities for many years to get rid of the effects of the curse. The sage Narada happened to pass that way and told him to take a dip in the lake called Kadamba. The prince did so and was completely cured. Indra, the king of the gods came to know of the *rishi's* wife's desire. He disguised himself as Rukmangada and procreated a son on her. The boy was filled with all noble qualities but was belittled by people because of his dubious birth.

He retired to the forest and performed strict *tapasya* standing on one toe and eating only dried leaves. Finally Ganesha appeared and gave him a boon or *vara* due to which he became a renowned *rishi*. Since Ganesha had given him a boon or *vara* at that place, he became famous as Varad Vinayaka — the Lord who bestows boons. This temple is situated in the town of Mahad, which is about one kilometre off the main road connecting Pune and Khapoli. The temple faces east and is carved of stone. There is a small pond behind the temple from which the present idol of Lord Varad Vinayaka is supposed to have been recovered in the year 1690.

The Thevoor temple to Sri Chintamani, is one of the most famous of the eight temples. It is situated on the banks of the river Mula-mutha that flows through the city of Pune. It is only twenty-two kilometres from Pune. The temple's main entrance is to the north but the idol faces east. It has a lot of historic importance also. The secret meetings of the Maratha rulers used to take place here during the Mughal period.

There are quite a few legends connected with this temple and why the Lord got the name, Chintamani. Prince Gana, the son of King Abhijeet was a brave warrior. Once he went to visit a great sage called Kapila Muni and saw a fantastic jewel called *chintamani* with him. This was the fabled stone, which was capable of fulfilling all the wishes of its owner. The prince coveted the jewel and asked the *rishi* to give it to him. When the sage refused, the haughty prince snatched it from him. Kapila was a devotee of Ganesha and appealed to Ganesha, who promised to get the jewel back for him. He killed Gana and brought the jewel to its rightful owner. However, Kapila refused to accept the jewel and begged

Ganesha to remain at this place instead. Ganesha agreed and remained beneath a Kadamba tree and took the name of Chintamani Vinayaka. The village came to be known as Kadamba Tirth.

The place called Lenyadri is about two hundred kilometres from Mumbai. It is on the top of a hill and one has to trek five kilometres from the village of Junnar. From here there is a climb of two hundred and eighty-three steps to the temple. Lenyadri means a mountain cave and the temple is carved on the slope of the mountain. It has a huge hall of about fifty-four feet tunnelled into the mountain with no pillars to support it. The idol looks quite shapeless and it is said that the Lord is sitting with his back to the entrance and is actually facing the other side. Many efforts have been made to dig from the other side in order to see the face but none of them have succeeded so far. There are about eighteen caves in this mountain but all are in total darkness.

The legend connected with this temple goes like this. One of the names of Parvati is Girija (the one who is born in the mountain). She desired to have Ganesha as her son. She practised *tapasya* for twelve years at this place. Ganesha agreed to become her son. The legend goes that he was born to her at this spot where the present temple is situated and spent fifteen years with his mother in these caves. Hence he is known here as Girijatmaja or the son of Girija. There is a large forest near the mountain, which was infested with demons that used to assault the sages and disturb their rituals. Ganesha destroyed them and allowed the sages to continue their worship unmolested.

The next temple in this series is the one of Vighneshwara at Ozar. It faces east. Once there was a king called Abhinandan. He wanted to perform a *yaga* (fire sacrifice) and conquer the heavens. When Indra, the king of the gods came to know of this he enlisted the support of the demon called Vighnasura, whose main job was to disturb the rituals of the sages and ordered him to obstruct the *yagya*. The king begged Ganesha to help him. Ganesha vanquished the demon that fell at his feet and begged for mercy. Ganesha forgave him and agreed to his request that the Lord should stay there and couple his name along with his. The place where he was defeated was Ozar and the idol here came to be known as Vighneshwara Vinayaka, the conqueror of Vighnasura.

The last temple in this series is the Sri Maha Ganapati temple at Ranjangaon. This town is fifty kilometres from Pune. The temple faces east. There is a basement below the temple in which you find a small idol of Ganesha with twenty hands and ten trunks. Apparently this is the original idol.

A man called Grudsamad was a great devotee of Ganesha. He had a son who was keen to conquer all the three worlds. His father told him to pray to Lord Gajanana if he wanted to be blessed. After a period of intense *tapasya*, Ganesha appeared to him and granted his wish that no one except Shiva would be able to destroy him. He also gave him three cities of steel, silver and gold and he became the demon known as Tripurasura. The *Shiva Purana* gives another version of this story. However, needless to say Tripura started to humiliate the gods and humans till finally they were forced to approach Shiva and beg him to kill the demon. Shiva had to worship Ganesha before he was able to kill the *asura*. The place where Shiva prayed to Ganesha came to be known as Ranjangaon.

A pilgrmage to all these eight temples is supposed to be a cure for all types of problems.

Sarvavigna haram devam,
Sarvavigna vivarjitam,
Sarva siddhi pradhataram,
Vandeham Gananayakam

"I worship Lord Ganesha,
Who removes all obstacles,
Who gives all siddhis (spiritual perfections)."

— *Sri Ganashtakam*

ॐ *Gam Ganapataye Namaha!*

CHAPTER THIRTEEN

VAKRATUNDA

Pujas for Ganesha

Jagat kaaranam,
Kaarana-jnanarupam,
Suraadim Sukhadim
Gunesham, Ganesham.
Jagatvyapinam,
Vishwavandyam suresham,
Parabrahma rupam,
Ganesham bhajema

We worship Thee who art the cause of the world,
The primal knowledge,
The origin of the gods,
The origin of bliss,
The Lord of gunas and the Lord of ganas
Thou pervadest the universe and art worshipped by all,
Thou art indeed the Lord of gods – the Supreme Brahman.

Bhakti is the Sanskrit word for devotion or love for the Supreme in all its many aspects. Worship of the form is often considered a lower method of contacting the divine. But Hindu *tantric* psychology has confirmed that it is a most scientific means to attain communion with the godhead as expressed in that particular form, which is being worshipped. It is not blind faith, as some would describe it. In fact blind faith leads to fanaticism and that is how all problems between religions arise. In Hindu devotional practices however the divinity within you is invoked and placed into the idol before you so that the idol becomes impregnated with the qualities of not just the deity but of the

Supreme. The mind expands and attunes to the cosmic wavelength and this in turn leads to our spiritual transformation. For many of us the idol is an effective means for invoking the Supreme. It is a wonderful tool for cultivating devotion. The devotee does not see the stone or the metal, which makes the idol but only feels the divine essence represented by it.

The method of making idols and their installation in temples is a special science discovered by the sages. After the installation there is a technique by which the deity is invoked and life is breathed into the idol. This is an esoteric secret known only to the initiates. These idols were installed in temples in order to help us to commune easily with God. The myriad forms you find in Hindu mythology embody different aspects of the divine power. When we worship the form of Ganesha we activate the obstacle-removing power of the Supreme and this influences our own life in a positive manner. Thus, idols are an effective as well as a beautiful means for bringing us closer to the Divine.

Every aspect of life vibrates to a certain throb that emanates from the primeval sound of "ॐ". Their permutations and combinations give rise to the infinite variety of forms. The fifty-one letters of the Sanskrit alphabet are symbolic representations of these major vibratory states. The science of *mantra*s is based on these letters and their corresponding sounds.

Ganesha, who represents the sound of "ॐ", is said to have fifty-one manifestations corresponding to the letters of the Sanskrit alphabet each symbolizing one divine power. Of these thirty-two are considered as very important aspects of Ganesha and allow us to realize most of our aspirations. Out of these the first sixteen known as the Shodasha Ganapatis are said to be the most powerful. Each of them has a special body colour and insignia.

Their names are given below:

1. Bala Ganapati.   The Boy Ganesha
2. Taruna Ganapati.   The Youthful Ganesha
3. Bhakta Ganapati.   The Ganesha of the Devotees
4. Veera Ganapati.   The Heroic Ganesha
5. Shakti Ganapati.   The Strong Ganesha
6. Dwija Ganapati.   The Twice-born Ganesha
7. Siddhi Ganapati.   Possessing Supernormal Powers

8.	Uchishta Ganapati.	The One Who is Worshipped through non-Vedic Rites
9.	Vignaraja Ganapati.	The Lord of Obstacles
10.	Kshipra Ganapati.	The One Who is Easily Pleased
11.	Heramba Ganapati.	Protector of the Weak
12.	Lakshmi Ganapti.	One Who is Joined with Lakshmi
13.	Maha Ganapati.	The Great Ganapati
14.	Vijaya Ganapati.	The Victorious Ganapati
15.	Nritala Ganapati.	The Dancing Ganesha
16.	Urdwa Ganapati.	The One Above

The main purpose of these forms is to evoke a type of mood in the devotee's mind that will enable him to attain certain exalted states of consciousness. But this does not mean that they are rigid. When one concentrates with great devotion on any one aspect naturally the other powers are also activated. Each form has a *dhyana sloka* or meditative hymn attached to it, which is meant to invoke a certain spiritual *bhava* or emotion in the devotee. This *bhava* or mental mood enables the limited human ego to efface itself and submit to the will of the universal ego. When the *pujari* or priest has completely submerged his ego in the universal ego, he is able to commune directly with the deity and and the *puja* he does in the name of the devotee will have great benefit.

The sect known as the Ganapatyas as has been said before, first started Ganesha worship. They consider the fourth day of both the bright and dark lunar fortnights and all Fridays as ideal for the worship of Ganesha.

The things needed for his worship are relatively simple. He loves the *dhruva* or *kusa* grass, which is actually a herb and grows prolifically all over India. He also loves the leaves of practically all fruit-bearing trees and plants. The informal manner in which Ganesha temples are constructed in every nook and corner of India shows his availability and approachability. In fact before the start of any *puja*, his form is invoked in a ball of turmeric powder or a lump of clay or sand and sometimes even in a lump of cow dung. Even *yogis* worship him since he is the presiding deity of the *Muladhara Chakra*. They consider him to be a *Maha Yogi*.

Kanaka *rishi* is said to have visualized the *mulamantra* of Ganesha as *Aum Sri Ganeshaaya Namaha*! The Vedas however give it as *Aum Gam Ganapataye Namaha!*

Actually Ganesha's worship became more popular during the Buddhist period under the growing influence of *tantrism*.

Normally the fourth day of the bright half of every lunar month is believed to be the day for Ganesha and is known as Siddhi Vinayaka Chaturti. The fourth day of the bright fortnight of the month of *Bhadrapada* (August/ September), is the most important and is known as Mahasiddhi Vinayaka Chaturti. This is the day on which Parvati created Ganesha and Lord Shiva accepted him as his son. Ganesha's birthday was celebrated on this day for the first time in Kailasa. It was on this day that he is supposed to have killed the demon called Sindur. If this day falls on a Tuesday or Saturday it is even more auspicious and is known as Varad Chaturthi. The full moon day of the month of *Vaishaka* (November/December) is also important for Ganesha.

The Vinayaka Chaturthi festival had been conducted in Maharashtra for centuries but it was the great leader Lokamanya Bala Gangadhar Tilak who made it into a national festival. He believed that when people got together to celebrate the birth of a god, they would forget their internal differences and become united in the Lord.

The *Mahabharata* gives the story of this festival. The Pandava king Yudhishtira once asked Krishna the reason why people who did many good deeds got no rewards. Krishna replied that Ganesha was the deity who had been specifically created for giving benefit to those whose good deeds had not been rewarded. He recommended that the fourth day of the bright fortnight of the month of *Bhadrapada* should be kept aside exclusively for the worship of Ganesha by which all those who feared that their good deeds were not being recognized, would get their just deserts.

The Varad Chaturthi vow for twenty-one days begins from the fourth day of the bright half of the lunar month of *Shravana* (July/August) and continues till the fourth day of the bright fortnight of the month of *Bhadrapada* (August/ September) – that is for eleven days in the month of *Shravana* and ten days in *Bhadrapada*. Lord Ganesha is fond of the number twenty-one. The devotee should smear a paste of sesame oil and powdered gooseberries on her body before taking a bath in the morning. A small shrine should be made by drawing the Ganesha *yantra* on the ground and scattering some rice grains over it. On this a bronze pitcher of Ganga water should be placed which is to be covered with two pieces of red cloth. A lotus flower with eight petals should be drawn on the pitcher with sandalwood or saffron paste. An idol of Ganesha should be kept on a wooden seat in front of the pitcher. The devotee should sit in front of this and chant the names of Lord Ganesha. There are eighteen important ones that are normally chanted.

ॐ Sumukhaaya Namaha!
ॐ Ekadantaaya Namaha!
ॐ Kapilaaya Namaha!
ॐ Gajakarnakaaya Namaha!
ॐ Lambodaraaya Namaha!
ॐ Vikataaya Namaha!
ॐ Vinayakaaya Namaha!
ॐ Vignanaashaya Namaha!
ॐ Dhumraketave Namaha!
ॐ Ganadyakshaaya Namaha!
ॐ Phaalachandraaya Namaha!
ॐ Gajananaaya Namaha!
ॐ Vaktratundaaya Namaha!
ॐ Shurpakarnaaya Namaha!
ॐ Herambaaya Namaha!
ॐ Skanda Purvajaaya Namaha!
ॐ Siddhi Vinayakaaya Namaha!
ॐ Sri Maha Ganapathaye Namaha!

With the repetition of every *mantra* one piece of *dhruva* grass is to be offered at the feet of the deity. His favourite number is twenty-one so one should offer these bits of grass twenty-one times. We can also offer twenty-one different types of flowers, fruits and sweet balls. The devotee should eat only fruits, milk or milk sweets during the course of this vow. The vow will finish on the fourth day of the bright fortnight of the month of *Bhadrapada*. It is only on this day that *tulasi* leaves can be used for Ganesha's worship. On other days they are prohibited. On the fifth day after the worship, the idol or *yantra* should be immersed in some holy water. On this day one should feed twenty-one Brahmins if possible. This vow is very good for the fulfilment of a wish or for gaining some spiritual benefit. This *puja* is normally to be done at mid-day and *prasadam* (food offerings) should be distributed to all after having fed the Brahmins. It is most auspicious to see an elephant on this day.

The story in the *Mahabharata* goes that Kunti, the mother of the Pandavas wanted to see an elephant on that day and asked her sons to fetch one. Gandhari, the mother of the hundred Kauravas had the same wish and asked her sons to fetch an elephant. The Kauravas searched and got the best elephant in the land for her before the Pandavas could find it. Arjuna then asked his father Indra (king of the gods) to send him Airavata, his royal elephant. Indra was agreeable but said he didn't know how to send it down. So Arjuna who was an expert archer formed a ladder of arrows by which the elephant came down. Needless to say Kunti was delighted to worship such an auspicious elephant and blessed her son.

TILI CHATURTHI VRATA

This is observed on the fourth day of the bright lunar fortnight in the month of *Magha*. On this day eleven sweet balls are made with white *til* (sesame) seeds to be offered to Ganesha. The devotee should fast the whole day and eat only these sweet balls at night after having offered them to the deity. This fast is usually kept for getting rid of some dire disease.

Dhruva Ganapati vow is kept when Vinayaka Chaturthi falls on a Sunday. After the usual Ganesha Chaturthi *puja* is done, the devotee should prostrate six times before the deity and circumambulate the deity six times and then offer six sprouts of *dhruva* grass along with six sweet balls (*modakams*).

VATA GANESHA VRATA

The banyan tree is known as *vata vriksha* and this vow is performed beneath a banyan or (*vata*) tree. This is observed from the fourth day of the bright fortnight of the month of *Kartika* (November/December) up to the fourth day of the bright fortnight of the month of *Magha* (December/January). In this the rituals should be performed in front of the whole Shiva family, consisting of Shiva, Parvati, Ganesha and Kartikeya. This ensures the good health of the whole family.

KAPARDI VINAYAKA VRATA

Kapardi is the Sanskrit term for cowry shells that were at one time very rare in India and used instead of coins. The devotee has to give cowries and some rice to all beggars in order to please Lord Ganesha. This is done on the fourth day of the bright fortnight of the month of *Shravana* (August/September). *Modakams* and rice pudding should be distributed to all at the end of the worship that is done in the way as prescribed above. Those who want to get rich can do this.

The most common *puja* is known as the *Shodashopachara puja* or the offering with the sixteen types of offerings. This type of *puja* is common to all deities. These sixteen offerings are water, flowers, leaves, incense, ghee lamp, fruit, cooked rice, pudding, clothes, bell, yak tail, fan, mirror, camphor, etc. The Lord is invoked as mentioned earlier and beseeched to accept our humble offering.

This *puja* is one that can be done to one's favourite deity everyday in the morning if one has the time and inclination. It is as good as meditation and establishes a strong rapport between the deity and the devotee. When you love someone you feel like showing your love in many ways. Human love is but a pale reflection of divine love and when the human being transfers the longing and love in her heart to a deity, she feels like doing something concrete to show this love. *Puja* satisfies this inherent need in the human heart to pour out the love within. Hinduism offers many types of rituals and *pujas* by which one can adore one's personal god in all types of ways. These *pujas* can be performed in our own houses or we can ask the temple priest to offer the *pujas* on our behalf. Even though we might not be expert in all the forms and rituals as described in the scriptures yet as Lord Krishna told Arjuna, "I am most happy to accept the humblest token of my devotee provided it is given with love. *Patram, pushpam, phalum, toyam, yo me bhaktya prayachati (Bhagavad Gita).*

We think that God is some distant Being who lives far away from us in some Heaven but actually he is the very life that pulsates in each of us, nearer to us than our own personalities. This is the Being whom we invoke in the idol to which we do *puja*. In fact the first step of the *puja* is to invoke the

Self, seated within us and transfer it into the idol that is kept before us and then continue to offer worship to it. At the end of the *puja* the final step is to take back the deity whom we have invoked externally and instal him back in our hearts so that we can commune with him all the time.

Dhruva grass (*cynodon dactylon*) is something that is special to Ganesha. It is always offered to him in all his *pujas*. It is an herb, which has many properties. If the juice is kept in the mouth after chewing the leaves, it helps to combat bacteria in the mouth and wards off infection. As usual there is a story connected with this grass. Analasura was a demon that created havoc on heaven and earth. The gods approached Shiva who told them to go to Ganesha. Ganesha swallowed the demon but was soon seen to be writhing in pain. The sage Kashyapa gave twenty-one stems of *dhruva* grass to Ganesha. After eating them his stomach pain disappeared. It is interesting to note that all the leaves used in the worship of the different gods, like *tulasi* for Vishnu and Krishna and *bel* leaves for Shiva, have medicinal properties.

The breaking of coconuts in front of Ganesha is a very special offering to him. This is done in all his *pujas* and is also done as a special vow when he has averted any trouble for us. There are two explanations to this. The coconut represents the *karma phala* or the fruits of our past actions which is what we are either enjoying or suffering now. Offering this to Ganesha is symbolic of offering our *vasanas* or inherent tendencies and begging him to deliver us from them.

The outer skin of the coconut represents the gross body that has an external show of beauty. But inside, it carries a lot of desires and attachments, which comprise the subtle body. We have to renounce all our desires except the desire to be united with the Lord. Before breaking the coconut in front of Ganesha we have to remove the stringy coir representing the body. Then we break the hard shell of our ego and expose the sweet kernel of our pure *sattvic* desire to become one with him. Finally the sweet water denoting our love is poured over him. It is common in South India to break a coconut for him if he averts some danger or accomplishes some desire.

Balasrag, kadali, chootha, panasekshu, cha modakam.
Balasuryamaham vande devam Balaganapatim.

"I offer my salutations to the Boy Ganapati,
Who is effulgent like the morning sun,
Who is adorned with a garland of tender flowers
And who holds a banana, mango, jackfruit, sugar cane and sweets in his hands."

ॐ *Gam Ganapataye Namaha!*

"May the dust of the lotus feet of Lord Ganesha, which is reddened by the garland of crimson flowers in the crown of Indra, remove all our obstacles."

"We take refuge in that one-tusked Lord who is the root cause of the world. He is manifest in the hearts of yogis and can be realised only by intense meditation."

"We seek refuge in that one-tusked Lord Ganesha who is the secret dweller in the hearts of all and by whose command this entire world exists and who enlightens us by his knowledge."

CHAPTER FOURTEEN

SHURPAKARNA

Mantras and Prayers

Dhumraketu ganadyaksho, bhalachandro Gajanana,
Dwadashaitani naamaani ya pateth srunuyanapi,
Vidyarambe vivaahe cha praveshe nirgame tada,
Sangrame sankate chaiva vignasthasya na jayate!

One who chants or hears the twelve names of Ganesha – Sumukha, Ekadanta, Kapila, Gajakarnaka, Lambodara, Vikata, Vighnanaasha, Vinaayaka, Dhumraketu, Ganaadhyaksha, Bhaalachandra and Gajaanana, at the commencement of studies, marriages, journeys and in the battlefield, will never have to face any obstacles.

The four paths for god realisation in Hinduism are *jnana yoga, karma yoga, raja yoga* and *bhakti yoga. Jnana yoga* is the path of wisdom, *karma yoga*, the path of selfless action, *raja yoga*, the path of following certain prescribed methods of body and mind control, and *bhakti yoga*, the path of devotion. Of these four, *bhakti yoga* is considered to be the easiest and most practical in this epoch known as *Kali Yuga. Bhakti* is love that is directed towards god. On this path, the longing of the heart is always turned towards a Supreme Spirit as embodied in our own personal deity. All actions are offered to that deity; all the yearning of the human heart for love is poured on the deity alone. Chanting of the names of god is an integral part of *bhakti yoga.*

The Puranas supply us with many *mantras* for the different deities which when used in the method called *japa* or repetitive chanting produces a tremendous change in our psyche. A *mantra* is the word symbol of the deity and encapsules the form of the deity within its sound. Every *mantra* has a presiding deity and a *rishi* who was the first to discover its use. Just as we automatically answer when our name is called, the deity answers the call of the supplicant when accompanied with love and devotion. Before starting *japa* we have to invoke the form of the deity in our minds. For this the Puranas give *dhyana slokas* or verses for meditation by which we can picture the form of the deity. It is only after we invoke him into our minds that we can start the *japa*. All the chapters of this book start and end with such verses, which can be used to invoke the deity in the heart before starting *japa*.

In the previous chapter we discussed the different methods of *puja* for Ganesha as well as for other deities. However, the chanting of the *mantra*s of the deity, which is known as *japa*, is the simplest and most effective form of personal worship of any deity. Lord Krishna says in the *Bhagavad-Gita*, "Yajnanaam japayajnyosmi" – "among rituals and sacrifices, I am *japa*". *Japa* is the repetition of the *mantra* of one's favourite deity. It can be done on a rosary or *japa-mala* or silently inside the mind. The latter is said to be even more effective but usually a rosary is used since it helps to keep the mind single-pointed on the *mantra*. A rosary of one hundred and eight beads is the best. This is suited to all people of all ages and castes and can be done even when travelling in a busy train or bus. Before starting the *japa* we should chant a *dhyana sloka* or a verse for meditation that describes the form of the deity. This will help to focus our mind on that particular deity.

Japa has certain advantages over *puja* and other forms of ritualistic communication with the gods. It does not need any external accoutrements or the physical help of a *guru*. Once we get the *mantra* from the *guru* we can practise it by ourselves wherever we are. No special training is needed except the correct enunciation of the Sanskrit *mantra*, which will be taught by the *guru* at the time of initiation.

Everyone knows that prayer is one of the most powerful forms of communication with the Divine. If the prayer is done with intense *bhava* or emotion, we can immerse our mind in the deity and actually materialise the form in front of us. This is due to the power of the *mantra*s, which are sound capsules that contain the form of the deity that is being worshipped. The ancient *rishi*s of India were masters of the science of sounds and they discovered many interesting things about the human nervous system and how it reverberates with the vibration of the cosmic sounds.

The findings of nuclear physics actually confirm these findings of the *rishi*s. Physics can change the energy force fields in a chamber and transform one element to another. If we knew the carbon *mantra* and say it properly we will cause that particular time-space-energy force field to occur and the result would precipitate some carbon particles. Some *siddhas* can do this with their minds and cause objects to appear. This is called materialization. This shows the relation between mind, sound and form. This is exactly what the *mantra*s teach. Each deity can be experienced in a *mantra* form. This is like remembering someone by their name rather than by their form. When we utter the *mantra* we conjure up the form of the deity. The great Gayatri *mantra* actually refers to a special 3-line Vedic metre, which is used for invoking a particular deity.

The human being is a microcosm in which all the details of the macrocosm are found in minute detail. The Vedic hymn to the Supreme Person known as the *Purusha Sukta* shows the different components of the cosmic person and how they are found in the individual also. The *Bhagavad-Gita* also gives us a vision of the cosmic person in the eleventh chapter. These poetic representations are given only to enable the human mind to grasp this amazing truth that the individual is only a reflection of the universal.

That part of our body that has the maximum representation of the universal is the nervous system with the spinal cord playing the most important role. The ancients postulated the existence of what they called *chakras,* which are closely connected with the astral world. The descent of consciousness into the material body is through these *chakras*. They are lotus-shaped whorls of spiritual energy situated in the astral body along the path of the physical spinal column. Since they are centres of spiritual energy, human instruments cannot detect them. Each *chakra* has its own sound, its own element, its own deity and quality. As mentioned earlier these *chakras* are in the form of lotuses. The first six *chakras* have fifty petals and each petal vibrates to the sound of one letter of the Sanskrit alphabet.

There are fifty-two primeval sounds which have always existed and from which the universe of forms have been created. The Sanskrit alphabet is the only one, which has all these sounds and thus most closely approximates these vibrations. All Sanskrit *mantra*s are made up of some of these sounds so when the *mantra* is chanted, that particular *chakra* starts vibrating to the sound if is is articulated properly with the correct intonation and with intense feeling. Hence we are told to chant these *mantra*s daily for a certain specific number of times. After many thousands of repetitions, the deity will deign to give us *darshan* (vision) of his form. It has been scientifically proved that predictable forms can be produced from sound.

When certain instruments were played it was found that their music could trace a corresponding form in the sand. Thus the *mantra*s of the different deities are capable of materialising the form of the deity. The *rishi*s perceived the potency inherent in the sound of thunder and the lightning. They decreed that even inanimate things emanated faint vibrations that could be heard by those whose ears were attuned to such subtle sounds as theirs were. These vibrations and sounds formed the universe and it is by these that it exists up to the present day.

The main deity in any ritual or fire sacrifice (*yajna*) is known as Brahmanaspati since he has the power of the Supreme Brahman. Thus it is that each god and officiating priest becomes Brahmanaspati when he pronounces these *mantra*s since they give him power over the things of heaven and earth.

Only when we understand this will be able to understand why Vyasa extols one particular god in each Purana to the exclusion of all the others. In fact the others pale into insignificance. The reason has already been given in the previous paragraph. At the time of worshipping a particular deity, he or she is supposed to represent the Supreme Brahman itself. When Ganesha is worshipped all the other gods including Brahma, Vishnu and Shiva lend their powers to him. Which god we worship depends on our particular need and nothing else can satisfy us. When we are thirsty only water can please us. Not the most delectable morsel can tempt us. Similarly when we want to get rid of obstacles only Ganesha can satisfy our need.

All gods are symbols of the energy of the Supreme. They provide us with strength as and when we need it.

We in India are indeed fortunate since we have so many *mantra*s which can be used during prayers and which are charged with the spirit of the deity. Ganesha *mantra*s are *siddhi mantra*s. They contain specific powers of the Lord. When chanted with sincere devotion they will ward off all evil and bless the devotee with abundant wisdom and success in all endeavours.

We will take a few of the *mantra*s to Ganesha here and give the specific purposes for which they are to be chanted. Of course all *mantra*s will take you to the Supreme if they are chanted without any ulterior motive but since most of us want some concrete result from our endeavours, their special purpose is given below.

The *mantra, Aum Gam Ganapathaye Namaha!* is to be used before starting any enterprise or journey.

If the *mantra, Aum Namo Bhagavate Gajananaya Namaha!* is used with faith and love for thousands of times, it will give us *darshan* of Ganesha.

Aum Sri Ganeshaya Namaha! is a *mantra* to be utilised by students for increasing their memory and passing their examinations.

Aum Vakratundaya Hum is a very powerful tool for removing negativity, and dishonesty on an individual, universal and international scale. The word *hum* calls forth an immediate response. This *mantra* has even been used for correcting spinal defects. Of course for this one has to make many repetitions, minimum would be a 1008.

 If some danger is coming your way the *mantra, Aum Kshipraprasadaya Namaha* asks for immediate action.

Those who long of physical and mental beauty as well as peace of mind should use the *mantra, Aum Sumukhaya Namaha!*

The *mantra, Aum Ekadantaya Namaha!* begs Ganesha to break the duality in which we are bound and make us single-pointed.

The *mantra, Aum Kapilaya Namaha!* will make our wishes come true. This is especially true in the realm of healing. If we wish to heal someone we should use this *mantra* regularly and supplicate Ganesha to heal the person.

The *mantra, Aum Gajakarnakaya Namaha!* gives us the ability to tune into the cosmic wavelength. We can sit anywhere and hear the voices of the ancestors, *devas* and saints.

When we use the *mantra, Aum Lambodaraya Namaha!* we become one with the universe. We experience the great truth that everything is within.

The *mantra, Aum Vikataya Namaha!* makes us realise that the world is a dream or drama in which we only play a role.

The word *vignam* as we have seen means "obstacle" and the *mantra, Aum Vignanashaya Namaha!* is a key *mantra* for Ganesha in as much as it is capable of removing every impediment in our life.

Vinayaka is the name of Ganesha in the golden age. So the golden age will come in our life and work if the *mantra, Aum Vinayakaya Namaha!* is chanted.

Dhumraketu means comet and the *mantra, Aum Dhumraketave Namaha!* is very effective when used in the face of national and international disasters.

If any group or country or nation needs help, the *mantra* to be used is *Aum Ganadhyakshaya Namaha!* We must focus our mind on the group and repeat the *mantra.* When a gathering of people chants this in unison there is greater force.

Ganesha's forehead is adorned with the crescent moon from which nectar drips so the *mantra, Aum Phalachandraya Namaha!* is good for conferring immortality as well as for healing.

The *mantra, Aum Gajananaya Namaha!* is excellent for eradicating one's ego. We should keep Ganesha's face in front of us and repeat the *mantra.* He is the one who gives us the fruit of our *karma.*

We often find people knocking on their foreheads with their knuckles when Ganesha *mantra*s are chanted or when they stand in front of the deity. This action stimulates certain nerves in the head and stimulates the flow of nectar from the *Shasrara Chakra* which flows down to the *Muladhara Chakra* at the base of the spine, which is Ganesha's seat. Thus the nectar flows over him in a formal libation. This knocking of the forehead is also a gesture of submission and beseeching forgiveness for errors.

People are also seen bobbing up and down before him and pulling their ears. This is an expression of humility. Pulling the ears draws the Lord's attention to the penitent devotee who is trying to efface his ego. Esoterically speaking, this action stimulates important nerves, which help to internalise our awareness before starting the *puja.*

Devotees always do *pradakshina* or circumambulation round the temple. This is only done in a clockwise direction. While we are doing this we are supposed to withdraw our awareness from worldly matters and direct it towards the divine. As we circle the Lord, subtle psychic worldly bonds that accumulate during the day in the human aura are broken. This type of circling helps to makes us single-pointed.

All the devotees of Shiva and therefore of Ganesha are seen to be wearing ash on their forehead. Ash denotes purity and also reminds us of the transitory nature of life. Ash has no qualities of its own. Whatever wood is burnt, whether sandalwood or faecal matter, all is changed to ash, which has the qualities of neither. Thus it is a symbol of the Brahman that has no qualities (*nirguna*). Moreover ash has a bright phosphorescent glow that is supposed to attract the deities.

The red dot, which many devotees apply in the middle of the forehead, is known as a *bindu*. It is placed at the exact spot where the third eye is supposed to be located. This is known as the *Ajna Chakra* and is the seat of the mind and intelligence. The person standing in front of you will be instantly drawn to this red mark on the third eye and thus during the conversation, he or she will be able to draw out the best in you. Thus we see that even the simplest thing which the Hindu does as a matter of routine, which might appear meaningless to the casual observer, is actually imbued with deep spiritual significance.

ॐ

Yadaksharam padam bhrishtam,
Maatrahinam cha yad bhaveth
Tat sarvam kshamyataam deva,
Praseeda Parameswara.

"O Great Lord, be gracious unto me,
And forgive me,
For any errors I might have committed
in the words and meter."

ॐ *Gam Ganapataye Namaha!*

ॐ
Guhaaya Namaha!

BOOK TWO

*K*artikeya

Tat Purushaya vidmahe,
Senamanyaaya deemahi,
Tanno Skanda prachodayaat!

I contemplate that Supreme Purusha,
I invoke the general of the gods,
May he enlighten me.

— *Kartikeya Gayatri*

Bala Subramanya with peacock (Illus. done in ancient Kerala
mural style using only vegetable dyes by K. Suresh).

ॐ

Skandaaya Namaha!

CHAPTER ONE

SKANDA

The Form of the Formless

Senaninam aham Skanda!

"Amongst generals, I am Skanda."

— Srimad Bhagavad Gita

Hinduism is a very complex religion and difficult to comprehend by most modern minds. Who can comprehend the meaning of these myriad deities, multi-armed, multi-headed with animal bodies and strange origins? The western world attuned to the morally perfect and orderly world of a Father in heaven and a devil seated in hell, was unable to make any sense of all this jargon and passed it off as the meaningless figments of the imagination of a bunch of queer *yogi*s meditating in the Himalayas. Hinduism with its plethora of symbols and images is endlessly complex and therefore endlessly misunderstood. But its true message is simple and universal – enlightenment. The goal having been fixed, any method of arriving at this goal was encouraged and explored by the *rishi*s. They realised the need of giving some form to the formless, so that the human mind, which is conditioned to handle forms alone, could concentrate and fix itself on something, which would be more comprehensible to it than the formless Brahman.

The gods and their symbols are all the outer coverings of an inner truth. One can never penetrate this camouflage without understanding the inner message. These symbols are only pointers or landmarks that help the aspiring soul to arrive at the ultimate goal. Having experienced the Absolute Truth, the *rishi*s also realised the absolute necessity of personal experience, before the individual could be liberated. They knew that future generations would not be able to comprehend this Reality, which was so simple that it missed the mark of the outer-oriented vision of the human being. Out of their deep compassion they made an attempt to pass on these truths in the form of symbols, stories, diagrams and forms, thus enabling this great esoteric knowledge of the formless Brahman, to survive during the vast passage of time.

Forms and qualities condition the human mind from birth. The mind cannot soar into the unconditioned and formless with ease. Thus the sages conceived of suitable forms that symbolise these sublime spiritual truths. Worship of the divine forms invokes those principles that they signify and thus function as conductors of divine energy and grace. The Vedas declare, *Ekam satyam, vipra bahuda vadanti*, meaning "Truth is one but the wise call it by many names." The *rishi*s found a way by which this Absolute Truth could be made comprehensible to the human mind through the worship of different forms of the gods and goddesses. The sublime truths of the Vedas and Upanishads were made available to the masses through the prolific and amazing stories of the Puranas. An earnest seeker will be able to find that the forms of the deities are pregnant with a profound meaning. Their several heads, weapons, garments and ornaments are all the outer accoutrements that veil lofty spiritual principles.

The Tibetan Buddhist tradition speaks of something called *termas* which are sacred texts that are disguised as a means of protecting them from destruction by scoffers and preserving them for those who would be interested in diving into their depths and discovering the secrets which were carefully hidden beneath. The figures and stories of the Hindu gods are similar. Their significance may not be immediately evident. The key to success in deciphering their esoteric meaning lies in the ability and intention of the seeker who studies it. To such sincere seekers, the gods themselves will reveal their secrets. Like the *koans* in Zen Buddhism, the figures of the gods baffle the mind to such an extent that the only way out is to break into the idols and come face to face with the reality which their figures mask.

Even though many of the Puranic stories are highly entertaining, that was not their sole purpose. They all have a hidden meaning that the devotee alone will come to know through diligent study. Many of the stories are meant to provoke and shock the mind and thus shake it out of its normal complacent belief in a god who is always in his heaven and a world where everything goes right. We are supposed to question and consider and discover the inner meaning for ourselves. These stories are basically meant to give us different facets of a many-splendoured Reality but unfortunately they don't give up their secrets that easily. We have to dig hard before they yield their treasures. Thus the elephant-headed Ganesha and the six-headed Kartikeya have a meaning, which is not obvious. In fact their meaning has to be deciphered within our own minds and not taken for granted in an obvious and over facile manner as the Westerners did when they first came to India. What the *rishi*s wanted to do through these stories was to communicate an alternate vision of Reality. They made use of contradiction, ambiguity and surprise in order to shake the mind out of its traditional ways of thought and life. Like a douche of ice-cold water on a sleeping man, these stories are meant to confound, confuse and disrupt the normal channels of thought and thus bring about a cataclysmic transformation in the sleeping psyche.

The life of the great *avatara*s as told in the Puranas actually demonstrate how the laws of nature that operate in the physical world can be utilised on the inward path of our ascent to divinity. Different aspects of a life of yoga are brought out and demonstrated by the manifestations of the Supreme Reality through their various *lilas*. The devotees who understand their right significance will be immensely benefited in their spiritual path. The modern mind loves to discover a reason for everything and may well ask the question as to why this Supreme should want to manifest itself in these numerous ways. The reason is beyond the ken of the human intellect. Hence the Puranas answer the question by saying that it is all HIS *lila* or play. Why does a child build sand castles on the beach and enjoy the sight of seeing them being washed away by the tide? Why does it paint pictures and throw them away? The child is only interested in playing and not hoarding or keeping for a future date. Why, if it comes to that, do eleven strong grown men run after a ball and rouse themselves to a passionate outburst of emotion? Thus the player, ideally, is only interested in the game and not the results. Hence the technique of living is to realise that all life is a game that can be played successfully only if we live in the present and concentrate totally on the game and not worry about the consequences thereof.

The six main sections of Hinduism are devoted to the gods, Vishnu, Shiva, Shakti, Ganesha, Surya and Skanda. Vyasa wrote eighteen Puranas depicting the life of all these gods. Of these eighteen, the *Skanda Purana* is the longest and has more than eighty-one thousand *slokas* or couplets. It is classified as one of the Maha Puranas and comes thirteenth in the list of eighteen Puranas. Puranas that glorify Vishnu are known as Vaishnava and are categorised as *sattvika* or having the predominant quality of *sattva* (harmony). Puranas pertaining to Brahma are known as *rajasika*. The *tamasika Puranas* glorify Shiva and his sons. Therefore *Skanda Purana* belongs to the *tamasika* category and brings out the glory of Skanda, the son of Shiva. Even though Vyasa's first work was the *Mahabharata*, the first Purana he composed is supposed to have been the *Skanda Purana*. It contains the main source of information about Skanda and gives an account of his amazing life. Actually it has two portions. The former gives only a brief account of Lord Skanda's *avatara* and the destruction of Tarakasura. The latter however gives a detailed account of his glorious deeds, his battles against the forces of evil and his marriage with Valli and Devayani.

In the beginning the supreme light of Brahman filled everything – that is to say it filled the ether. From there it passed on to become air, fire, water and earth. This is the etymology of Subramanya's birth – the descent of the formless Brahman into the forms of the five great elements (*pancha bhutas*) of Nature. Thus the Purana says that he was born from the seed of Shiva that was ejected into etheric space. It was transported through the air or *vayu* to Agni, the fire god who dropped it into the waters of the river Ganga. She deposited it upon her banks into a clump of reeds. Thus the five elements of ether, air, fire, water and earth combined in order to nurture the *tejas* or seed of Shiva in the world. Thus Kartikeya's birth is actually the story of creation.

He was born out of the union of *Purusha* and *Prakriti* – or Shiva and Parvati – the Supreme Person and Nature. There is an essential link between the two. They are irrevocably bound to each other. Creation takes place only because of this union. The first emanation from this union of *Purusha* and *Prakriti* is the cosmic *ahamkara* or ego which contains the three *gunas* of Nature known as *sattva, rajas* and *tamas* which are the three strands which are absolutely necessary to bind the *Purusha* to *Prakriti*. It is on this platform that the cosmic drama can take place. *Ahamkara* is the *param tattva* as represented by Kartikeya. The

Vedas represent the *sabda* or sound form of the universe and the peacock symbolises the universe. The cosmic drama, in which the *Purusha* appears to be bound to *Prakriti*, is set in motion through ignorance and can only come to an end with the birth of knowledge. Kartikeya is the one who wields the spear of knowledge and fights against this abysmal ignorance. The cock on Kartikeya's banner is *nivritti* or the path of wisdom leading to knowledge of the Self. His crowing ushers the dawn and the radiance of the sun, which dispels the darkness of ignorance.

The two great forces in Nature are gravity and electromagnetism. As we have seen, Ganesha is the force of gravity. The second great force is electromagnetism and Kartikeya is the god of this force. His power is electric. He instigates revolutionary changes and then brings order out of the chaos. His *Shakti vel* or spear of power, works deeply within us like the powerful force that binds electrons and neutrons together. This power emanates from his spear like energy expanding through the universe in the form of radio, and light waves. We are always experiencing the dualities of light and dark, positive and negative, which are the electromagnetic forces that issue from Muruga's realm. This is analogically represented by the *devas* and *asuras*. If we take the analogy of fire we can say that Shiva is the fire, Shakti, the heat of the fire, Ganesha, the red colour and Muruga, the light of the fire.

Muruga works in conjunction with Ganesha to unite us to Shiva. He is the material manifestation of the mind, which comes from the cosmic *ahamkara*, whereas Ganesha is the one who guides the elemental forces or *gana*s that maintain order in the cosmos as well as create obstructions.

The Supreme Brahman is denoted as *sat, chit* and *ananda* – Satchidananda, which means existence, knowledge and bliss. Shiva denotes *sat* or existence and Parvati, *chit* or knowledge and Skanda, *ananda* or bliss. In his form as Shanmukha or the six-faced deity, he has both the aspects of Shiva and Shakti in him. His five faces stand for the five-faced Shiva and the sixth face for Shakti or Parvati. The fact that he came out of Shiva's third eye shows that he is the incarnation of pure wisdom since Shiva's third eye is the eye of wisdom. He was born to destroy the demonic forces of the world; therefore he had to come from the seed of Shiva who personifies the destructive aspect of the trinity.

Swami Krishnananda says, "The cumulative force, which combined the forms of the five elements impregnated with the divine power of Shiva, manifested itself as a six-fold divinity with six faces. The child contained within himself both the manifest as well as the unmanifest worlds. This child of Shiva had a mysterious birth and a mysterious up-bringing, under mysterious circumstances in order to fulfil a mysterious purpose which the gods alone knew."

In the *avatara* of the Supreme, as Skanda, what is portrayed is the eternal struggle between ignorance and knowledge, between the lower demonic forces and the higher divine principles, which operate both on a cosmic scale as well as on the individual platform. Six-headed, twelve-armed and seated on a peacock, Kartikeya is the symbol of youth, beauty and valour. He also denotes Supreme Knowledge, which alone can destroy the nescience of ignorance.

In most of his icons, Subramanya is shown as a young boy with one head and two arms or with six heads and twelve arms. He always holds the *vel* or spear. He either rides on a peacock or has one standing beside him. The bird holds a snake under its claws. A rooster is displayed on his banner. The cock announces the approach of the sun, or the light of knowledge, which alone can dispel ignorance. The cock also denotes *Sabda Brahman* or sound, which is the original form of the Supreme while the peacock stands for the diversified and multifaceted universe. Skanda has conquered the materialistic world of pride, egoism and vanity and thus rides on the peacock. There is another esoteric aspect of the peacock. It is the most beautiful of all birds. It reveals its inner bliss by dancing and displaying its gorgeous plumage. In this dance it shows perfect balance. The heavy body is delicately balanced on its slender feet. In esoteric language you can say that the peacock symbolises the mental equipoise of the liberated person, who is capable of keeping up the delicate balance between material and spiritual.

When mental equipoise is achieved, the mind becomes content and peaceful. The spear or *vel* is pointed at the end and very long. It is a symbol of the mind that has to be single-pointed if it wants to slay the demon of ignorance. It also stands for knowledge and is always clasped to his breast to show the importance of knowledge. It is with this *vel* or the power of knowledge that he slew the demon Taraka who represents ignorance. The Puranas describe him as the Son of God, begotten to save the world from the cruelty of demons like Taraka. The serpent crushed under his foot shows that he has completely subdued *maya*.

The face has all the five *jnanendriyas* or organs of knowledge. These five along with *buddhi* or the intellect are the six gates through which a person gains knowledge of the external world. It is through these six orifices that the inner consciousness flows out. Thus Subramanya, who portrays the inner consciousness, has six heads. The six faces also stand for the six *chakras*. In the story of his birth it is said that he was taken out from six lotuses growing in a clump of *shara* reeds. In *Kundalini yoga*, the adept has to pierce the six lotuses or *chakras* before reaching the state of ultimate wisdom in the seventh *chakra* known as *Sahasrara*. Hence Shanmukha is ever in a state of bliss, having gone beyond the six *chakras*.

These six heads also represent his six divine attributes, which are the *bhagas* or qualifications of one who is called Bhagavan, or the Supreme Lord. These are *jnana* or wisdom, *vairagya* or dispassion, *bala* or strength, *kirti* or fame, *shree* or wealth, and *aiswarya* or divine powers. Only one who has all these six attributes is fit to be called Bhagavan. The six heads also imply that he is all-pervading – there are four cardinal points and two others, above and below. They also correspond to the six seasons thus proving that he was the master of time. It is said that the six systems of Indian philosophy emanated from his six heads.

In his *nirguna* aspect he is depicted as Dandapani. He wears only a loincloth and carries the spear alone and is not accompanied by his wives. This symbol shows that he is free from *maya*, without the forces of desire and action, carrying only the spear of knowledge.

"I take refuge in Lord Guha of six faces,
The son of Shiva and leader of the army of the gods,
Who is knowledge infinite and has a deep red colour,
And rides on the divine peacock."

— *Skandopanishad*

ॐ *Sharavanabhava!*

ॐ

Shanmukhaya Namaha!

CHAPTER TWO

SHANMUKHA

The Historic Concept

Shadananam chandanalepitangam,
Mahorasam divyamayoora vahanam,
Rudrasya soonum suralokanatham,
Brahmanayadevam sharanam prapadye

I bow to Lord Subramanya, the son of Shiva,
The Lord of the kingdom of heaven,
Who has six faces and is covered with sandal paste,
Who rides on a peacock and is full of strength.

The concept of a war god is one that has been found in all religions and Hinduism with its rich imagery and thousands of gods was no exception to this. Even though he is not mentioned in the *Rig Veda*, certain ideas that were found in the Vedas were crystallized into what later turned out to be the god, Kartikeya.

The earliest mention of Skanda-Kartikeya is in the *Chandogya Upanishad* where the sage Sanatkumara is identified with Skanda. He is supposed to have taught the sage Narada how to overcome ignorance and attain supreme wisdom. Thus in the post-Vedic literature, Skanda is shown as a religious teacher whereas in the epics like the *Ramayana* and *Mahabharata* he is prominently depicted as a war god. In the *Bhagavad-Gita*, Lord Krishna declares that he is Skanda among generals. This proves that the concept of Skanda as the general of the gods was prevalent long before the advent of the *Gita*, which comes in the middle of the *Mahabharata*.

According to an early Buddhist text called *Mahamajuri* of the 1st century, images of Shakra, Shiva, Skanda, Narayana, Kubera, Chandra, etc. were shown to the infant Siddhartha who later became the Buddha. This shows that at that period, the Skanda cult was popular in the north and that he was only next in popularity to Shiva and Vishnu.

Kalidasa's "Kumara Sambhava" is a great Sanskrit poem on the birth of the war god. The famous poem called "Thiruppugazh" is by the Tamil saint and devotee of Skanda, known as Arunagirinathar. His "Kandaranubhuti" and "Kandaralankaram" are the two other renowned poems that describe his personal experiences of God as Skanda. These are great classics both in Tamil literature as well as in the world of spiritual writing. The "Kumara Tantra" also gives many aspects of the worship of Skanda. The *Mahabharata* recounts his principal deeds. His birth is also mentioned in the *Valmiki Ramayana*.

During the Kushana period in the first century BC, he was very popular in the north. This might be because the Kushanas were a martial race. A number of images of Kartikeya have been discovered in Mathura, which had been a stronghold of the Kushanas. The image of the war god Skanda is also found in many of the coins of the Kushana king called Huvishka (AD 106-138).

A large number of inscriptions have also been discovered in Bihar, which bear the name of Kartikeya and has his emblem, the peacock. The tribe called the Yaudheyas in Rajasthan and Punjab also worshipped Kartikeya with six heads. On one side of the coin it is written, "Brahmanya, the divine lord of the Yaudheyas". Brahmanya is another of the names of Kartikeya. Some coins show Kartikeya on one side and Lakshmi on the other.

The city of Rohtak in Haryana was known as Rohitaka and was connected with the Kartikeya cult. It was a very prosperous country during the time of the *Mahabharata* in which it is mentioned that one of the sons of Pandu attacked the mountainous country of Rohitaka.

Many of the seals of the Gupta period also have the emblem of Kartikeya. Some of the Gupta rulers where named after him, thus showing his popularity. Skanda Gupta, Kumara Gupta and Mahasena Gupta are some examples that prove the prevalence of his worship in those times.

In North Bengal and the Kumaon district in the Himalayas, his cult was very popular especially in Baijnath in the Almora district. Many inscriptions of the 9th and 10th century AD have been discovered as to the existence of a famous city called Kartikeyapura. North Bengal also has a number of places connected with Skanda worship in the early AD 967.

However due to some reason his popularity waned after the Gupta Age and soon he was mentioned only in association with his father Shiva. In the medieval period he was seldom given a separate shrine and was clubbed together with the rest of Shiva's family.

Since his cult is closely associated with Shiva, he was invested with many of his father's attributes. He came to be called Mahayogi, a healer, teacher and lord of the elements. Shiva continues to be an ascetic despite the fact that he was married to Parvati so also Subramanya, the husband of Valli and Devasena is considered to be an ascetic.

Some of the oldest epithets of Skanda are Brahmanya, Brahmasaya and Brahmanishta all of which mean the one who is the Absolute Brahman incarnate.

As with all Hindu gods, his names are many and each of them denote a certain aspect of his personality. In North India he is most popularly known as Skanda and Kartikeya. In the south he is known as Muruga, Andavar, Subramanya, Kumara and Swaminathan.

He is called Kartikeya because the six Krittikas or the constellation known as the Pleiades nursed him. Since he was nursed by six mothers he is known as Shan Matura or the one with six mothers. He produced six faces and sucked the milk of all six mothers so he is known as Shanmukha or the one with six faces. Since he was born of the dissipated semen of Shiva, he was known as Skanda (that which has slipped out). He is known as Kumara since he is the killer of evil as denoted by Tarakasura. The word *ku* stands for evil and *mara* means to kill. He is also known as Kumara since he was a *brahmachari* (celibate). He is known as Shastipriya or the one who is fond of the sixth day of the lunar month. According to the legend of his birth he killed Tarakasura on the sixth day of the bright half of the lunar month of Kartika. Skanda was consecrated as the commander-in-chief of the divine army in this month and thus he is also known as Devasenapati – commander of the army of the gods.

Since Agni, the god of fire was the first to catch the seed as it fell from Shiva; he is known as Agnibhu, Agneya, Pavaki or Pavakeya. He is also mentioned as *hutavaha tanaya*. All these names mean, the son of Agni. Fire and sun have a close connection so Kartikeya is also connected directly with Surya, the sun god. The *Svetasvatara Upanishad* says, "He comes riding in the sky on his beautiful peacock after conquering the hosts of *asuras* and showers his grace on his devotees."

The bluish-green peacock is an allegory for the sky and Lord Subramanya, whose form is red, corresponds to the sun. The sun's action in dispelling darkness and bringing light can be compared to Kartikeya's grace in removing the veil of *maya* and showering us with Supreme Knowledge. The peacock stands for *maya* and you find that it always has a serpent crushed under its claws denoting the conquest of *maya* by Kartikeya. Shikhivahana means the one who rides on a peacock.

Subramanya's spear is known as the *shaktiayuddha* and is fashioned from chiselled pieces of the sun. The sun god's wife was Samjna, the daughter of the divine architect, Vishwakarma. Due to the intense heat radiating from him, she was unable to live with him. Her father promptly chiselled off bits of the sun's effulgence so that his daughter could live in comfort with her husband. These pieces were made into a spear for Kartikeya. Another reason for his connection with the solar deity is his association with the cock. The crowing of the cock announces the arrival of the morning sun and everyone wakes up. The sun dispels darkness, which stands for ignorance. The crowing of the cock announces the coming of Kartikeya who puts an end to the darkness of ignorance.

He is known as Gangaputra or the son of Ganga since the river Ganga carried the seed of Shiva for a while. However Ganga found that even her icy waters could not bear the heat of Shiva's seed so she deposited it in a clump of reeds known as *shara*. Hence Skanda is known as Sharavanabhava. This word has six syllables in Sanskrit and means the one who was born in the reed forest of *sharas*. It is his special *mantra*.

He is known as Kraunchabheda since he pierced the mountain called Krauncha where the *asuric* forces had taken shelter. He is also known as Guha. *Guha* means cave in Sanskrit and he is the one who hides in the cave of our heart. So this name actually means "the hidden one".

His mother Parvati is supposed to have presented him with his chief weapon – the spear or *vel*. Hence he is known as Velayudha or the one who has the lance as his weapon. Like his father he is also known as Yogeshwara or the Lord of yoga.

Skanda is also shown as Mahasena or the god of war when he appears in full battle regalia. He is sometimes known as Vishaka. At first Vishaka was considered to be his brother and there is a legend of Indra piercing the right side of Skanda with his thunderbolt and Vishaka coming out of it. Later on they were fused into one god called Kartikeya.

Shiva is supposed to have created twelve *grihas* or planets to assist Skanda. Out of these five are male and seven female. These female goddesses are known as the *saptamatrikas* or the seven mothers who are a class of fierce deities responsible for miscarriages in pregnant women and infantile diseases. They are intimately connected with Kartikeya. Realising his great power, they begged him to accept them as his mothers. Many of them are supposed to work with him. Skanda's association with them shows that he was originally the deity of a tribe that worshipped mother goddesses under various names. Like Ganesha he was non-Vedic and non-Aryan. Worship of the mother goddesses was prevalent even during the time of the Indus Valley Civilization.

Eventually the mother goddesses were united and came to be known as the goddess, Revati. She is the personification of the sixth day after the birth of a child and has another name Shasti or the sixth day of the lunar month. Shasti is also the name of Devasena who was one of the wives of Skanda. Once a demon threatened to destroy the gods and they begged Skanda to help them. He sent Revati who assumed the form of a she-wolf and devoured the demon. According to the *Devi Bhagavatam*, Revati is called Shashti Devi because she represents a sixth part of *Prakriti* or Mother Nature. She is the presiding deity of children and grants offspring to childless couples and is worshipped on the sixth day after the birth of a child. The sixth month of pregnancy is still considered dangerous for the mother and special ceremonies are conducted for the safe delivery of the child.

Even though Skanda is supposed to be the General of the armies of the gods, his nature is gentle and yielding. In fact in character Ganesha seems to be the more aggressive of the two. Even when they were young boys and playing in Kailasa with their parents, Kartikeya was always out-witted by the wily Ganesha. He is depicted as having a guileless nature, easily hurt and full of love.

It is strange that after having held sway over North India for a considerable period of time, the cult of Kartikeya was totally wiped out. However it re-appeared in all its glory in the south and is still prevalent.

"I know not logic and dissertation,
I don't know grammar and syntax,
But in my heart shines the six-faced luminous light,
And thus marvellous words flow from my mouth of their own accord."

— *Subramanya Bhujangam*
by Adi Shankaracharya

ॐ *Sharavanabhava!*

"You who are desirous of achieving your object,
Should tempt the mind of Shiva, firmly fixed on contemplation,
To the beauty of Parvati, like iron to a magnet."

— *Kumara Sambhava*
by Kalidasa

ॐ

Subramanyaaya Namaha!

CHAPTER THREE

SUBRAMANYA

Taraka

Jajwalyamaanam suravrindavandyam,
Kumara-dharatada-mandirastwam,
Kandarpa rupam kamaneeyagatram,
Brahmanyadevam sharanam prapadye

I bow to the son of Shiva with a handsome form
Who looks like Cupid,
Who is worshipped by the gods.

— *Sri Subramania Pancharatnam*

As we have seen the enmity between the gods and the demons was a continuous affair. At times the gods were victorious and at other times some mighty demon would appear on the scene, made powerful with boons given by the gods themselves and then defeat the gods and reign over the heavens. This is the *lila* or play of the Supreme. Evil and good have to co-exist even though they are mutually antagonistic. This is the very basis of the cosmic drama and it has its human counterpart in the world below. As above so below is the way of Nature.

Exchange is the very foundation of life. We exist only because we take and give with every passing moment. We take in oxygen and give out carbon dioxide. The plants take in carbon dioxide and give out oxygen without which we could not live. Those who do not take part in this great universal exchange are known as *asuras*. Their life is only for their own benefit. They are incapable of understanding the needs of others. This is the main difference between the character of the *devas* and the *asuras*. The *asuras* offered sacrifices into their own mouths while the *devas* realised the necessity of offering sacrifice to an external source. In their arrogance the *asuras* thought, "Why sacrifice to anyone else? We are the greatest!" But the *devas* went on making offerings to the Supreme Being. The recognition of the presence of something greater than them was all that distinguished the *devas* from the *asuras*. Sacrifice or *yajna* is the law of Nature as Lord Krishna pointed out to Arjuna in the *Bhagavad-Gita*. The whole of Nature unselfishly offers her wealth to the Supreme and expects nothing in return. The human being who has more of the *asuric* nature in him always expects and demands the fruit of his labour to be reserved exclusively for him. Hence he is always on the sea-saw of joy and sorrow.

In this continuous battle between evil and good as depicted by the *devas* and *asuras* we always find that even though the gods are virtuous they are never able to defeat the vicious demons! What is the mystery behind this? This is truly a mystery that few people are able to comprehend. We wail that the virtuous are always being trampled upon and vice seem to be stronger. To find out the reason for this we have to understand that virtue by itself can never confront vice. This is because it is only a counter correlative of vice. Vice can only be overcome by a power that transcends both and not one that is merely ethical or moral. Evil is not afraid of mere morality and ethics. Mere goodness is helpless against vice. We have to enlist the force of the Divine within us. The Supreme force is above both virtue and vice. It is an integrating force, whereas virtue is only a part of that duality which is contradicted by vice. Virtue cannot exist without vice and vice versa. That is why in Semitic religions God and the devil are postulated as existing side by side. One cannot exist without the other. Unlike Hinduism, these religions did not progress beyond these irreconcilable opposites to a Supreme Reality from which both emanate. If there is nothing called bad, then there can be nothing called good either. They have to exist side by side since duality is the face that Nature shows to us. The Supreme however transcends both. So we always find that in the Puranas when the forces of evil start to assault the forces of good, the *devas* are compelled to turn for aid to the Supreme as embodied in Shiva, Vishnu or Brahma.

No doubt gods are far superior to humans in virtue, knowledge and goodness but by themselves they are unable to withstand a vicious power like

Taraka. Similarly none of us, however good, can withstand the force of evil that is threatening to swamp the world. Unless the Supreme is invoked there is no hope for the planet. The solution for the evils of the world today lies in appealing to God and not merely in increasing the number of good people. Lord Shiva, ever immersed in *samadhi,* who portrays the universality of consciousness, was the only hope for the gods.

The *asura* called Taraka was the embodiment of vice and Kartikeya took birth in order to kill him as well as his two brothers. There are many stories told about Taraka's birth of which we will take a few. The great sage Kashyapa had two wives. The eldest was known as Diti and the second, Aditi. Diti's sons were the *asuras* who were also known as *daityas* or demons and Aditi's sons were the *devas* or the gods. The first two sons of Diti were known as Hiranyaksha and Hiranyakashipu. They were so powerful and harassed the gods to such an extent that Vishnu had to take two incarnations in order to kill them. He took the form of a *varaha* or a boar to kill Hiranyaksha and the form of Narasimha or half-man, half-lion in order to destroy Hiranyakashipu.

Diti was naturally extremely upset at the death of her invincible sons and begged her husband to give her another son. He gave in to her wishes and she performed many austerities and eventually begot a son called Vajranga. At her bidding, he captured Indra and some of the other gods and incarcerated them in a dungeon. When Kashyapa admonished him, Vajranga released them. Actually he had a pious nature unlike other *asuras* and had no personal animosity towards the gods so he was glad to release them. He then asked Brahma to instruct him on the true nature of Reality. Brahma was so pleased with his sweet nature that he created a beautiful woman called Varangi and gave her to him as his wife. Vajranga had a *sattvic* disposition but his wife had a true *asuric* nature, cruel and spiteful and filled with hatred for the gods. However she served her husband so faithfully that he thought she was a changed woman and asked her to choose a boon. Immediately she asked for a son who would be able to destroy the gods and cause misery to Vishnu. Vajranga was horrified when he heard this. As a man of honour he could not go back on his word but he knew that if he gave in to her wishes the rest of the world would suffer. What was he to do? Finally he propitiated Brahma and asked for a son who would be strong and valorous but who would also practise austerities.

Varangi conceived and produced a son who had a gigantic body and enormous strength. At the time of his birth evil portents were seen. Comets and shooting stars appeared in the sky. Earthquakes shook the world and fire and floods erupted everywhere. The moon and sun were eclipsed. Tempests and typhoons raged and jackals and hyenas howled eerily. Blood oozed from the udders of cows instead of milk and they started lowing piteously.

This child was called Taraka. When he became a youth he begged his mother to allow him to do penance. But his penance was not to gain enlightenment but to conquer the gods and rout them from the heavens. He undertook unimaginable tortures of the body in order to propitiate Brahma. He stood for long stretches of time on a single toe, gazed fixedly at the sun for days, sat in the midst of five sacrificial fires and hung himself upside down from a tree. Due to the power of his *tapasya*, a scorching fire sprang from his head and threatened to engulf the whole universe. Fearing for the safety of the world, Brahma appeared before him and asked him to choose a boon. As is usual with the *asuras* the boon he chose was for immortality. Of course Brahma said that he was powerless to give such a boon. So Taraka craftily asked for a boon that he would die only at the hands of a son of Shiva. He knew Shiva to be a supreme yogi and was quite sure that he would never beget a son.

As soon as he got these boons from Brahma, Taraka formed an army of the demons and went to Indra's heaven and proceeded to drive the gods out of their abode. They were unable to resist him and took to their heels and hid in caves and forests.

After the death of his first wife Sati, Shiva had become an ascetic and wandered about the icy peaks of the Himalayas and meditated in inaccessible caves so that none dared to approach him. Due to his intense *tapasya*, the rivers dried up and the earth lost its glory. The hearts of all beings became dried up and lost their ability to love. All creatures were immersed in an ocean of sorrow from which there appeared to be no reprieve. Disease and famine stalked the world. The only creature who appeared to be prospering was this fiend called Taraka.

The world was shuddering under his inequities. He appeared to be invincible since he had got a boon from Brahma that only the son of Shiva could kill him and Shiva appeared to be a confirmed celibate so the world was sunk in gloom and the gods doomed to wander about homeless. They went with Indra at their head to Brahma and begged him to deliver them from this new plague.

"A mighty demon called Taraka, grown insolent because of the boon given by you, has risen to torment the worlds like a spiteful comet. All nature is at his command. The sun sends his rays only to awaken the lotuses in his lake, the moon waits on him with all his digits at all times, the wind blows gently over him like a fan and the seasons wait upon him as if they were his gardeners. The sea offers its precious jewels to him. Though served in this way he continues to harass the three worlds!"

Brahma pondered over the matter and said that it was very doubtful if they could ever find a woman who could lure a yogi like Shiva into marriage. So they trouped off to Vaikunta to approach Vishnu who had a solution for every problem. Vishnu told them that the great goddess (*Parashakti*) alone would make a fitting bride for Shiva and told them to pray to her and she would certainly oblige them.

The gods started to worship her and at the end of their *tapasya*, the goddess deigned to appear before them and said:

"O Devas!" She said, "I know your desire and I will incarnate myself in the house of Himavan, the king of the Himalayas. I shall marry Shiva and beget a son who will destroy the demon, Taraka." The gods were very happy to hear this and waited anxiously for this event.

"What can I compare to your six faces?
If there be six full moons free from blemishes
And if those moons are shining on all sides,
They would be no match for your effulgent faces!"

— *Subramanya Bhujangam*
by Adi Shankaracharya

ॐ *Sharavanabhava!*

CHAPTER FOUR

PARVATI NANDANA

The Cosmic Alliance

Dwishadbhujam dwadashadivyanetram,
Trayitanum Shulamasim-dadaanam,
Sheshavataaram kamaniyarupam,
Brahmanya devam Sharanam prapadhye

I take refuge in Lord Subramanya,
Who is the incarnation of Shesha,
Who is handsome with twelve hands and twelve eyes,
And who carries the spear.

— *Sri Subramanya Pancharatnam*

Himavan had married Mena, the daughter of the manes and the great goddess was born in her womb. She is Tripurasundari, the most beautiful in all the three worlds and naturally the child was the most entrancing baby. As she grew up she became the darling of her parents. When she reached adulthood, she was so entrancing it appeared that no one who gazed on her could take his eyes off her loveliness. Kalidasa gives a most wondrous description of the exquisite beauty of Parvati.

He says, "She was created by the Creator of the universe with great effort as if with the desire to see all beauty combined in one form, by gathering together all the standards of comparison and combining them in one delectable form."

When she came of marriageable age, the sage Narada came to the royal household and prophesied that she was meant to be the bride of Shiva who would even share half his body with her because of his intense passion for her.

The mountain Lord now went to the place where Shiva was meditating and worshipped him with all due rites and left his daughter with her two attendants to wait on him. Shiva remained totally oblivious of her ministrations. Nothing daunted, she kept worshipping him day after day with great devotion and love. The self-centred gods watched anxiously for they were waiting for the day when he would wed her and give them a son who would vanquish Taraka. They became more and more impatient as each day passed and the great yogi showed no signs of succumbing to Parvati's overtures. They were unable to understand how anyone could withstand the intoxicating sight of her budding youth. They decided to employ Kama, the god of Love to help them.

Indra called Kama and said, "My friend, I have only two weapons with which to subdue my enemies – my thunderbolt and you. My thunderbolt however is powerless against those with great ascetic power, whereas you can go unchallenged everywhere and can accomplish everything. We desire to get a commander of our forces who will be capable of vanquishing this terrible Taraka and only the son of Shiva can do it. You are the only one who can churn the mind of the great ascetic and make him fall for Parvati's charms. She is assiduously worshipping him so you should go there and choose a fitting time to tempt him."

Kama was proud of his prowess and agreed with alacrity. He went to Shiva's Himalayan abode accompanied by his timorous wife, Rati who was full of misgivings about this foolhardy enterprise. As soon as Kama entered the icy slopes of the Himalayas, the vernal season manifested itself. Trees began to put forth their tender shoots and bees started to buzz around in great joy, inebriated with the honey dripping from the flowers. Deer ran about intoxicated by the beauty of the season. The cuckoo cooed softly, calling its mate. The ascetics who were living in that forest near Shiva saw the untimely intrusion of spring and could hardly control their own minds. Wherever Kama stepped along with his wife, all living beings became drunk with passion and started forming into pairs. Shiva alone remained undisturbed and submerged in meditation.

Kama hid in the bushes and waited patiently till Parvati, the daughter of the mountains, like a tender lotus bud, decorated with spring flowers in her hair, approached Shiva's abode and started her daily worship of the Lord. Parvati had made a rosary of lotus seeds for him and shyly offered it to him in the hope that he might open his eyes and accept her gift of love. Luckily for Kama, Shiva opened his eyes at that precise moment and gazed at the exquisite Parvati who was shyly standing there in the full bloom of her youth. Kama sent his flower arrow unerringly at this exact moment. Shiva found that his mind was perturbed for some reason and cast his eye around to discover the source of this disturbance. He saw Kama standing proud and erect, ready to shoot his next arrow. His clenched fist was resting at the corner of his right eye; his shoulders were bent forward and his left foot drawn in, his beautiful bow was bent into an arc. He was poised to let fly his next arrow.

As Shiva turned his gaze on him, a blazing fire with mounting flames sprang from his third eye and consumed Kama in the very act of shooting his arrow. The gods who had been anxiously watching from behind the bushes quivered with fear while Rati mercifully swooned.

Having destroyed the source of his annoyance the great Lord disappeared along with his retinue leaving Parvati utterly bereft.

She was greatly agitated and returned home with her attendants, not knowing what to do. She cursed her beauty, which was unable to fulfil her heart's desire. She decided to do rigorous penance in order to get the great yogi as her husband. Obviously he was immune to her charms? Would he succumb to her austerity? However, just as a lotus flower looks beautiful even in the midst of slime so did her loveliness shine through her matted locks and clothes made of bark tied with a girdle of grass! Her rose-tipped hands held a rosary instead of flowers. She, who had been wont to sleep on the softest of silks now slept on the hard earth using her slender arm as a pillow!

When she saw that even this was not enough to attract her Lord she resorted to harsher and harsher forms of *tapasya*. In summer she sat in the midst of four blazing fires and gazed at the sun. During the monsoons she slept in the open in the rain. In winter when the wind turned to sleet she stood in the icy waters of the lake, impervious to the biting cold. She subsisted on the leaves that had fallen from the trees and hence got the name Aparna. All the sages extolled her and came to pay obeisance to her. At last one day an ascetic with matted hair came to the grove and started to question her.

"O Mountain born Lady! Why have you abandoned all bodily comforts and taken to a life of such austerity? Is heaven your goal or do you crave for a husband!

He, on whom you have fixed your heart, must indeed be cruel that he cares not to look at you. Tell me his name and I shall berate him."

Parvati dared not say his name but her friends who were with her told the sage the whole story of her ordeal and that she was hoping to win Shiva, the great yogi by her extreme asceticism.

The sage laughed in scorn when he heard this and started belittling Shiva.

"What would a high born beauty like you want with such a person? His parentage is obscure and his wealth is his nudity covered with ashes! Snakes are his necklaces and goblins his sole friends. His beloved habitat is the burning *ghat*! Give up this ignoble desire of yours and return to the lovely palace of your parents and look for a husband who is worthy of your charms."

Parvati was furious when she heard this. She turned on the sage like a tigress defending her young.

"O thou of depraved soul!" She cried, "What can one like you know of the greatness of my Lord! He is the Supreme Being himself and I will take none other for a husband. However I am not interested in arguing with you. Let him be what you say he is. My heart is filled with him alone and no one can persuade me to change my mind. I will not stay here and listen to this vile talk about my beloved!"

So saying she turned away in utter scorn and was just going to run away, when the sage who was none other than Shiva who had come to test her resolve, caught her by the hand and showed his true form to her.

"O Uma! Henceforth I'm your willing slave! Command me as you will."

Parvati shyly said that he would have to ask her parents for her hand and marry her with all due rites!

Shiva then sent the seven sages to go to the mountain god and ask for his daughter's hand in marriage since the gods had requested him to produce a son who would be able to kill the demon Taraka.

The sages were delighted to do his bidding and went to the king of the Himalayas and said. "Lord Shiva, the wearer of the crescent moon, the witness of all and the giver of all desired objects has sent us here to ask for your daughter in marriage. You would do well to give her to him for it will result in peace for the world and happiness for your daughter."

The mountain god was only too pleased to accept these words but he first looked at his wife Mena in order to get her approval. She gave a reluctant assent since she did not want to displease her husband and daughter.

The wedding day dawned. Many were the preparations, which were made in the city called Oushadiprastha, the capital city of the Himavan. The bride was anointed with perfumed oils and given a ceremonial bath with scented water poured out of golden pitchers to the accompaniment of soft music played by her maids. After this she was smeared with unguents and then clothed in fabulous garments and decorated with jewels. Her hair was tied in a charming knot twined with a garland of jasmine flowers. She looked so beautiful that no comparison could be made to anything, which would do justice to her exquisite charm.

In the meantime the gods were trying to do the same to Shiva in the bridegroom's mansion. They begged him to discard his usual mode of dressing and put on something more suitable for a bridegroom. The Lord laughed and just touched all the paraphernalia with his hand. Immediately the ashes on his body became a white unguent, the elephant hide in which he was usually clad became a silk garment and his third eye appeared as a *tilaka* mark on his forehead. The snakes that were twirled round his neck and body changed into different ornaments suitable for their proper places. His hair did not need a jewel since the moon itself was always adorning it in all its brilliance. Thus decorated and seated on his bull vehicle, Nandi, he appeared before the gods and announced that it was time to depart to the marriage hall.

The sun held the ceremonial umbrella over his head. The rivers, Ganga and Yamuna assumed visible forms and held yak tail fans on either side of him. Brahma and Vishnu attended on him on either side. Thus they came to the city gates where the king of the Himalayas was awaiting him. He was led with all due honours to the wedding platform. Then the wives of the sages brought in Parvati. Her father kept her trembling hand, pink-tipped and laden with bangles, in Shiva's hand. The priest now led them thrice round the sacrificial fire to the chanting of *mantra*s.

Brahma pronounced a blessing on her, "O fortunate One! May you be the mother of a hero!" The gods heartily endorsed this blessing.

"Seated on a peacock,
You are the essence of the Word.
You have a most handsome physique,
And are enthroned in the hearts of the sages,
You are the essence of the four Vedas,
O Son of Shiva!
You are the Lord of the Universe!"

— *Subramanya Bhujangam*
by Adi Shankaracharya

ॐ *Sharavanabhava!*

"Becoming the bee on the lotus of Parvati's lips,
He (Shiva) lived on the slopes of the Mandara Mountain,
Where the stones are marked with the impression of,
The bracelets of Vishnu."

— *Kumara Sambhava*
by Kalidasa

ॐ

Tarakasura samhaarine Namaha!

CHAPTER FIVE

KUMARA

Birth of the War God

Surari-ghorahava-shobhamaanam,
Surotthamam shakti-dharam Kumaram,
Sudhara-shaktyayudha-shobhi-hastam,
Brahmanya devam Sharanam prapadhye

I take refuge in Lord Subramanya,
Best of gods whose hand is adorned with the spear,
And who annihilates the enemies of the gods.
                              — *Sri Subramanya Pancharatnam*

After spending a few nights at her paternal home, Shiva took his bride away to the cold and frosty slopes of Kailasa that was his abode. At first he ignored her totally but she was not put off by this apparently callous treatment and served him faithfully as she had done before. At last he decided that he had tested her enough. In order to satisfy her wishes and those of the gods, he carried her to their conjugal bed, which was an autumnal cloud, tinged with the rosy hues of sunset. There he sported with her for aeons. It is said that a hundred celestial years passed in this fashion without his discharging his seed.

With Shiva, excess was always his norm. He either went into deep mediation, which lasted for centuries or was, locked in the embrace of his wife for ages.

Thus was the seed of Shiva nurtured through the great love he bore for Parvati. Theirs was an eternal romance undiminished by familiarity. It appeared to be an endless wooing which knew no boredom. The most important thing, which emerges from these stories, is the fact that Kartikeya was born of the intense love of Shiva and Parvati for each other. In an earlier age the Great

God had danced in grief and rage bearing her dead body in his arms. In this life Parvati had stood on one foot for sixteen years eating only dried leaves in her passion to get Shiva as her husband. Their love is unparalleled in the Puranas. What wonder that it should have produced a child who was to be the saviour of the world?

Kartikeya was thus the product of this seed that had been nurtured for aeons by the love of Shiva for Parvati and hers for him. Even though he was not born in her womb, yet he was in truth her son – loving and kind even though born to be a war god.

The gods were getting desperate. They were anxiously awaiting a happy conclusion to their schemes but Shiva seemed quite content to dally with his beautiful wife. Then it is said that the gods went to Brahma and begged him to stop this amorous sport of the Great God (Mahadeva).

"No woman will be capable of bearing this seed which has been nurtured in a divine dalliance which has lasted for centuries," said Brahma.

So they went to Vishnu and begged him to come with them and put an end to Shiva's long drawn out romance.

"Unless we do something to provoke him, Shiva might well wait another aeon before producing a child," said Vishnu musingly.

They went en masse to Kailasa and found the entrance to the cave guarded by Nandi who had been warned to keep everyone out. After waiting for an unconscionable period of time they began to get impatient and started eulogizing Shiva. They begged him to come out and grant their plea for a child who would save the world. They made such a noise outside with their hymning that he was forced to loosen his hold on Parvati and come out holding her hand. She was furious with the gods and cursed them that they would all be childless since they were the cause for having interrupted Shiva just at the moment when he had agreed to give her a child.

Shiva asked them, "My seed has already been dislodged from my heart. Who is it who is capable of receiving this vital fluid?"

As he spoke the seed that he had been withholding for centuries flew out like a fiery comet and fell on the earth where it oozed like hot lava and threatened to cover the whole earth. The gods feared that the earth might crack with the heat of this amazing fluid so they begged Agni, the god of fire to gather it. But the heat was too much even for Agni so the gods begged Ganga, the other wife of Shiva to keep it in her bosom and cool it. Ganga took on a delectable form. On seeing this delightful form, the seed of Shiva melted on all sides and slipped into her.

But even the cooling waters of Ganga were unable to carry this fiery seed and she cried out in agony to Agni.

"I am unable O shining one, to carry the seed of Shiva which has been intensified by your own heat."

The wives of the six sages had been turned into the constellation known as the Krittikas or the Pleiades, which is found in the sign of Taurus. The seed divided itself into six portions, which Agni took and planted in the womb of these six women. It was impossible for one womb to contain the heat of Shiva's seed that had been made extraordinarily potent by such great *tapasya*. Part of the fluid slipped on to the earth and turned into gold and silver. Distant areas were turned into copper and iron and its dross turned into tin and lead. In this way Shiva's *tejas* turned into various metals.

The wives of the sages now delivered and threw the foetus back into the Ganga since they could not bear its burning heat. Mother Ganga deposited it into a clump of reeds known as *sharas*. Here the foetus turned into a lovely baby boy. On the sixth day of the bright half of the lunar month of *Margashirsha* (Nov/Dec) the son of Shiva, who was meant to be the saviour of the world, was born. Since he was the product of six wombs he had six faces and sucked the breasts of all six mothers simultaneously so as not to disappoint any of them. Hence he is known as Shanmukha or the one with six faces. Since he was born of the Krittikas he was called Kartikeya. Since he had slipped into the womb of the Ganga he was called Skanda. Since he was born among the reeds he was also known as Sharavanabhava, which is a *mantra* that has six syllables and is very important for Kartikeya. He was also known as Kumara, the son of Shiva.

The jealous gods who had been selfishly watching the development of the seed into a bonny boy now grabbed the baby from his mothers much to their dismay and wafted him off to Kailasa and presented him to Shiva and Parvati as their son.

When Parvati saw the baby, milk started to ooze out of her breasts for she knew it to be her own.

"You are the product of Shiva's *tapasya* and my bliss. Even though you are not born from my womb, you exist because Shiva caressed me."

She hugged and kissed him and then passed him on to Shiva's lap where he played with the snakes round his father's neck. Within minutes he changed into a beautiful bonny boy of six years.

The selfish gods hardly gave a chance to the delighted parents to enjoy their child. They clamoured that he be crowned immediately and made their general and sent to accomplish the deed for which he had been born.

Water from all the holy rivers of the land was brought and consecrated with *mantra*s and herbs. Skanda was seated on a golden throne and this water was poured over his head to the chanting of Vedic hymns.

The gods blessed him and gave him all types of weapons and insignia. He chose the spear, which his mother had given him as his special weapon and the peacock as his vehicle and the rooster as the emblem on his flag. Shiva now told the gods that they could accept him as the general of their army and thus he got the name Devasenapati.

Heading the army of the gods, Kartikeya proceeded to Shonitapura, the capital city of Tarakasura. Indra came on his elephant, Agni on a ram, Yama on a buffalo and Varuna on a dolphin. This strange array struck terror into the hearts of Taraka's forces but he rallied them. Brandishing his sword and letting out a fiendish laugh he rushed into the fray.

Skanda was riding on the peacock. The moon god Chandra held the royal umbrella over his head. All the other gods accompanied him on their respective vehicles. Taraka was also seated in a beautiful chariot. Shiva's attendants fought valiantly with the ranks of Taraka's army. But it became increasingly clear to Vishnu that the gods were being thrashed especially since Taraka had started to use all his black magic arts. Vishnu requested Kumara who was only a boy of six to go to the front and fight with Taraka.

Taraka laughed mockingly and taunted the gods, "How shameless of you to send a mere boy to fight with me. But what can you accept when you have a coward like Indra for a king!"

Indra was furious at this deliberate insult and hurled his thunderbolt at Taraka who retaliated with his own weapon and felled Indra to the ground. Kumara, looking like a veritable war-god now confronted Taraka. A fearful duel was started between them. At one time the demon managed to fell Skanda from his peacock and a great wail rose up from the ranks of the celestial beings that had come to watch this cosmic event. Kumara sprang up and comforted the watching beings and promised to kill the wicked one. He hurled his spear at Taraka's chest and felled him. The lance now pierced the earth from which a gush of water bubbled out. Kumara took his sword and severed Taraka's head. The gods and sages were jubilant. *Apsaras* danced with joy and the celestial beings rained flowers on the head of the wonder child. Parvati took Kumara on her lap and hugged him. Thus was his reason for his birth fulfilled.

"O conquerer of Taraka!
I worship your broad chest,
Reddened by the saffron on the breast,
Of Valli whom you embraced,
Thus do you shower your grace on your bhaktas!"

— *Subramanya Bhujangam*
by Adi Shankaracharya

ॐ *Sharavanabhava!*

"Parvati stroked her lover (Shiva) with a golden lotus,
He closed her eyes with the water from his hands,
She sported by the heavenly Ganga in the sky,
With a girdle of fish encircling her."

— *Kumara Sambhava*
by Kalidasa

CHAPTER SIX

GUHA

Other Birth Stories

O Kumara! Son of Lord Shiva, who destroyed Tripura,
Do thou manifest before my eyes,
Holding the spear in thy hand,
Wearing silk garments,
With necklaces of brilliant rubies on thy chest,
And thy cheeks bright with the earrings dangling from thy ears.

— *Subramanya Bhujangam*
by Adi Shankaracharya

The nine planets are the Earth, Moon, Mars, Jupiter, Saturn, Mercury, Venus, Rahu and Ketu. These celestial bodies revolve round the Sun and once in every sixty years they return to their original positions. They influence the minds and bodies of all creatures without our knowledge. There are twelve houses in the zodiac and the planets move through these houses and individually and jointly influence everything in the world whether animate or inanimate. They influence the thoughts and actions and the health of every human being. The *rishi*s were able to gauge their effects on human beings and thus compiled the science of astrology, which is only now coming to prominence. The gods and the demons were constantly fighting with each other and each took the help of the planets. Thus the gods had Jupiter or Brihaspati as their preceptor and the demons had Venus or Shukra as theirs. The war between the army of the gods headed by Skanda and that of the demons headed by Taraka, Surapadma and Simhamukha could thus be called an inter-planetary war. Skanda was born to help the gods or the forces of good.

The birth of Kartikeya is described in many Puranas like the *Ramayana, Devi Purana* and *Shiva Purana*. The great poet Kalidasa gives a most entrancing description of the dalliance of Shiva and Parvati, which resulted in the birth of Kartikeya. He was born to redeem the world and purify it from the scourge of the dreadful demon known as Taraka. The demon stands for ignorance and Skanda was born to conquer ignorance.

In the beginning Indra, the king of the gods, was himself the general of the divine army but due to his over-indulgence in wine, women and song, he lost a lot of his powers and he began to seriously consider engaging a permanent general for his army. This desire was made more urgent by the atrocities of the *asura* called Taraka.

In the "Balakanda" of the *Ramayana*, it is said that the *devas* approached Brahma to give them a general for their army since Shiva, who used to play this role had taken to a life of seclusion. Brahma said that the only one amongst them who could have a son was Agni and he suggested that Agni should be asked to beget a son from Ganga. Thus Agni is said to have produced Kartikeya out of Ganga. So he is a product of the two main elements of fire and water and contains both their qualities of destruction and sustenance.

The *Mahabharata* also consistently mentions him as the son of Agni. He is called Agniputra, Agneya and Pavakatmaja.

Another unusual version of Kartikeya's birth is given in the *Matsya Purana*. Shiva and Parvati were locked in an embrace, which lasted for centuries. The celestials sent Agni to disturb the couple by his intense heat. The heat generated by Agni was so great that Shiva released his hold on Parvati and at that moment his *tejas* (seed) that he had been withholding for aeons slipped out instead of falling into Parvati's womb. Shiva became angry and ordered Agni to drink the semen. Shiva's *tejas* was so potent that even Agni couldn't contain it for long. It burst out of him and created a lake. After some time the lake became filled with lotuses and other water plants. One day Parvati happened to take a bath in it. Feeling thirsty she pulled out a lotus and started to drink the water in it but this was not enough to quench her thirst. At that moment the six stars known as the Krittikas came out of the lake carrying pots of water. She asked them to give her some water. They did so but made a condition that the son born to her would be given to them and called after them. Parvati was dying of thirst and agreed to their condition. Soon after drinking the water that had been impregnated with Shiva's seed, Parvati became pregnant. Before long a baby came out of her right side. He was as resplendent as the morning sun. His glory filled all the three worlds with its light.

In the *Vamana Purana*, Skanda is known as the son of Agni and Kutila who is supposed to be another daughter of the Himalayas. According to this version, Agni carried Shiva's seed for five thousand years and then Kutila bore it for another five thousand years before Skanda was born.

In some Puranas he is compared to the sun god or Surya, "arising in the midst of red clouds". In the *Mahabharata* he is called Deeptavarna and Diptashakti. In the *Brahma* and *Skanda Puranas* his name is included in the one hundred and eight names of Surya. In the early Vedic literature, Surya was often connected with Agni. In fact Surya is only another aspect of Agni. The inference is obvious. Skanda was always connected with Agni from birth and since Agni is a form of Surya, naturally he is also connected with Surya.

Another story in the *Skanda* and *Brahma Puranas* mentions that Skanda was sometimes seen as an exceedingly handsome youth who had the ability to attract all women by his charisma. He often dallied with the wives of the other gods who found him irresistible. When the gods complained to Parvati she reprimanded him and tried to dissuade him from these frolics. He refused to listen to her but she played a trick on him and the next time he went to seduce a woman he found the form of his mother instead. This put an instant stop to his amorous ways and he began to see his mother is all women. This made him turn into an ascetic. It is suspected that this story in a later interpolation when Skanda was worshipped in Tamil Nadu as Muruga who is often portrayed as a god of love and revelry.

The *Mahabharata* gives a different version of Kartikeya's birth. Indra was seated on the mountain deep in thought when he heard the distressed cries of a young girl. The girl was being forcibly abducted by a demon called Keshin. Indra rescued her and asked her how she came to be there. She said that she was the daughter of Prajapati Brahma and her name was Devasena. She had come to the lake along with her sister Daityasena who had been ravished by this demon. However, her sister appeared to like the demon and had gone with him whereas she had resisted his advances. Actually the word *devasena* means the army of the gods and the word *daityasena* means the army of the demons. In other words, Devasena was the storehouse of all noble qualities and her sister Daityasena the depot of the qualities of evil.

Devasena begged Indra to find a husband for her who was invincible, handsome and who was capable of conquering both celestials and demons alike.

Indra was not too sure how he could manage to get a man like this for the Prajapati's daughter. Just at that moment, he witnessed a solar eclipse. Agni, the god of fire was making oblations and was seen to enter the solar orb. Indra now came to a decision that only a son of Agni would make a fitting mate for Devasena.

He went with her to the hermitage of the seven sages where a fire sacrifice was going on. Agni had just come out of the solar orb in order to transport the sacrificial offerings to the respective gods. At that time he saw the wives of the *rishi*s and fell in love with them. They would have none of him so he went away to the forest to nurse his disappointment.

Svaha, the daughter of Prajapati Daksha was Agni's actual wife and when she saw her husband's condition she decided to fulfil his desire. First she disguised herself as Shivaa, the lovely wife of the sage, Angiras. One by one she took on the form of six of the wives of the sages. The fire god was only too pleased to have an amorous dalliance with these beautiful ladies, thinking them to have fallen for his charms.

However she did not want any blame to be attached to the wives so each time she had intercourse with Agni, she cast his seed into a golden pit which was inside a clump of reeds called *sharas*.

The seventh sage was Atri. His wife Arundati was the embodiment of fidelity. Svaha found that she could not take on her form since she was totally protected by her great chastity.

The seminal fluid of Agni collected and became a child on the very first day and was named Skanda. The child grew very fast and by the fourth day his body and limbs were fully formed and he was called Guha. By the sixth day he had six heads, twelve ears, twelve eyes and twelve arms and was called Kumara. The sixth day of every lunar month is known as *Shasti* and it was on this day that Kumara killed many demons.

When Svaha in the guise of the wives of the *rishi*s was returning home after her dalliance with Agni, some *gandharva*s (celestial musicians) noted her and reported the matter to the *rishi*s who believed that their wives had been unfaithful to them and discarded them. The six wives complained to Skanda about the unjust behaviour of their husbands and begged him to raise them to the heavens. Skanda knew that they were innocent and raised them to the heavens and made them into the stars known as the Krittikas (Pleiades). Arundhati, the purest of them was also made into a star after her death. She is one of the brightest stars in the firmament.

Svaha was aware of all that was going on and felt rather jealous that the wives of the *rishi*s had been raised to the position of mothers and she herself was unknown. She approached Skanda and told him that she was his actual mother. She confessed the whole story of her secret passion for Agni. Skanda felt sorry for her and declared that in future every time the priests made an oblation into the fire their incantations would have to be preceded by her name, which would be used as a *mantra*. Thus it is that to this day all oblations into the fire are followed by the word, *svaha*! Thus Svaha was able to dwell with Agni all the time.

Prajapati Brahma now told Skanda that he had been born for the good of the world. Shiva had entered into Agni and Parvati into Svaha and thus he was actually the son of Shiva and Parvati.

The *Skanda Maha Purana* gives another story of Tarakasura and Kartikeya. Taraka practised severe penance to Brahma and asked for the boons of immortality and invincibility. Brahma refused the former but told him that he would be invincible in fighting. He conquered the heavens and drove the gods to exile. As usual they approached Vishnu who advised them to encourage Shiva to get married to Parvati, who was doing penance in order to get Shiva as her husband. The rest of the story is similar.

Shiva married Parvati and then retired with her to his solitary abode, Kailasa. Here they were locked in each other's embrace when the gods accompanied by Vishnu approached him to remind him of his promise to get a son who would kill Tarakasura. Parvati had also petitioned him for a son. Shiva was pleased with her extreme devotion and decided to fulfil her wishes. Just at this time the gods appeared on the scene. However, Nandi refused to allow

them to enter the sacred presence. The gods begged Agni, the god of fire
to do something about this. Agni escaped the ever-watchful gaze of Shiva's
doorkeeper, Nandi and stole into the sanctum sanctorum without permission.
He came as a mendicant and begged for alms. Shiva was enraged and aimed
the trident at him. Parvati in the meanwhile had gone to get alms for the
mendicant. When she returned she saw that the beggar was Agni in disguise.
Parvati was quite enraged to see this and cursed him that he would become
all-devouring. She also cursed all the gods that they would reap the consequences
of their slyness and would never have any issue.

Shiva's seed that had already been released came out as an all-devouring
fire that was capable of consuming the whole universe.

Agni fled from the scene and reported all that happened to the anxious
gods who were waiting outside. Hardly had he finished speaking when all the
gods found that they were writhing with labour pains. They begged Vishnu
to help them and Vishnu promptly sent them to Shiva himself. The gods now
started to pray en masse to Shiva. At last Shiva, whose anger had already cooled
down, appeared and asked them to bring up the rays, which seemed to be
troubling them. They did so and the rays took the form of a mountain of
shining gold.

Agni was still writhing with the burning sensation and did not know how
to get rid of it. Shiva told Agni to deposit the rays carefully in the womb
of some good woman. Agni was very doubtful about this.

He said, "O Lord! Your splendour is unbearable. I doubt if there is any
lady in the world who is capable of bearing it."

At that time the sage Narada advised him thus: "O Agni you will be able
to deposit the semen of Shiva into the wombs of those women who take
their early morning baths in the month of *Margashirsha*."

Agni was shining with Shiva's effulgence and was burning by the banks
of the Ganga when the wives of the seven sages came in the early hours of
dawn for their ritual dip in the holy waters. It was the month of *Margashirsha*,
(November/December) and they felt bitterly cold. They approached the burning
fire to warm themselves. Only Arundhati, the wife of Vasishta refused to go
near the fire and even warned the others not to go. However, they disregarded
her and approached the god of fire and he immediately impregnated them

with the radiance of Shiva, which he was carrying. These rays burnt into every pore of their bodies and Agni himself was released. When they returned to their *ashrama*s, the *rishi*s immediately realised that they had been impregnated and cursed them.

The wives felt very sorry for their ignorant action and brought out the rays in the form of a foetus on to the Himalayan slopes. Only then were they relieved of their burning sensation. But even the mountain was unable to bear the heat and started getting scorched. He hurled it into the Ganga. The Ganga now deposited that unbearable semen in a forest of *shara* grass. On the sixth day of the bright half of the lunar month of *Margashirsha* (November/ December), the son of Shiva was born. He appeared as a six-faced, six-mouthed infant who had six names – Kartikeya, Gangeya, Shaka, Vishaka, Atibala and Mahabala.

At that time the great sage Vishwamitra came on the scene and was delighted to see this brilliant child. The child laughed up at him and told him to perform his purificatory rites. Then Vishwamitra told him that he was not a Brahmin but a Kshatriya. But the divine child told him not to worry and that from then onwards he would be given the status of a Brahmarishi or a sage of brahminical origin. So now he was deemed fit to perform his purificatory rites. These rites have to be performed soon after the birth of a baby.

Now Agni appeared on the scene and seeing his son he claimed him as his own and gave him a miraculous weapon, the *vel* or spear. Skanda took the spear and climbed up the peak and hit the peak with his spear and the peak broke. Ten thousand demons came to attack him but were killed on being struck with the spear. Indra now came and was frightened that this boy might usurp his place. Of course he did not know his identity at that time. He hit his right side with the thunderbolt. A mighty personage called Shaka came out. Then he hit him on his left side and another huge being called Vishaka came out. Then Indra struck Kartikeya on the heart and another person called Naigama appeared. All four of them rushed to attack Indra who ran away to his own region.

At that time the six ladies known as the Krittikas came there for a bath and saw the lovely boy. They all wished to suckle him so he assumed six faces and drank milk from all their breasts. Thus all of them were satisfied. They continued to suckle him and give him the choicest of food. Once they took him to the assembly of the gods where he showed his wonderful feats. On seeing him all the gods were surprised and asked him to reveal his identity. He immediately returned to his abode and remained concealed. That is how he got the name Guha (one who is concealed).

In the meantime Parvati asked Shiva, "How is it possible that your semen should have gone unfertilised. It must have become a child and I'm sure it is being hidden by one of the gods."

Shiva now called the gods and told them to search for the child and find out who was guilty of having hidden him. One by one the gods narrated the story of the various roles they had played in the cosmic drama and how they had transferred the semen to different spots due to its unbearable héat. Now the wind god and the Sun and the Moon took up the tale and described the whereabouts of the semen and how it had been nurtured by the Krittikas and was hiding in the clump of *shara* grass. Shiva sent his emissaries headed by Nandi to escort Guha to Kailasa. He was met by all the gods and taken in state to Shiva and Parvati who were anxiously waiting for him. She gathered him to her bosom and nursed him at her overflowing breasts. Then Shiva took the baby on his lap where the child started to play with the snakes.

Afterwards at the request of the gods, he was installed as the Devasenapati, commander of the gods. He was formally anointed by Brahma with waters from many holy lakes and rives. Vishnu gave him a crown and bracelets as well as his own garland known as Vaijayantimala, which was a garland of never-fading flowers. He also gave him his discus.

Shiva gave him a trident, the bow Pinaka, the axe, the arrow known as Paasupata as well as all wisdom.

Brahma gave him his holy thread, the Vedas, the *Gayatri mantra,* a water pot, the weapon known as Brahmastra and the knowledge of how to destroy the enemy.

Indra gave him his elephant and the thunderbolt.

Varuna gave him a white umbrella and a necklace of gems.

The sun god gave him a chariot with the speed of the mind and a coat of mail.

The Moon gave a vessel filled with nectar. Yama, the god of death gave him a staff as well as his daughter Devasena as his consort. Thus equipped Kartikeya went at the head of the army of the gods and accomplished the work for which he had been born by killing Taraka.

"Suganda hill is as sacred as Mount Kailasa,
Skanda stays on Ganda Madana Hill only to proclaim,
That whoever ascends that hill ascends Mount Kailasa,
Lord Shanmugha stays on top of that hill,
Let him remain there to bless me."

— *Subramanya Bhujagam*
by Adi Shankaracharya

ॐ *Sharavanabhava!*

"The lotus although it closes its petals for the night,
Remains for a while with a hole in the middle, as if,
To give entrance to the bees that desire to reside within."

— *Kumara Sambhava*
by Kalidasa

ॐ
Shikhivahanaaya Namaha!

CHAPTER SEVEN

MAHASENA

Birth of the Asuras

Ishtartha-siddhipradamisha putram,
Ishtannadam bhusura kaamadhenum,
Gangodbhavam sarvajanaanukulam,
Brahmanya devam Sharanam prapadhye

I take refuge in Lord Subramanyam,
The son of Shiva, who gives all desires,
Born of Ganga for the sake of all people.

— *Sri Subramanya Pancharatnam*   ॐ

We will now take up the story of Taraka's brothers who were known as Surapadma and Simhamukha, to kill whom Kartikeya took on a human form.

In his previous birth, Surapadma had been a virtuous king called Prabhakara ruling over a prosperous kingdom. Sage Agastya once came to his court and told him about the proposed advent of the Lord as Kartikeya. He also proclaimed that only a person who had done a lot of austerities would be able to take birth as his vehicle, the peacock or his standard bearer, the rooster. The king was fired with the ambition to become Kartikeya's vehicle so he did severe *tapasya* to Shiva who agreed to include him among his *gana*s. He came to be known as Surapadma.

In the meantime Taraka and Simhamukha also desired to become the carriers of the Divine Mother and Maha Shasta, who had the lion and the elephant as their vehicles. They also performed severe *tapasya* and came to be enlisted into the team of *gana*s of Lord Shiva.

Once during a war with the *asuras*, the *gana*s under the leadership of Surapadma, Simhamukha and Taraka defeated the *asuras*. The king of the *asuras* then appealed to Shiva and complained about the unfair treatment meted out to his people by his *gana*s under the leadership of these three. Shiva promptly cursed them to become *asura*s and hence they were born as three demons with the same names.

Another story about their previous lives can also be mentioned here. Once the gods had assembled at Kailasa to witness the Tandava *nrittya* (the dance of creation) of Lord Shiva. They left their vehicles at the foot of the mountain. Brahma, Vishnu and Kartikeya went to witness the Lord's dance. Brahma's swan, Vishnu's eagle and Kartikeya's peacock and rooster were left at the foot of the mountain. The three *gana*s of Shiva, known as Surapadma, Simhamukha and Taraka were also there and they instigated the birds to fight amongst themselves. The peacock and the cock were on one side and the eagle and the swan on the other. The three *gana*s joined the rooster and the peacock and inflicted severe injuries on the other two. When the gods returned, Vishnu and Brahma complained to Kartikeya. He promptly cursed the *gana*s to be born as *asura*s as a punishment for their cruel actions and to torture the gods and eventually be killed by him with his spear. Thus the three took birth as *asura*s. They were abjectly apologetic and begged Skanda to release them from the curse. He said that this was not possible but if they wished he was prepared to give them a boon. They begged him to allow them to become the flag bearers and vehicles for the gods in another birth. Thus Surapadma became the peacock and flag bearer of Skanda, Simhamukha became the lion vehicle of the Maha Devi, and Tarakasura became the elephant vehicle of Maha Shasta.

The previous history of Ajamukhi, the sister of the three *asura*s is also given in the *Skanda Purana*. In her previous birth she had been a lustful woman called Chitrarekha. Despite the fact that she was married to a very good man, she continued to have affairs with many other men. Once it so happened that the sage Durvasa came to their house. Compelled by her promiscuous nature, Chitrarekha proceeded to solicit the sage. Durvasa is known in the Puranas for his irascible nature. He turned the full force of his wrath on her and was just about to curse her when she ran and hid amidst a flock of goats. The irate sage soon ferreted her out and bade his disciple to tie her to the branch of a banyan tree. The sage cursed her that she would be born into the clan of the *asura*s with the face of a goat and thus she was born as Surapadma's sister.

Now that the cause for the birth of the *asuras* has been described we have
to go into the actual story of how they were born on earth. As we have seen
the gods and demons are ever balanced on the sea-saw of duality. Sometimes
the gods are victorious and at other times the demons. Once the king of the
*asura*s had a daughter called Surasai. She was most upset to see how her father
had been defeated by the gods and determined to find a method of suppressing
them. She went to Shukra, the preceptor of the *asura*s and begged him to
teach her all the magic arts at his command. Very soon she became such an
adept that Shukra changed her name to Maya. She decided to beget sons through
a great sage so that they would have immense power and be able to subdue
the *devas*. She went to the forest where the sage Kasyapa was in deep meditation.
By her magic spells, the forest, which had been dark and gloomy, changed
into an entrancing glade where she sang and danced in front of the sage. At
last one day the sage opened his eyes and fell for her charms. She begged
him to marry her and he gave in to her wishes, fully aware of the consequences
of his action. He knew that her children would give further scope for the Lord's
play. The sages knew everything and they only played the part of instruments
in hastening the process of another *avatara* of the Supreme.

The first son of their alliance was called Surapadma, the second, Simhamukha
since he had the face of a lion and the third was Taraka who had the face
of an elephant. She also gave birth to a girl called Ajamukhi who had the face
of a goat.

When they came of age, the boys begged their parents to give them some
advice on how to conduct themselves. Kasyapa advised them to lead virtuous
lives spent in *tapasya* and thus gain liberation. He then left the family and
penetrated deeper into the forests in order to continue his interrupted *tapasya*
for he knew that the time had come for his sons to play their part in the
drama of Kartikeya's birth.

Maya however secretly drew the boys to her side and told them they should
go north and propitiate Lord Shiva and gain boons from him by which they
would become invincible and gain control over the heavens. The boys went
to the Himalayas and started rigorous *tapasya*. When they saw that Shiva did
not respond they redoubled their efforts and started sacrificing their limbs one
by one into the fire. Even then Shiva did not appear. At last Surapadma decided

to make the final sacrifice of his own body and jumped into the fire. The other two brothers also decided to follow suit and were just preparing themselves when Shiva, who is noted for his kindness, appeared and stopped them from throwing themselves into the flames. He brought Surapadma back to life and granted them all the boons they asked for except that of immortality. However he assured them that they would not be defeated by anyone except a child and that too one who came from his own loins!

They returned in triumph to their mother who was delighted at their success and sent them off to their preceptor, Shukra for further studies. He told them to enjoy themselves to the utmost and live a sensuous life of extravagance and unbridled passion since Shiva himself had granted them all the boons they wished for.

"Overthrow the *devas*. Strip them of their riches and make them your slaves!"

The boys were delighted at this advice, which was just what they wished to hear. They went off and carved out huge portions of land for themselves and built fantastic cities. Surapadma's capital was in the south and was known as Mahendrapuri. Simhamukha's capital was known as Asuram and was in the north and Taraka built his capital near Emakudam. The divine architect, Visvakarma, built all three cities.

After this Surapadma sent his son Banukopan to capture the gods and to make Indra and his consort prisoners. Indra and his wife fled in the guise of parrots and dwelt in South India. But his son Jayanta was captured and brought to Mahendrapuri, Surapadma's capital and made to work as a fisherman. The rest of the gods were also made into slaves. Brahma was made into a priest at their temple, Vayu, the god of winds was made the sweeper of the city streets and Varuna had the noble task of sprinkling water on the roads! The golden orb of the sun god, Surya, was given to his son Banukopan to play ball with. Thus the *devas* had to suffer untold insults and ignominy at the hands of the brothers.

In the meantime Indra left his wife under the protection of Maha Shasta and went to Kailasa to beg Shiva to intervene. During his absence Ajamukhi, the sister of Surapadma, tried to abduct Indra's wife, Indrani and take her to her brother. However, Maha Shasta thwarted her attempt and wounded her. She swore to take revenge.

The *devas* who were undergoing untold misery at the hands of the ferocious brothers decided to go to Kailasa and persuade Lord Shiva to come to their aid. When they reached Kailasa they found their way blocked by Shiva's mount, Nandi who told them not to go in since Shiva was closeted with the four boy sages, called Sanaka, Sanatkumara, Sanatana and Sadananda. He was instructing them on the four stages of *sadhana* called *yama, niyama,* yoga and *samadhi.* As an explanation of the last stage, Shiva closed his eyes and went into *Maha Mouna* or the great silence of *samadhi.* Thus he demonstrated the fact that this last stage could not be explained but only experienced.

The *devas* were terribly disappointed and did not know what to do. At last they persuaded Kama, the god of love to go and shoot his flower arrows at the Lord and wake him from his deep trance. Kama crept in for he could pass through locked doors and shot his arrows with unerring accuracy. Disturbed in his meditation, the Lord opened his third eye and out shot a wave of terrible heat and light, which turned Kama to ashes. The *devas* rushed to the presence and fell at his feet and begged him to save them from the *asuras* and from his wrath. Shiva's anger was always short-lived and he assured them of his help. Rati, the wife of Kama now took the opportunity to beg for the life of her husband, which was granted. He was given a form that could be seen only by Rati and not visible to anyone else.

The *devas* were delighted by Shiva's pledge and returned to their drudgery as slaves of the *asuras*, waiting for the day on which Shiva would be pleased to come to their aid.

"*Jnana* or wisdom is the perception of non-difference.
Dhyana or meditation is to extricate the mind from sense objects.
Snana or bath is the cleansing of the impurities of the mind.
Shoucha or purity is the controlling of the senses."

— *Skandopanishad*

ॐ *Sharavanabhava!*

Shaktidaraya Namaha!

CHAPTER EIGHT

DEVASENAPATI

General of the Divine Army

Ya shloka-panchakamidam padathiha bhaktya,
Brahmanya-deva viniveshitamanasa syad,
Prapnoti bhogamakhilam,
Bhuvi yadyadishtam,
Ante sa gachati muda guhasamyameva

Those who chant these five verses to Lord Subramanya with devotion,
Will attain all their desires,
And eventually reach his abode.

— *Sri Subramanya Pancharatnam*

Shiva married Parvati, daughter of Himavan and retired to Kailasa. He appeared to have forgotten the promise he had made to the *deva*s. So once again they went to Kailasa to remind him of his promise. Shiva took on a form with six faces. A spark, like a meteor shot out of each of these faces. The *deva*s were terrified and did not know how to handle the situation. They begged Vayu, the wind god and Agni, the god of fire to carry these six sparks and deposit them in the Ganga. Agni and Vayu could hardly carry the sparks and quickly deposited them into the Ganga. She was requested to take the sparks to a lake known as Sharavana filled with reeds known as *shara*. When the sparks reached the lake they changed into six divine babies who were incredibly beautiful. Each baby was lying on a lotus. The six stars known as the Krittikas took on human forms and came to give suck to the six divine infants.

The *deva*s had been closely following the sparks and when they saw this wondrous sight they apprised Shiva and Parvati about this and all of them came to the spot to see this extraordinary spectacle. Parvati was delighted to see the babies and gathered them altogether into her arms by which they became one single baby with six faces and twelve hands. She was wondering how she could cuddle a baby with six faces and twelve arms when once again there was a transformation and he became a lovely baby with just one head and two arms and nestled close to her breast. Parvati was delighted. However, many other aspirants now appeared to claim parentage of the divine baby. Agni said he was his son as he had held the sparks. Ganga said he was hers since she had carried him in her waters, the clump of reeds claimed him as theirs since he was born in their lap and the Krittikas demanded that he be given to them since they were the ones who suckled him.

The four main characters responsible for Skanda's birth were Shiva, Parvati, Ganga and Agni. Shiva intervened and tried to pacify the various claimants. He declared that as the son of the clump of reeds he would be known as Sharavanabhava, as the son of the Krittikas he would be called Kartikeya, as Ganga's son he would be known as Gangeya, as Parvati's son he would be known as Skanda and as his own son, Kumara. To satisfy all parents, the boy took different forms when he approached them. He appeared as Shakha before Parvati, as Vishaka before Ganga and as Agneya in front of Agni. The Ganga originates in the Himalayas and Parvati is the daughter of the Himalayas. Thus Ganga is not only her elder sister but also her co-wife since she resides in Shiva's locks. Agni is another aspect of Shiva therefore in all ways, Shiva can be considered to be Kartikeya's father and Parvati his mother.

To the amazement of the *deva*s another nine divine heroes emerged from the lake of reeds. Shiva told the gods that these were his special *gana*s headed by Veerabahu, who had been created to assist Kartikeya in his stupendous task of routing the *asura*s.

After the *deva*s had worshipped him, Shiva and Parvati took him back to Kailasa where he spent a very short childhood before the *deva*s once again appeared to ask him to lead their army.

Parvati objected, "He is only a child. What can he do against those mighty demons?"

Shiva laughed and said, "He may be only a child but he is born of my divine spark and he will be irresistible in battle. Have no fear."

One story goes that Indra was not sure if the boy could actually defeat the demons. He sent some of the gods to fight with Kartikeya while he was playing in the hills and dales of the Himalayas. Kartikeya defeated them and the frightened Indra foolishly declared war on Skanda and challenged him to a fight. As was to be expected Skanda routed Indra's army in no time. Infuriated at being defeated by a mere child, Indra hurled his thunderbolt at him. It pierced his right side and out of the injury sprang another being known as Vishaka. At first Vishaka was considered as a brother of Skanda but later on he appears to have merged into him and Vishaka became another name for Skanda. After this show of strength, Indra and the other celestials requested Kartikeya to become their king but Skanda refused this offer. Instead he agreed to become the commander-in-chief of their army.

Shiva summoned his son and gave him many formidable weapons. Parvati gave him the spear and all the other gods gave him their most invincible weapons. At last when everything was ready the army led by Kartikeya set out with the blessings of Shiva and Parvati and cheered by the other gods.

Kartikeya who was leading the host of the gods now met a demon called Krouncha, who had been cursed by Agastya to become a mountain since he had been guilty of killing many innocent people. Krouncha tried to stop the approach of the army, so Subramanya threw his spear at him and delivered him from his mountainous form.

Agastya had been told by Shiva to go south carrying a pot of water from the heavenly Ganga (*akasa* Ganga). On the way this *asura* called Krouncha who had assumed the shape of a mountain had tried to deflect him from his mission. Agastya guessed his identity and cursed him that he would remain in the shape of a mountain until Kartikeya delivered him.

Agastya continued his journey and after crossing the great mountain known as the Vindhyas, he reached South India. He had been carrying the river Ganga in his water pot and Ganesha was given the task of making him empty the pot so that South India would become fertile. Ganesha took the form of a crow and upset the water pot and this was the source of the great river Kaveri that is one of the most fertile rivers of the south.

Krouncha had been a great friend of Taraka and when he heard that he had been destroyed Taraka was furious. He rushed at Subramanya holding aloft the *Sudarshana Chakra* of Lord Vishnu to prove that he had defeated Vishnu. There ensued a fierce battle between the two of them in which Taraka tried every trick in the art of warfare to kill his enemy but to his dismay he found that none of his weapons had any effect on Kartikeya. At last he took up the dreaded weapon given to him by Shiva, known as the *Pasupata-astra* and hurled it at Shiva's son! Such was the stupidity and audacity of the demon! Skanda saw it coming and immediately meditated on Shiva and received the weapon on his chest where it changed into a harmless flower. Then he retaliated and hurled his famous weapon – the spear – with deadly accuracy at Taraka's chest.

After vanquishing Taraka, Skanda proceeded on his way to the south and eventually reached the famous spot known as Tiruchandur on the seashore. There is a beautiful temple of Subramanya at this spot. News of the death of their brother was carried to his brothers, Surapadma and Simhamukha. They re-doubled their atrocities against the gods and this news in turn was taken to Subramanya who was camping in Tiruchandur.

Skanda now sent his general, Veerabahu to Surapadma's capital commanding him to release Indra's son, Jayanta immediately and stop all further atrocities against the gods. Surapadma's capital was fully guarded by innumerable demons with strange faces and grotesque bodies. However, Veerabahu was determined to enter the fortress and managed to reach one of the gates. He killed the elephant-faced demon that tried to stop him and entered the city incognito. He was astonished to see the beauty of the city and felt sorry that it would soon be reduced to ruins. He was amazed that these demons were capable of such *tapasya* that they could wrest favours from the gods! While he did his tour of the city he chanced upon the prison in which Indra's son, Jayanta was imprisoned. He comforted him and promised him a speedy release and then proceeded to investigate the rest of the city. He was dazzled by Surapadma's audience hall, which was unrivalled even in Indra's heaven. Veerabahu was now spotted as an enemy spy and dragged before the king. Veerabahu bravely declared the reason for his visit and told the *asura* that his master had ordered him to release Jayanta and return their heaven to the gods. If not, he would incur Skanda's wrath. He had already killed Taraka and would soon despatch him to the same realm!

Surapadma refused to listen to such nonsense and declared that he was hardly going to be deterred by such threats especially when administered by an arrogant boy!

"Tell your master that I will certainly not buckle under such childish threats and will make mincemeat of him at our first encounter."

He ordered Veerabahu to be caught and incarcerated with Jayanta but he outwitted the guards and returned safely to Tiruchandur where he reported the whole matter to his master.

Surapadma immediately called a council of war and made careful plans for attack and defence. Some of his ministers tried to point out to him, the pitfalls of his plans but he would not listen to any of them.

"Skanda is an incarnation of his father, Shiva. It would be far safer for us to give in to his wishes and release Jayanta and come to a compromise with the gods. To disregard Skanda would be tantamount to insulting Shiva and will bring nothing but ruin upon our clan."

But the *asura* king was doomed and refused to pay any heed to such salutary advice.

Hearing about these doings from Veerabahu, Skanda shifted his army from Tiruchandur to a place near Emakudam, which was the capital of Simhamukha. When he heard about this manoeuvre, Surapadma sent a battalion headed by his son, Banukopan to rout the enemy. Banukopan was helped by his grandmother, Maya who gave him a magic weapon that made Veerabahu and the other generals of Skanda's army fall into a dead faint. Having finished this work, the *astra* (weapon) winged its way back to Banukopan who disappeared from the battlefield and reappeared in his father's capital. His report of the battle enraged his father so much that he decided to go to the battlefield himself on the second day.

Skanda had not yet entered the fray but when he heard about this magic weapon he sent a counter missile called the "Mohanastra", or the weapon of illusion and restored to consciousness all his warriors who had swooned.

In the fierce battle that followed, Simhamukha's son was killed. Infuriated by this, Taraka's son fell on Kartikeya's army and killed many of their invincible leaders. Veerabahu rushed to intercept the *asura* prince and in the fierce fight that followed he managed to kill him. Incensed by this, Surapadma rushed to the scene and proceeded to annihilate eight of Veerabahu's brothers. He then turned the full force of his fury against Veerabahu and hurled his dreaded *danda* or club at him. It struck him on the chest and he fell to the ground bleeding and unconscious. Taking him to be dead, Surapadma now proceeded to decimate the remaining army. Many died and the others fled from the field.

Kartikeya now entered the scene and came face to face with the triumphant king. He sent a series of missiles, which cut off all the weapons and insignia of Surapadma, one by one. Then he hurled the discus that had been given to him by Vishnu and annihilated hundreds of *asura*s. Surapadma found that none of his usual weapons had any power against Skanda and at last despatched the deadly *Pasupata-astra*, which he had received as a gift from Shiva. He confidently waited for Skanda to fall since this particular weapon had never been known to fail. To his amazement, Shanmukha, the son of Shiva, now calmly took the weapon in his hands as if it was a toy and kept it aside. It was only now that Surapadma realised the power of the being that he had disregarded as a mere boy! Taking recourse to his illusory powers he disappeared from the field for the day.

The next day was the third day of battle and Banukopan set out determined to rout the army of the gods. He came face to face with Veerabahu and a grim battle ensued between the two which both realised would be a fight to the finish. Once again Banukopan employed the magic arts he had learnt from his grandmother and launched an *astra*, which put everyone in the army to sleep. Many of them fell into the sea. Skanda immediately hurled his spear, which revived the fallen leaders, and the *asura*s found to their dismay that all the fallen generals of Skanda's army were back in their old positions.

Skanda now decided to take the offensive and told Veerabahu to force an entrance into Surapadma's capital. The fortress was strongly defended by his second son, Hiranyan. However Veerabahu slowly but surely pushed the prince and his army back and thrust his way into the fortress. Hiranyan realised that he was fighting a losing battle and disappeared from the field and lived in concealment at some far off place.

Another son of Surapadma known as Agnimukha took his place. He inflicted many casualties on the enemy host but at last was forced to concede to Veerabahu's superior might. He begged his favourite deity, Kaali to help him.

The goddess came and dealt a crippling blow to the army of the gods. When the goddess came face to face with Veerabahu, he stood with folded palms and prayed to her. She smiled graciously at him and disappeared from the field. After this even though the prince fought valiantly he was overpowered and killed by Veerabahu. Seeing this, Surapadma's other sons came forth to fight, but Veerabahu routed them all very easily.

Now Banukopan made his third and final appearance. When it appeared that he was losing, he, once again called upon his grandmother, Maya, to help him. He disappeared from the scene and flew up into the air from which vantage point he rained arrows at the vulnerable host of the gods. Veerabahu was furious at these illusory tricks and sent his *jnanastra*, or weapon of knowledge and forced Banukopan to reveal himself and come down to earth for a hand to hand fight. At last with a superhuman effort and praying to Kartikeya for help, Veerabahu cut off Banukopan's head, which now rolled helplessly on the ground.

Surapadma was devastated when he heard this and rushed to the battlefield and gathered the remains of his dear son and brought it home to his castle. He called his brother, Simhamukha to come to his aid immediately. The latter ravished the enemy hosts but again Veerabahu mowed down all his sons single-handed. Infuriated by this, Simhamukha bound Veerabahu and all the rest of the leaders of the army and wafted them away to a hill far away from the battlefield. He then entered the camp and killed many of the *gana*s there.

On hearing this news, Skanda realised that Simhamukha was indeed a worthy opponent and immediately came on the scene. He brought back those who had been wafted to the hill then turned to face Simhamukha himself. There ensued a grim battle in which he put an end to his opponent's life.

Surapadma was stunned to hear the news of his invincible brother's downfall. Nothing daunted he rallied the remnants of his forces and sent to the nether worlds for further reinforcements. Veerabahu and others immediately tried to block Surapadma's advance. The *asura* king fought valiantly and at last found himself face to face with Shanmukha. The duel that ensued was most memorable – as great as the duel between Rama and Ravana. Surapadma knew that defeat was inevitable if he fought according to the rules. So he employed every devious trick taught to him by his mother, Maya. He brought back to life all the *asura* warriors who had been killed and also obtained a magic chariot. He assumed many forms including that of animals and birds. But it was all in vain for Shanmukha was the Supreme Being himself who was beyond all illusion (beyond *maya*). Maya herself would have been powerless against him, what to speak of her son! With one twang of his bow he despatched all the revived *asura*s back to the nether world from where they had been brought. With another twang he took over the magic chariot for his own use. Surapadma was mortified to see the chariot that he had brought for his own use being used by his archenemy. Next Skanda smashed his vehicle. Surapadma promptly took the form of a huge bird and swooped down upon him. The Lord tore the bird to pieces but Surapadma escaped from the bird's body just in time and saved himself.

Kartikeya was filled with admiration for the way in which the *asura* was fighting. He admired his courage and also felt compassion for him for he knew the story of his previous lives. Before killing him, he revealed his cosmic form in all glory before the demon king. At this enthralling vision, all the illusions he had learnt from his mother fell away from him and he prostrated full length before that Supreme Person.

The Lord now assumed his original form. Once again Surapadma was overpowered by delusion and resumed the fight. He took the form of a huge tree. The Lord took his spear and cleft the tree into two. Unable to escape his doom, Surapadma took his real form and with a roar of anger he rushed at Subramanya with the desperate idea of crushing him in his arms and bringing him down to the ground. The Lord in his mercy wanted to put an end to the *asura*'s miseries and took his spear and cut him in two. In commemoration of this fight, the Lord ordained that the peacock and the rooster whose forms Surapadma had assumed would become his vehicle and the emblem on his flag. This was in keeping with the promise he had made to him in is previous birth.

Thus ended the life of the powerful king of the demons. The gods got back their lost kingdom. He is supposed to have killed Surapadma on the sixth (*shasti*) day of the bright fortnight of the month of *Margashirsha* (November/ December). This is the sixth day after Diwali and is known as *Skanda Shasti* and is a very important day for the worshippers of Skanda.

After the Great War, Kartikeya set about destroying the last remnants of the demonic hoards that had either fled or were hiding. Bana was a cowardly demon that had fled from the scene of the great battle. Now he started harassing the mountain Krauncha who had been subdued by Kartikeya and who now begged him for help. Kartikeya killed Bana and delivered Krauncha.

Another time he heard the news of the terror and destruction caused by a goat-headed *asura*. This was Ajamukhi, the sister of the Surapadma who had a goat's face. She was bent on avenging the death of her brothers. He chased her and caught hold of her horns but out of mercy he made her into his subsidiary vehicle instead of killing her.

The esoteric significance of this story as with most puranic stories is the same – the estrangement of the *jivatman* or the embodied soul from the *Paramatman* or the Supreme Soul and its journey back to its source. The three *asura*s were the sons of Maya or delusion. These three represent the three *gunas* of *maya* or Nature known as *sattva, rajas* and *tamas*, which bind the immortal spirit through ignorance, to the mortal body. Subramanya incarnates himself in order to help the forces of good (*deva*s) who had been incarcerated in the prison of the three *guna*s!

Surapadma despite his intense *tapasya* was unable to enjoy the fruits of his austerity for long. The *asura*s are those who have taken a turn away from the light and are being dragged down to the depths of hell, which is a place of their own making. In its journey back to its original state, the *jivatman* has to undergo many hardships. The *guru* of the *asura*s is Shukra, the lower mind, which brings forth many arguments to justify its inclination towards carnal pleasures. This would have ended in ruin but due to the grace of Subramanya, the *asura* was released from his ignorant state and restored to a place of grace as the Lord's standard-bearer and vehicle.

"O spotless son of Parashakti (mother of the universe),
You stay on the seashore to proclaim to devotees,
That they will cross the ocean of *samsara* (transmigratory life),
And be free of all worldly worries,
If they worship you at this spot (The temple of Tiruchandur)."

— *Subramanya Bhujangam*
by Adi Shankaracharya

ॐ *Sharavanabhava!*

CHAPTER NINE

UMASUTA

Wives of Kartikeya

Yatabde taranga layam yanti tungaha!
Tadeva padasannidhou sevatham me.

Just as huge waves in the ocean disappear on reaching the shore,
So also those who have recourse to your feet will be freed from enormous
worries.

In the north Kartikeya is supposed to be a celibate since he saw his mother
in every woman. In the south he is seen as the personification of masculine
beauty and virility and is always flanked by his two wives, one from heaven
and the other from the earth. In the south, Ganesha is the eternal celibate (*nitya
brahmachari*) because he never found a woman to compare with his mother.
Thus we find that descriptions of the wives of the sons of Shiva vary from
north to south. Actually none of the gods have wives. They are pure beings
made of consciousness and light. Basically they are neither male nor female.
Their consorts are not separate from them but aspects of their being – their
shakti or power. Valli and Devayani, the consorts of Muruga signify the *ida*
and *pingala nadis*, male and female currents. But the Puranas delight in making
stories so we will take up the stories of Skanda's marriage as given in both
the *Shiva Purana* and the *Skanda Purana*.

The story as given in the *Shiva Purana* says that when the two sons of Shiva,
Ganesha and Kumara came of marriageable age, the parents decided to get
them married. Now the question arose as to who should marry first. Shiva
declared that the one who should go round the universe first should have first
choice. Kartikeya wasted no time and immediately set off on his peacock. The

wily Ganesha knew he was sadly handicapped by his bulky body and tiny vehicle. "Why should I undertake such a dangerous journey crossing rivers and mountains, oceans and valleys?" Instead he thought of a brilliant method of getting his own way without resorting to all these difficult tasks. He took his purificatory bath and made his parents sit on a golden throne and solemnly circumambulated them thrice and demanded that he should have first preference. When questioned about his strange behaviour, he replied that Shiva and Parvati constituted the whole universe of movable and immovable things and hence going round them was tantamount to going round the universe. Thus as we have seen, Ganesha's marriage was solemnized even before Kartikeya got back. He was furious when he returned and found that his brother's marriage was over. He went away to the Krauncha Mountain as a protest and remained a *brahmachari.* This incident coincides with the exit of Skanda from North India after a glorious career as a martial deity.

The story in the *Skanda Purana* is a little different. This Purana extols Skanda as the Supreme Person and not just the son of Shiva. During the short while that he had resided at Kailasa, Skanda had met the two daughters of Lord Vishnu who were called Amrutavalli and Sundaravalli. They had both fallen in love with the handsome son of Shiva but at that time he was unable to marry either of them. Skanda had promised to marry them in another age when they would be born again – one as the daughter of Indra, king of gods and the other as the daughter of a hill tribe of South India. Accordingly, Amrutavalli had been born as the daughter of Indra and Sundaravalli as the daughter of a tribal chieftain called Nambi who was the head of the tribe called the Veddas.

After the successful completion of his *avatara,* which was to vanquish the three demons, Lord Skanda returned to Tiruchandur with his victorious army and released all the gods who had been made prisoners.

Indra took this opportunity to approach Skanda and ask him to accept the hand of his daughter, Devayani in marriage. Skanda remembered his promise to Amrutavalli in another age and agreed. It was to be conducted at the famous pilgrim spot known as Tiruparankunram, which is a little north of Thiruchandur. When the guests came Skanda felt very unhappy that his parents had not been invited. However, the moment he thought of them Shiva accompanied by Parvati and Ganesha now appeared much to the delight of all concerned. The marriage was conducted with all the usual accoutrements and the delighted gods now retired to their own abode.

The *Shiva Purana* describes the tiff between Skanda and his parents that was the reason for his having left Kailasa and gone to the south. When the two boys, Ganesha and Kartikeya were staying in Kailasa with their parents, the sage Narada came and brought a pomegranate fruit for the children. However he said that this was the fruit of cosmic wisdom and could not be cut into two. Only one of them could have it. As usual to test his children, Shiva said that the one who went round the universe first should have the fruit. Kartikeya immediately set out on his peacock. Ganesha knew his limitations. Neither he nor his mount was noted for speed. He was too corpulent and the mouse too slow. There was no way that he could outdistance the slender Kartikeya mounted on the peacock. As usual he thought of a clever strategy by which he could win the race as well as get the blessings of his parents. He took his ritual bath and made Shiva and Parvati sit on a golden throne. He then prostrated to them and went round them thrice. At the end of the ritual he once again prostrated to them and demanded the fruit. They were very pleased at his intelligent reply that as far as a child was concerned his parents were the beginning and end of his universe and so he deserved the fruit since he had gone round them thrice and not just once as requested. The two sons of the cosmic mother, Parvati denote the two aspects of the evolved human being – strength and wisdom.

When Kartikeya returned, he was shocked to see that the fruit had been given and eaten by his shrewd brother. He was quite angry at this unfair treatment and declared that he was going to leave Kailasa and go and settle at some lonely place in order to meditate and get the fruit of supreme wisdom. He asked Shiva to give him permission and it is said that Shiva told him *palam nee*, which in Tamil means, "You yourself are the fruit!" This statement has the same meaning as the great Upanishadic statement, *Tat twam asi*, "That thou art." The esoteric import of this statement is that the embodied soul (*jivatman*) and the Supreme Soul (*Paramatman*) are one and the same. Shiva pointed out to Skanda that he was indeed the Supreme Soul and thus he had no need to eat the fruit that gave supreme wisdom!

However, Kumara was not to be pacified and he left Kailasa and went south to the hill called Palani (*palam nee*), where he practised penance in order to discover this truth. The shrine at Palani is one of the most inspiring shrines to Kartikeya in India. In fact it was here that he was given the name Muruga or the divine youth.

Parvati was so unhappy at the separation from her eldest son that she begged Shiva to go south. He agreed and they came and took up their residence at the famous *jyotirlinga* called Sri Shailam where Shiva is known as Mallikarjuna. From here Parvati found it easier to visit her beloved son.

The story of his courtship and marriage to Valli, a tribal girl is one that has delighted all his devotees through the ages. It is the story of the love between a god who chose to stay on the earth because of the great love he bore for a simple tribal girl. Both literary and oral traditions confirm that Valli was a historical personage. She is a mysterious twelve-year old who seems to have spanned the passage of time from pre-historic times to the present day. Chief among her admirers is Subramanya himself. The intensity of her love for him is supposed to have kept him on this earthly sphere to this present day.

The age-old romance of Valli and Muruga is filled with all the traits of a great romantic novel. It is said that Valli was found as an infant in the jungle by the chief of a tribe known as the Veddas who were actually worshippers of the boy god, Muruga. The Veddas are a tribe found in the north of Sri Lanka at the place, which is presently known as Kataragama.

The Hindu Puranas delight in narrating the story of the previous birth of this baby who had been miraculously found in the middle of a jungle. It is said that one of the *avatara*s of Lord Vishnu known as Upendra once went to Vaikunta, the abode of Vishnu in order to have his *darshan*. Vishnu was seated with Lakshmi. Upendra came to them and begged to be allowed to worship them. Vishnu agreed and all three were engrossed in the worship when the sage called Kanva entered the hall. None of them noticed him and therefore none of them welcomed him or gave him the honours due to a sage. One might wonder why the sages always seemed so quick to curse people. The sages are renowned for their ability to foresee the future and are always anxious to bring about another aspect of the *lila* of the Lord. It is to be noted that it is always for this purpose that they pronounce their curses. This seems quite strange to others who do not know the reason. Kanva therefore cursed all three of them that Vishnu would be born as a dumb sage devoted to Shiva and Lakshmi would be born as a deer roaming in the forest and Upendra would be born as a hunter for many births. When Vishnu asked him to mitigate this curse, he agreed to bring it down to one birth instead of many births. He also said that all three of them would be restored to their original status at the marriage of Skanda and Valli. Thus we see that the whole aim of the game was to bring about this endearing chapter in the story of Muruga.

In course of time Vishnu came to the world as Shivamuni, a dumb saint and roamed about the forests of Sri Lanka, which was a part of India at that time. Upendra also took birth in the same forest as a hunter. Lakshmi in her form as a deer roamed around in this very forest. As ordained by the sage, when Shivamuni saw the deer he felt a deep and passionate longing in his heart, since it was none other than his consort through eternity. The deer reciprocated the love and always kept close to him. Eventually the deer conceived and delivered a human child. Seeing the infant to be totally different from herself, she abandoned the little baby girl to her fate in a clump of creepers. The hunter, Upendra now appeared on the scene and took the baby girl home to be brought up as his daughter. The Tamil word for "creeper" is *valli* and thus he named her Valli since she was found amongst the creepers. The child grew up hearing stories of Muruga and gave her heart to him from a tender age. She took a solemn vow that she would never marry a mortal but would wed only Muruga, the tutelary deity of her tribe.

"The Lord Murugan shines in the little village,
On the sides of the high hill where,
The white rivulet sounds.
The men wear clusters of Vanaki flowers, dripping with honey,
They dance with their women in the street,
Keeping time with the Tondago drum."

The sage Narada now reminded Skanda of his promise to Sundaravalli while in Kailasa, that he would marry her. He told him that she was being brought up as the daughter of a tribal chief and had made a vow that she would wed none but him. Skanda immediately left for the forest where Valli resided. The Veddas were a forest tribe who lived on nuts and fruits and flesh but once a year they would make a clearing in the jungle and cultivate millet. Somebody was always kept in the field to guard against the assault of animals, birds and other marauders. That year Valli had been sent to the millet field in order to safeguard the field. She stayed in a small hut that was normally built for the person who was appointed to look after the field.

Muruga came to the field disguised as a hunter and made advances to the maid. Even though she was only twelve years old, the child had already sworn to wed none other than Muruga so she repulsed him and ordered him to clear off. He refused to comply, and told her that he had come there only with the express purpose of winning her hand. She was quite outraged at his audacity and called out to her brothers for help. Her seven brothers rushed to her aid but the wily hunter changed himself into a tree much to Valli's amazement. The brothers chided her for calling them without any reason and returned to their work. As soon as their backs were turned the tree became the hunter once again. This time Valli decided that self help was the best help and took a stick and chased the hunter off.

After a while she saw an aged ascetic tottering towards her. Valli very kindly offered him some of her fruits and water. After he finished eating she was amazed to hear him make a declaration of love for her and request her to marry him. She laughed contemptuously and told him very sternly that she had taken a vow to marry none other than Muruga. Instead of revealing himself he decided to tease her a little and requested Ganesha to help him. Ganesha in his form as an elephant came charging into the clearing. Valli was terrified at seeing the mad elephant and rushed into the old man's arms and begged him to save her. He agreed on condition that she promised to marry him. The terrified Valli clung to his arm and agreed to everything and the elephant disappeared as mysteriously as it had appeared.

As soon as it disappeared she shook free from the old man's arms and refused to keep her promise since it had been extracted under duress. No sooner had she said this than the elephant came charging again. She was so frightened that once again she gave her solemn word to marry the old man if he chased the elephant off. The old man laughed and waved the elephant off and revealed himself as Muruga the handsome war god, carrying his inevitable spear. Needless to say she was thrilled to see her idol in front of her physical eyes and agreed to have a *gandharva* (clandestine) marriage with him. This type of marriage was one of mutual consent and did not need the permission of the parents. Their love blossomed with the ripening millet and the couple spent an idyllic honeymoon in the little hut in the field. When the millet was ready for harvesting her brothers came to call her. Unfortunately they came when Muruga had gone out and she was too shy and afraid to tell them anything. However she was most unhappy and drooped and pined and refused to eat. No one could make out what the matter was. At last her mother called a soothsayer who proclaimed that she was possessed of an evil spirit and that she would have to perform a type of dance ceremony to appease Muruga and dispel the spirit.

Meanwhile Muruga returned to their love nest in the field and found the little hut empty and his beloved gone. He was frantic and searched for her over hill and dale. The great poet Arunagiri, in his book *Kandar Anubhuti*, touchingly describes this scene of the great warrior wandering amidst the mountains and forests and rivers and hills frantically searching for his beloved. At last he traced her to her home and stole into her house at midnight and asked her to elope with him. The tribals woke up and chased the hunter who vanquished them with a flourish of his spear. Valli begged him to bring her relations back to life. He did so and to their amazement they saw Muruga's cock emblem on the hunter's head. They were overjoyed to see their beloved god in their midst and were only too happy to allow Valli to marry him.

To their great joy, the sage Narada now appeared and the divine marriage was conducted in true tribal style with dancing and music, followed by a feast of fruit, honey, millet cakes and venison. The Great God stayed on in the forest amidst his kinsmen, enjoying the simple pleasures that they offered, tied to them by the intense love that Valli bore him. In keeping with her name she had entwined herself round him so that he could not move away from her!

In the book *Kandar Anubhuti*, Arunagiri says that Muruga, whose lotus feet are placed on their heads by Brahma and other gods, placed the lotus feet of the hunter's daughter on his own head! The great love that Valli bore for Muruga was equalled only by the love he bore for her. Hence every devotee of Muruga feels that if they could also make a vow like Valli that they would wed none but Muruga, he would condescend to bless them in a similar fashion.

This legend shows that Subramanya is also the god of those tribes whose modes of worship are primitive and crude. Thus he was prepared to confer knowledge on all, regardless of the level of their understanding and spiritual attainment. According to ancient records, the Veddas were a tribe in the north of Sri Lanka. This story is told in the annals of the famous temple of Kataragama in Sri Lanka.

All puranic stories are imbued with esoteric significance so let us try to understand the inner meaning of this great romance between Valli and Skanda. His two consorts, Valli and Devayani represent *iccha shakti* or the power of desire and *kriya shakti* or the power of action. These two also portray the two different types of devotees. One is the conservative type who rigidly and sincerely observes all the rules and injunctions given in the scriptures. Devayani, daughter of Indra, whom Subramanya married in the orthodox and regular way, following all the rules, portrays this type. Valli, the daughter of a tribal chieftain, on the other hand represents those *bhakta*s or devotees who are totally carried away by the tide of their love and are not even conscious of the injunctions of the scriptures. It is the overwhelming force of their love that impels the divine to come and rescue them despite the obstructions kept in their way by their relations.

The *vel* or spear denotes *jnana shakti* or the power of knowledge. When the *jiva* has *iccha shakti* or intense desire for liberation, the Lord in the form of the *guru* comes and gives it *jnana shakti* or the power of knowledge. With this knowledge it uses its power of action (*kriya shakti*), and eventually attains liberation.

Valli represents the *jiva,* which has been separated from its original status of eternal bliss. It roams in the wilderness of the forest of the world due to its ignorance of its original nature. She spends her time throwing stones at the birds that peck at the grains in her field. The esoteric meaning of this story is given here.

The dark forest is *tamas* or ignorance; her brothers are *rajas*, in whose grip she has been caught. Her dedication to guarding the grains shows her intense commitment to her spiritual practice. She keeps the catapult of discrimination (*viveka*) in her hands and shoots the pebbles of dispassion (*vairagya*) at the birds that come to disturb her spiritual practice (*sadhana*). Subramanya is the

Paramatman, the source of bliss from which the *jiva* has separated due to its ignorance. The *guru* in the form of the sage Narada arrives to join the two who have been separated and thus they are married. The *jiva* in the form of Valli possessed unflinching devotion to the Lord and thus she was able to realise her ambition in spite of all obstructions.

"Let my mind be a bee and hover round thy lotus feet,
Which are pink in colour and full of nectar
And which are adorned with anklets with tinkling bells and beads."

— *Subramanya Bhujagam*
by Adi Shankaracharya

ॐ *Sharavanabhava!*

"O destroyer of Taraka,
The very sight of your sacred ashes,
Makes demons run in fear and,
Destroys all illnesses,
Like leprosy, fever and madness."

— *Kartikeya Stotram*

ॐ
Amruthaaya Namaha!

CHAPTER TEN

GANGEYA

Curse of the Snakes

O Jagannatha! I offer my prostrations to thy six heads,
Wearing crowns with brilliant rubies which protect all creatures,
Which did Shiva kiss with joy, uttering this mantra six times.
"O child! You were born from my seed,
May you live long!"

— *Subramanya Bhujangam*
by Adi Shankaracharya

ॐ

Once it is said that the gods along with Brahma and Vishnu came to Kailasa to have *darshan* of Lord Shiva. All of them paid their respects to the boy hero, Shanmukha. Brahma alone who was always obsessed by a sense of his own importance refused to bow before a child. In fact he deliberately averted his eyes and refused to even look at him. Kartikeya decided to teach him a lesson and invited all the gods to his special audience hall. When they had taken their seats, he put a series of questions to Brahma. In the final question, Kartikeya asked Brahma to explain the importance of the *pranava mantra, Aum.*

Brahma was unable to give a satisfactory explanation and so Kartikeya ordered that he be put into prison in order to cool his pride. From that time onwards the work of creation was taken over by himself.

The gods felt sorry for the grandsire and asked Shiva to accompany them and beg Kartikeya to release Brahma even though he was a conceited ass! Kartikeya said that a god who did not know the significance of *Aum* was not fit to function as the creator of the world. However, under pressure from his father, he released Brahma.

Since he declared Brahma's explanation to be wrong, Shiva now asked Kartikeya to explain the meaning of the *pranava mantra*. Shanmukha accepted the challenge and proceeded to expound the meaning of this great *mantra* to his own father. Shiva, who knew everything was delighted with his son's exposition on the subject and gave him the name of Swaminathan, or the one who was the teacher of his own sire.

Another account of Brahma's defeat goes that it took place at Palani. When the gods came there to meet him after he had defeated the demons, Skanda said that the victory was due to his invincible *vel* or spear. Brahma however insisted on taking credit for the victory since he was the creator and he was the one who had made the spear. Skanda was angry at this show of pride and cursed Brahma that he would lose his powers of creation and be born on earth as a human being.

Many stories of Subramanya show his connection with snakes. The peacock that Kartikeya uses as his vehicle is famed for being the enemy of snakes. In those regions where peacocks reside, snakes are hardly ever seen. In many places in Tamil Nadu, Subramanya is connected with the Naga (serpent) cult.

In South India, Muruga is widely worshipped as the serpent deity and the one who can overcome all the demerits that accrue to us for having harmed or killed snakes. This is known as *sarpa dosha*. Since he is the Lord of snakes he has control over them so that those who suffer from *sarpa dosha* normally approach him for redemption. It is believed that leprosy is the result of *sarpa dosha*. These are not mere superstitions but have a scientific aspect. It is noted by astrologers that when five of the seven planets in a person's horoscope come under the sway of Rahu and Ketu, which are the malignant serpent planets, the person is said to be having *sarpa dosha*. This is said to have come through the sin of having killed a serpent in this life or in another, intentionally or otherwise.

A look at the planetary movements during the last century show an enhancement in the influence of Rahu and Ketu on the planetary positions resulting in this *dosha* and causing a lot of suffering to a number of people on the planet. Many great personalities who have performed wonderful deeds during their lifetime are said to have suffered from *sarpa dosha*. To mention a few – Abraham Lincoln, Rani Lakshmibai of Jhansi, Rani of Chittoor, Pandit

Jawaharlal Nehru, Emperor Nero, Ghenkinz Khan, Jesus Christ, Mussolini, etc. Although these great personalities achieved great things in their life, their end was terrible.

This *dosha* is said to be the cause of many of the difficulties that we face in life like continuous loss in business and continuous ill health, miserable married life, childlessness, skin diseases, diseases of the eyes, ears and throat, poverty, improper development of the organs, loss and litigation and constant worry. Those who have built their houses after destroying snake hillocks are bound to have ill health and unhappiness as long as they live in that house.

Worship of Muruga is said to be a cure for the curse of the snakes since he is their patron deity. Soon after he had killed Taraka, Kumuda, the son of the snake, Shesha, sought refuge with Kartikeya, since he was being harassed by the *asura*, Pralamba who had been an ally of Taraka. Skanda killed Pralamba and delivered Kumuda and gave him leave to return to his own abode of Patala (the nether world). The grateful snake blessed him and begged him to become their patron deity. He also proclaimed that anyone who worshipped Muruga would be freed from the threat of snakebite. In the temple of Trichengode, Skanda is worshipped in the form of a serpent. The sixth day of the lunar month, or *shasti* is sacred to both Subramanya and to the serpent gods.

In South India snakes are supposed to be charmed beings that have the power to curse the person who kills or harms them. Hence, snake worship is pretty prevalent all over the south. In olden days most big houses had a special place in the compound that was reserved for snakes. Here they were worshipped and given milk to drink. They were supposedly fond of this beverage. The strange thing is that in those houses where snakes were given harbour and worshipped there was never a case of anyone dying of snakebite. In present times with the breakdown of the ancient family system all the old houses have also been broken down. The images of the snakes were transferred to temples where they are worshipped. In some cases when this was not done the family members suffered from strange calamities and diseases, which rightly or wrongly were attributed to the curse of the snakes that had been abandoned. The curse also falls on those who deliberately harm or kill snakes especially serpents like the cobra. Even today there are many snake hills to be seen in Karnataka, Andhra Pradesh and Tamil Nadu. If these are found in the middle of a place where the government wants to build a road, the builders take special pains to circumvent the little mound so that the snakes remain unmolested.

In Kerala there are two famous temples dedicated to snakes in which many miracles happen. Newborn babies of the family are left at a special place where the chief snake is supposed to come and bless them. In one of these temples a lady who has miraculous powers at her command, does the *puja*.

Most South Indian temples keep idols of serpents somewhere in the compound. Each type of idol is a remedy for a particular type of *dosha* or for fulfilling a particular wish of the devotee. The *pujas* or rituals to overcome these *doshas* are many. However, they have to be performed by people who are well versed in such matters. These rituals entail a lot of expenditure so not everyone can afford them. Thus the Puranas declare that worship of Subramanya is the best and simplest method for overcoming all the different types of calamities that can accrue to us due to *sarpa dosha*, since he is the Lord of serpents. As one can see from his pictures, the peacock has a snake crushed under its foot. Esoterically speaking, the snake is the symbol of ignorance, which Kartikeya eradicates with his vehicle, the peacock.

"O son of Shiva!
Your six smiling lotus faces,
Shine like a group of swans,
Your eyes glance sideways, moving like a row of bees,
Over your red lips overflowing with nectar."

— *Subramanya Bhujagam*
by Adi Shankaracharya

ॐ *Sharavanabhava!*

ॐ

Abhayaya Namaha!

CHAPTER ELEVEN

VELAYUDHA

Palani

O son of Parameshwara!
O merciful Lord!
When you have twelve large eyes, stretching to your ears,
What will you lose by casting a side glance at me for a minue?

— *Subramanya Bhujagam*
by Adi Shankaracharya

Once when Shiva gave a discourse on yoga, every creature in the world rushed to Kailasa. As a result of this mass exodus, the whole world started to tilt towards the Himalayas. All wisdom and knowledge had gone to the north. There was nothing to keep the balance of the world. Shiva told Agastya, the wisest of his disciples to proceed south, carrying with him all the sacred and secular lore that he had taught. Agastya agreed but begged Shiva to give him something that would remind him of the Himalayas. Shiva gave him two huge mountains, called Shivagiri and Shaktigiri, to take to the south. *Giri* means "mountain" and these mountains were called Shiva and Shakti since they represented Shiva and Parvati. The demon, Ettumba was designated to carry them. He made a huge bow and tied the hills on either side and carried them across his shoulders. When he reached the place called Palani, he kept the mountains down and went to the river. When he returned he found them rooted to the spot. Try as he might he could not uproot them. He looked around and saw a handsome young boy sitting on one of the hills. The boy was sitting with one leg over the other and waving it about. He had a mischievious look on his face. The demon became very angry since he suspected that the boy had a hand in this. He ordered the boy to get off the hill so that he could carry it to its destination. The boy refused and Ettumba became furious. They had a fight in which Ettumba was killed.

Just then Agastya came on the scene and recognised the boy to be none other than Kartikeya. He bowed low before him and Kartikeya said, "I shall keep these mountains here for they remind me of my home in the North." Ettumba's wife now came and begged Muruga to bring her husband back to life. Pleased with her devotion Muruga revived Ettumba. He begged Muruga to keep him as his sentinel at the entrance of his abode. Thus we can see the shrine of Ettumba half way up the hill. He also begged Muruga to bless all those who came to the hill carrying a bow with some offering hanging on either side as he had done. This wish was also granted. Agastya was happy to comply with the Lord's wish that the Palani hill should be left where it was and thus Kartikeya resided on the hills of Palani and Agastya on the plains. The balance of the cosmos was restored.

Ettumba carrying the two hills like a bow across his shoulders is still remembered in Palani and one of the biggest offerings here is for the devotee to carry something called a *kavadi* which is a curved bow-like structure on either side of which is hung some milk or fruit or some offering to the Lord. This is taken on the shoulder of the devotee while she or he climbs up the mountain and kept in front of the idol as a gift. The pole, which supports the *kavadi,* has an esoteric significance. It is compared to the spinal column with the *Muladhara Chakra* at one end and the *Sahasrara Chakra* at the other.

The other story of Palani has already been related. The celestial sage Narada could forsee the future exploits of the boy hero in South India and with a view to hastening the time for his departure from the Himalayan regions he brought a fruit to Kailasa which was to be given as a prize to the child who would go round the earth first. As we have seen Ganesha won the prize with his sagacity. His sense of justice inflamed, Kartikeya stormed out of Kailasa and went south. Clad only in a loincloth and carrying a staff he went to the spot where modern Palani stands and decided to stay there. The story goes that Shiva and Parvati followed him since Parvati couldn't bear to be parted from him. Shiva tried to console him by telling him that he himself was the Supreme fruit of the Vedas and thus he did not need any material fruit. The words in Tamil are *palam nee* which mean, "You are the fruit." Thus the spot where Subramanya resided came to be known as Palani. Here Kumara is in the form of a young boy and is the very embodiment of renunciation. He wears only a loincloth and is divested of all ornaments. He carries a staff in his right hand and his left hand is placed on the hip. He is known as Palaniandi or Dandapani.

Palani is one of the most important places of the worship of Lord Subramanya. The shrine is at an altitude of 1,550 feet and is open to all castes. The orthodox way to go there is by carrying a *kavadi* and climbing the steps. Now most people prefer to go by the cable car. Though the temple is in the state of Tamil Nadu, the Lord faces the state of Kerala, so he is equally adored by both states.

Most of the deities worshipped in the shrines of Tamil Nadu are made out of granite. But here the image of Muruga is strikingly different. It is a strange amalgam known as *navapashanam*. It is a unique combination of nine kinds of medicinal minerals, some of which are even poisonous. These are blended in an exclusive proportion known only to its maker who was the great sage and *siddha* – Bhogarnatha whose story will be related below. The idol of the boy, Kumara, is naked except for a loincloth, he has a shaven head and holds a spear. He is known as Velayudha, the one who carries a *vel* or spear.

According to the Indian version there are six important shrines to Kartikeya each of which is connected with some aspect of his life. All of them are found in South India in the state of Tamil Nadu. They are Palani, Thiruchandur, Thiruparankunram, Thiruttani, Pazhamuthirsholai and Swamimalai. However, another legend in Sri Lanka says that Kataragama in Sri Lanka is the most important shrine of Muruga since he met and married Valli at that place and all his fights with the demons took place here. The tribes there are still known as Veddas.

Thiruchandur is a very important shrine connected with Muruga. A place on a hill or near the sea is supposed to be the best spot for a shrine of the war god. Thiruchandur is close to the sea and it is said that when Murugan came to this town he found it too small and asked the celestial architect Visvakarma to enlarge it. The beautiful sculpture on the right wall of the temple shows him on a peacock fighting the *asura* Surapadma and the figure on the left wall depicts him seated on an elephant with Devayani.

Swamimalai temple is supposed to be the one in which Skanda gave a discourse to his father on the mysteries of the *pranava mantra* and thus he got the name Swaminathan or the one who taught his father. The temple is on top of a hill as is usual with Subramanya temples while Shiva's shrine is at the bottom of the hill as befitting a disciple. Here his vehicle is that of an elephant instead of the usual peacock. The story goes that Indra, king of gods presented his elephant, Airavata to Subramanya in gratitude for having saved him from a demon.

The sacred geography of Tamil Nadu is closely connected with these *Aaru Patai Veettukal* or the six war camps of Muruga, which are associated with particular episodes in his career. These are scattered across the length and breadth of Tamil Nadu and thus relate the whole state with the career of Muruga. The number six is a significant number in numerology and closely connected with Subramanya. It signifies the six rays of the *shat-kona yantra* in which two triangles intersect each other. These six points refer to the six cardinal directions of space. These are the six rays that emanated from Shiva and coalesced and integrated to become Kumara, the personification of perpetual youth.

The story of sage Bhogarnatha who was the greatest devotee of the Lord of Palani is well worth repeating here. His name is also closely connected with the shrine of Kataragama. A description of the great *rishi*s of ancient India was given in the first chapter. Most people may not even believe that such men actually existed. To prove the truth of this, the details of the life of the great sage called Bhogarnatha who lived in 3102 BC is given here. We know of his life from the poem called "Bhogar Jnana Saagarama" which means the "The Oceanic Life Story of Bhogar". This is such an incredible story that it is not comparable to even the fables and fairy tales of olden days.

In this book Bhogarnatha states that he was the disciple of the great *siddha* known as Kalangi Nathar who was himself a disciple of the ancient sage, Agastya. Kalangi Nathar was born in Varanasi. He attained *swarupa samadhi* (left the physical plane) at the age of three hundred and fifteen years and then took his astral body to China, which then became the centre of his activities. He belonged to the ancient tradition of the *Nava* (nine) *Nath Sadhus* who traced their lineage to Lord Shiva. There are nine important shrines associated with this tradition, five of which are in the Himalayas. Amarnath is the place where Shiva first taught this great yoga to Parvati. The others are Kedarnath, Badrinath, Kailasanath (Tibet) and Pasupathinath (Nepal).

Bhogarnatha practised *Kundalini Yoga* in four stages. He chose the Palani hill as the site of his intensive yogic practices for the final stage. Through the grace of Lord Muruga, the eternal youth, Kumara Swami, as he lovingly called him, he became an adept in yoga. Even though he went to many places, he kept this sacred place as the centre of his activities. His poem describes the countries that he visited sometimes physically, sometimes astrally, as well as through transmigration. In one of his songs, he claims to have flown to China in a sort of plane, which he built himself. He held discussions with Chinese *siddhas* before returning to India.

His visit to South America has been confirmed by accounts left by the Muycas of Chile. They called him Bocha. Here is an extract from one of their texts.

"Bocha, who gave laws to the Muycas was a white-bearded man wearing long robes, who regulated the calendar, established festivals and then vanished in time like others! (Presumably other remarkable teachers had come across the Pacific according to the numerous legends of the Incas, Aztecs and Mayans.)

Bhogarnatha convened a meeting of many *siddhas* just before the beginning of the present *Kali Yuga*, 3102 BC to determine the best way for humanity to progress along the path of spirituality in the coming Age of Kali. *Bhakti Yoga* or the yoga of love and devotion was chosen as the best means. Bhogarnatha was entrusted by the other *siddhas* with the task of defining the rituals for the worship of their favourite deity, "Palaniandi" or the Lord of Palani. Many of these rituals are continued to this very day. In fact he was the one who made the idol, which is worshipped today. He made it from a substance that was expected to last throughout the Age of Kali. Even idols made of granite, the most resilient of stones is known to wear and crack if different types of ingredients are poured over the deity day after day for thousands of years, in the *puja* known as *abhishekam*. So Bhogarnatha fashioned an idol out of nine secret herbal and chemical ingredients known as *navapasham* which made it harder than granite. Eight of these ingredients were combined in a mould of the idol. The ninth was added as a catalyst in order to solidify it.

In recent times scientists who attempted to determine the composition of a small sample taken from the idol were startled to find that it vanished when heated. Thus the composition of the idol remains a mystery to date. Devotees believe that traces of this substance are contained in the water and other liquids with which the idol is bathed and which when consumed will give great benefit both spiritually and physically.

At one time, Kalangi Nathar, Bhogar's *guru* who had migrated bodily to China wanted to enter into a period of *samadhi* (mystic trance), for three thousand years. He summoned his chief disciple Bhogarnatha telepathically to come to China and take over his mission there. Bhogarnatha chose to travel in a boat by sea, following the normal shipping trade route.

In China his *guru* instructed him on all aspects of the *siddha* form of medicine, which included the preparation, and use of something called *kaya kalpa*, which is a formula for promoting longevity and extending human life to an incalculable period of time. When Kalangi Nathar entered into his trance of *samadhi*, Bhogarnatha continued his mission. To make it easier for himself he transferred his vital body into the physical body of a deceased Chinaman and took on the name of Bo-Yang. "Bo" is actually a derivation of the word *bhogam* which means bliss, both material and spiritual. He proclaimed that this bliss is experienced when the *Kundalini Shakti* or the *yin*, feminine energy as the Chinese call it, awakens and passes to the crown of the head, the seat of Shiva, which is the masculine *yang* according to the Chinese.

Now Bhogarnatha decided to overcome the limitations of the body with its degenerative tendencies and prolong its life for a longer period, through the use of the *kaya kalpa* herbs as instructed by his *guru*. This would give him ample time to totally master the *Kundalini Yoga* techniques and enable him to go into the state of *swarupa samadhi* which his *guru* had practised and which he had taught him. In his poem he vividly describes what happened after carefully preparing a tablet using thirty-five different herbs.

Before taking the tablet, he chose three of his best disciples and his faithful dog and took them to the top of a mountain. He first offered the tablet to the dog which ate it and immediately dropped down. He next offered it to his leading disciple, Yu, who also sank to the ground. When he offered the tablets to his two remaining disciples, they were very nervous and promptly hid their tablets instead of swallowing them. Bhogarnatha swallowed the remaining tablets and fell down unconscious. The two disciples were panic-stricken and hurriedly went down to get material to bury the bodies. When they returned they found a note in Bhogar's handwriting, which said:

"The *kaya kalpa* tablets are working as I was sure they would. After waking up from my trance, I restored to life, the faithful Yu and the dog. You have missed your golden opportunity to become immortal."

In his own words he describes what happened to him after eating the tablets. "With great care and patience I made the tablet and swallowed it. I became as immortal as any human being can become. I lived in the land of the foreigners for twelve thousand years and fed the *ojas* (spiritual energy) with the *ojas vindhu*. I received the name Bhogar. The body developed the golden colour of the pill. Now I'm living in a world of gold."

After having transformed his Chinese body, Bhogarnatha lived for over a period of 12,000 years during which time the body developed a lustrous golden colour as described in his poems. During this time he perfected the *Kundalini Yoga* technique that would enable him to leave the physical body and yet remain alive (*swarupa samadhi*).

After the incident with his Chinese disciples, Bo-Yang became known as Lao Tzu, and was accessible for nearly two hundred years in China and became well known as a great teacher. He trained hundreds of Chinese disciples in tantric yoga practices, where semen and sexual energies are conserved and sublimated into spiritual energy.

In the 5th century BC the great Chinese sage, Confucius met Lao-Tzu Bo-Yang and said of him:

"I know a bird can fly, a fish can swim and an animal run. To catch that which runs, a net can be fashioned, for that which swims a line can be strung, but the ascent of a dragon on the wind into heaven is something that is beyond my knowledge. Today I have met Lao-Tzu who is perhaps like a dragon." (Among the Chinese, the dragon is the symbol of the *Kundalini Shakti*).

At the end of his mission to China about 400 BC, Bhogarnatha, with his disciple Yu, to whom he gave the Indian name Pulipani and other close disciples left China by the land route. As recorded in Taoist literature, at the request of the gatekeeper at the Hjan Ku Mountain pass, Lao-Tzu crystallised his teachings. He did so in two books, the *Tao Ching* and the *Te Ching*.

In the second book he says, "Do good to him who has done you injury." This was also said by the contemporary Tamil *siddha*, Tiruvalluvar as well as by Jesus Christ. Taoist tradition continues to seek physical immortality using techniques remarkably similar to those taught in *Shaiva Siddhanta Yoga*, which was obviously taught to them by Lao-Tzu alias Bhogarnatha.

Along their way Bhogarnatha and his disciples visited several shines in the Himalayas including Kamarupa, modern Kamakhya, the famous tantric shrine in Assam. He composed his greatest work of 700,000 verses near mount Kailasa with the blessings of Lord Shiva. It was later abridged into seven thousand verses and is known as "Bhogar Sapta Kandam". He then visited Arabia and then returned to India. When he came back to Tamil Nadu he introduced the Chinese salts and chemistry that he called *cheena-charam* and also the art of porcelain making at which the Chinese excelled. He submitted his manuscript for evaluation to his *guru* Agastya and to an academy of *siddhas* who had gathered there. It was endorsed by all of them as being a divinely inspired book.

After this many *siddhas* became his disciples to study the sciences of *kaya kalpa* and *Kundalini Yoga*. He eventually turned over his teaching mission to his Chinese disciple, Pulipani.

After doing *tapasya* at Sthula Giri and Shiva Giri, he went to the place known as Kataragama in Sri Lanka to perform more *tapasya* and gain the grace of Lord Muruga. He established the famous *yantra* representing the thousand and eight petalled lotus at Kataragama. Some people say that his disciple Kalyana Giri established this *yantra*. Then he went to Palani, his favourite spot on earth and decided to go into *swarupa samadhi*. The Bhogarnatha *samadhi* is a most impressive place in Palani.

Later he is said to have taken another form and returned to Kataragama where Mahavatar Babaji Nagaraja met him around AD 211.

Much later after a period of six dynasties (AD 220 to 590) Bhogarnatha returned with some Tamil disciples to China. During the construction of the Brihitswarar Shiva temple in Tanjore, around AD 900, Bhogarnatha advised its builders on the method of raising the eighty-ton capstone (*shikar*) to the top of the temple more than 200 feet high. The instructions to his Tamil disciples were sent through a novel method. They were despatched through homing pigeons. He suggested making a sloping ramp five miles long by which the stone was pulled to the top of the temple. This was one of the most remarkable engineering feats of those times. He also advised the king of Tanjore to build a small shrine dedicated to one of his chief disciples, Karuvoorar, behind the Shiva temple.

Though Bhogarnatha is said to have left the physical plane at Palani, he continues to work on the astral plane inspiring his disciples and devotees all over the world. In rare instances he even transmigrates into another physical body for certain specific purposes.

In the last century he identified himself as a Tamil *siddha* known as Swami Ramaiah.

We are indeed fortunate that he left behind some record of his remarkable life. Perhaps he did this so as to impress the modern mind of the great abilities that the ancient *rishi*s of our land had achieved. As was said in the first chapter, these remarkable men did not leave any account of their amazing lives and thus we have to depend only on oral tradition as well as the teachings of the Vedas to prove their existence. But here the sage himself, has given us an autobiographical account, which though incredible has to be accepted.

"O Lord! When the emmissaries of Yama,
the Lord of Death approach me,
And try to frighten me,
Do thou hasten to appear before me,
Riding on the peacock and carrying the spear,
And encourage me not to be afraid."

— *Subramanya Bhujagam*
by Adi Shankaracharya

ॐ *Sharavanabhava!*

Pavakatmajaaya Namaha!

CHAPTER TWELVE

SWAMINATHAN

Kataragama

Hail Guha!
During the last moments of my life,
When I would have lost control of my senses,
When I would have lost consciousness,
When I would be unable to move my limbs,
When I would be frothing from my mouth,
When my body would be trembling with the fear of death,
When I would have none to protect me,
Do thou hasten to give me darshan!

— *Subramanya Bhujagam*
by Adi Shankaracharya

In South India it is said that all the exploits of Kartikeya took place on the Indian continent but according to the Sri Lankan version his journey took him from Kailasa to Kataragama on the island of Sri Lanka. Strangely enough both these places lie on the same line of longitude. He is supposed to have crossed the straits to Sri Lanka and then gone on foot to the hill of Katirmalai from where he led the host of the gods and defeated the demons. The *Skanda Purana* also indicates that Murugan fought the demons at this place.

Kataragama is sometimes known as Dakshina Kailasa or the Kailasa of the south. Kailasa in the Himalayas and Kataragama in the far south constitute a north-south axis not merely in yogic lore but also in geography. They both lie on the same line of longitude – 80.10 degrees east. This fact was well known to all the *yogis* who lived in Kataragama. This axis refers to the *sushumna nadi* or subtle nerve centre that runs through the human spine. All the seven *chakras* or subtle centres of psychic energy are located along this nerve. Kailasa in the

Himalayas corresponds to the *Sahasrara Chakra* or the thousand-petalled lotus, which is the seat of Shiva, while Kataragama is likened to the *Muladhara Chakra* situated just above the anus in the human body. The *Devi Kundalini* lies curled up just above the *Muladhara Chakra* and is the point of entry for those who want to practise *Kundalini Yoga*. She has to be awakened by yogic practices and forced to rise up through all the *chakras* until she attains union with Shiva in the *Sahasrara Chakra*. This axis is also likened to the light, which was emitted from the Supreme at the start of creation.

So esoterically speaking the descent of Skanda from Uttara Kailasa to Dakshina Kailasa or Kataragama is an allegory for the descent of Spirit into matter. This is further enhanced and made into the story of Muruga and Valli. Muruga, the Supreme Spirit comes to earth to woo and wed the yearning human soul as portrayed by Valli. The very name of the place *katir-kaman* supports this idea. *Katir* means effulgence or light and *kaman*, passion or love. The effulgence comes from Kailasa and kindles into the flame of passion – that is to say the *Paramatman* descends into the human form and weds the aspiring *jivatman*.

In ancient times when sacred geography played an important role in the construction of important towns, a configuration of seven hills was considered to be an ideal location for the capital of a state or for the construction of a temple. Notable examples in Europe are Athens, Rome, Constantinople and Jerusalem. In India the famous temple of Thirupathi is located on seven hills and the same applies to Kataragama, which is also on seven hills. The number seven signifies the reversal, return and integration of the soul to its original status of innocence. This is the object of all those who follow Kumara or Muruga.

Bhogarnatha as well as many other *siddhas* and saints are connected with this shrine. But strangely enough there is no icon or idol of Muruga in this place. His aspect as pure consciousness alone is worshipped here. The sanctum sanctorum contains a small casket with the *shat-kona yantra*, which is a mystic design in which two triangles interlock. The six points thus created refer to the six cardinal points of space. Thus the six-faced Shanmukha is the Lord of Space. He is the conscious presence abiding at the source and centre of our three-dimensional world, which is a field of infinite possibilities. The Sri Lankans believe that Kartikeya's entire career took place on this hill for it is here that the six cardinal points of space collapse and return to their undivided singularity.

The most well known and romantic incident in Murugan's career took place here. This was his secret courtship and marriage with Valli Amman, the daughter of the chief of the Veddas who were the indigenous tribes of the forest. From a conventional point of view this union of a god and a tribal girl, almost an outcaste is a gross mis-match. But as we have seen, this combining of the two, represents the union of the Supreme Spirit with the earth bound soul that craves for this merger.

The legend attached to this temple is as follows. Lord Muruga had taken an incarnation in South India by the name of Kataragama. His wife's name was Tevayani. This name is actually the Sri Lankan distortion of the name Devayani or Devasena, who was Subramanya's first consort. It so happened that Kataragama had a quarrel with Tevayani and left her and went to the island of Sri Lanka. He proceeded to the hill called Katirmalai, which was the abode of the tribe called the Veddas. This hill is just above the present day shrine of Kataragama. One day when he was out hunting, he met the adopted daughter of the Vedda chief known as Valli. The rest of the story is the same as the romance of Valli and Subramanya described in the previous chapter with a few differences that will be given below.

In the Hindu tradition, vows play an important role in the relationship between the deity and the devotee. Though a child, Valli had made a vow that she would marry no man but Murugan himself. This is the core of the legend of Kataragama. In Sinhalese folklore Lord Kataragama also makes a solemn vow that he would ever remain at Kataragama to help and protect his devotees. Murugan's devotees are famous for making difficult vows in order to gain his grace. They pierce their cheeks with arrows and walk barefoot on hot coals. But strangely enough none of them seem to get hurt.

The story of their romance is most intriguing. Murugan knew of Valli's vow but he did not approach her in his own form but in a series of disguises. As we have seen in Kataragama temple there is no idol. Only the *yantra* is worshipped. Thus in this place Murugan is regarded as formless. Therefore, whatever form or face he chooses to show is only a guise. His true devotee is expected to penetrate the disguise and realise that he is indeed formless. Due to his tricks and methods of teasing his devotees, the Lord of Kataragama, like Krishna is lovingly called a thief and a rogue!

Kataragama found Valli in the millet field and approached her as a handsome young hunter and proposed to her in a brazen attempt to make her violate her vow. She adamantly refused to succumb to his charms. Next day he took the form of an old Brahmin and tottered in front of her and begged for some food. She offered fruit and honey, which was all she had, but he said he needed water to wash it down. She agreed to show him the way to the well. On the way he asked her if she was not afraid of living in a field in the midst of the jungle all alone when the men were away hunting.

She said she was afraid of nothing except elephants. Immediately Ganesha appeared in front of them as an elephant and Valli clung to the old man and begged him to save her. He said he would do so only if she agreed to marry him. She promptly agreed and he brought her back safely to her village. When her family saw them they rushed to attack Kataragama whereupon he changed himself into a tree. The Veddas proceeded to cut down the tree but at the very first blow, blood gushed out of the wound so the Veddas discovered his identity. They realised that he was Murugan, the god they had been worshipping for centuries so they joyously agreed to the marriage. Thus Kataragama and Valli lived happily together for many years.

In the meantime Tevayani was tired of her lonely existence and sent Kataragama's teacher who was known as Muttulingam Swami as well as a Muslim called Mohammed Navi, to search for her husband. They knew that he had gone to Sri Lanka so they followed him and eventually came to the region of the Veddas. However they were unable to locate him even though they wandered in the forest for a long time. They were on the point of giving up the task when Muttulingam Swami discovered that someone else had smoked the opium pipe that he had used and left on the hill the previous day. He knew immediately that only Kataragama would have dared to do such a thing. Once again they started searching for him even more earnestly and very soon discovered him. They insisted that he accompany them back to India. The thought of forsaking Valli was inconceivable, so he refused to go.

Instead, he persuaded his *guru,* Muttulingam to stay behind but the Muslim, Mohammed Navi returned to India and blurted out the whole story to Tevayani.

She was determined to get her husband back and went post haste to Sri Lanka. She found Kataragama and pleaded with him to return to their home in India but he refused. So she decided to stay on with the Veddas. It appears that the Muslim, Mohammed Navi had also followed her. The Veddas accepted all of them and they lived amicably together till the end of their lives. When they died the Veddas built a temple for Muttulingam Swami and a mosque for Mohammed Navi on either side of the temple of Valli. They also built a shrine for Tevayani.

Obviously the mosque was built in order to effect a reconciliation between the two religions. Muslims are allowed to visit the shrine at all times except the time of the main *puja*, since Mohamed Navi was the one who had betrayed Kataragama. If any Muslim is found inside at that time, he is severely beaten. However at other times all castes and religions are welcome to Kataragama, which has become a Mecca for Muslims as well as a Kailasa for Hindus. Lord Muruga in his form as Kataragama is available to all, irrespective of caste, creed or social status. His grace is abundantly given to all.

Kataragama has all the three points which all sacred shrines are supposed to have – *murti*, or idol, *sthalam* or holy spot, and *teertham* or holy river. The sacred *yantra*, or mathematical figure imbued with spiritual power is kept in the place of the idol. The *sthalam* or place is the holy hill known as Katirmalai and the *teertham* or river is called the Manika Ganga or the Ganga of gems.

Kataragama has an amazing ambience. The atmosphere is filled with mystery and magic. Countless miracles keep taking place here. The main temple has two apartments. The sanctum sanctorum is heavily veiled with seven curtains. This does not have an idol of Kataragama. Instead it has a casket, which contains the mysterious *yantra* (mystic diagram), which is embossed on a golden tablet studded with gems. This is where the divine power is supposed to reside. The Lord in his *nada bindu* form (form of letters and sound) is enshrined in the *yantra*.

The great sage Kalyana Giri who was a disciple of Bhogarnatha made this *yantra*. By his intense *tapasya* he made Murugan available to every devotee through this *yantra*. He is supposed to have come from North India and done intense *tapasya* for twelve years chanting the great *mantra* of Muruga (*Aum Sharavanabhava*) without sleeping. When he went into *samadhi* the Veddas were supposed to have looked after him and thus got the blessings of Kataragama. The place where the sage had sat for his *tapasya* is the sanctum sanctorum of the temple where the casket containing the *yantra* is kept.

After he left his body, two other sages also known as Kalyana Giri, are supposed to have taken over the *puja* of the *yantra*. The priests who came after them still conduct *pujas* according to the rites as established by them, which is what was originally taught to them by the Veddas. So it is tribal in character. They tie up their mouths with a white cloth when they offer the *pujas* so as not to defile the articles used in the ritual with spit, which might fly from their mouths. They also offer fruits and honey from the jungle rather than elaborately cooked foods.

The Kataragama Mahadevale temple is on the left bank of the Manika Ganga, which is the holy river, which flows near Kataragama. It is here that Murugan is supposed to reside. The place is shrouded with mystery. It is a modest single storey building and is said to have been built in the 2nd century BC by the Sinhalese king Duttugemunu who was directed to build the temple by Lord Kataragama himself. *Yogis* who meditate here say that the temple has actually seven stories – three above and three below apart from the ground floor, which everyone can see. These correspond to the seven *lokas* or astral worlds that lie above this planet. In fact the temple is a microcosm of the hierarchical cosmos described in Indian tradition.

Certain places on earth are believed to exude a mystic power since they are in direct contact with their subtle counterparts in the astral worlds. The Mahadevale temple is one such place.

Another interesting feature of Kataragama is the famous *pada yatra* or pilgrimage on foot. It is a tradition, which has been inherited from the island's indigenous forest dwellers – the Veddas. The devotees start from the far south of the island. They take about forty-five days to two months to reach the Kataragama shrine in the remote north-eastern jungle. The *yatra* is timed so that the devotees can reach the temple in time for the biggest festival there. This custom existed long before the arrival of the other major religions associated with this shrine.

The *pada yatra* is not a mere walking journey but a spiritual passage through subtle dimensions that are revealed only to the devout participant. The pilgrims traverse through the shadowy world of outward appearances and penetrate into the effulgent realm of *katir kaman* or "light and delight". Only one who is imbued with faith can appreciate what it means to cross the threshold of ordinary time and plunge into the realms of sacred time and sacred space. The voyage to the innermost sanctum is a spiritual journey into one's own metaphysical centre.

The festival for which the pilgrims come, starts on the new moon day of the Tamil month of *Adi* – July/August and ends on the full moon day of the same month (*Adi*), which comes in August. Thus the worship of Murugan is connected with the lunar cycle. The new moon marks the beginning of the ritual associated with Murugan and ends with the full moon denoting fulfilment. Each night during the festival, the sacred casket enclosing the *yantra* is placed on the back of an elephant and taken round in a procession round the temple. It is said that when it reaches the shrine of Tevayani the drums beat very loudly in order to drown her cries of protest! Apparently she has not stopped her supplication of Kataragama, entreating him to return with her to India.

Devotees of Muruga undertake many vows. One of the strange sights here is that of pilgrims carrying earthen pots with burning camphor on their heads while they follow the procession. Strangely enough none of them seem to get their heads burnt by this unique offering. A day prior to the termination of the festival, there is a fire-walking ceremony. Only devotees, who are inspired by the deity to be a vehicle for the exhibition of divine power, dare to take part in the ceremony. In the early hours of the morning they bathe in the sacred water of the Manika Ganga or the river of gems, and then step barefoot on to the forty feet track of burning embers fearlessly. To the amazement of spectators none of them who have thus been inspired ever get burnt. "Those who come to scoff remain to pray!"

There are other indigenous forms of worship here that are even more amazing to behold. Some pilgrims go round with their mouths gagged so that they cannot talk or eat. Others have their lips and cheeks pierced with silver-headed pins. Some votaries hang themselves on hooks to a tree that is specially reserved for this purpose. The hooks are pierced through the flesh of their backs! These types of customs might seem barbarous to the modern mind, which is the western mind, but it must be realised that whatever form of self-punishment is undertaken as a fulfilment of a vow, the devotee is found to be unscathed at the end of the process. This can only be called miraculous.

Sometimes inexplicable trances and possession by the spirit of Kataragama are found amongst the pilgrims. No scientific explanation is feasible for the doubting modern mind. Another common experience during the festival is for children to get lost but invariably they are always brought back to their parents in a mysterious manner. Murugan in the form of Kataragama is supposed to answer the prayer of sincere devotees in many mystifying ways. He appears in various human forms and gives them advice. But when they search for the person later, he is never to be found. The history of Kataragama abounds with innumerable episodes of this nature.

Ancestral memory and present day happenings bear witness to the thousands of miracles that have been enacted on this stage by the divine play of Lord Kataragama. Millions of boons have been received through his ever-abounding grace. The subtle presence of many *siddhas* who have lived here many years ago are felt by people even now.

Naga puja or snake worship existed here from about 220 BC and still continues. As we have seen, worship of Muruga is considered the best way to alleviate the effects of *sarpa dosha* or the curse of the snakes. Many cures are affected here of people getting cured after having been bitten by the poisonous snakes that abound in the neighbouring forest.

The sacred *vibhuti* or ashes in this temple is obtained by digging at a place called *vibhuti malai*. This again is another divine mystery since no one knows how it got there. Indeed there are many such inexplicable happenings in this extraordinary temple.

Till very recent times the only way to reach Kataragama was by foot. The path led through thick equatorial jungle, infested with snakes and wild animals. It was very similar to the pilgrimage to Sabarimala, which will be described later. Only the intrepid and the faithful could make this hazardous journey and return home alive. Even today there are a few people who still follow this ancient trail and go on foot. Now of course the town has been connected by road to all major cities of Sri Lanka so most people prefer the safe method of going by some motor vehicle.

Even in this age of scepticism, Kataragama is an extraordinary place where strange things happen which appear to defy the laws of science. Most Hindus believe that the pilgrimage to Kataragama is feasible only if Murugan himself issues an invitation.

"O Shanmukha!
I worship thy twelve arms.
That punished Brahma,
That governs the world through thy lila,
Those arms that killed Yama, Surapadma and other enemies of Indra,
Those arms that are matchless in protecting the universe.
And which are a terror to thy enemies."

—— *Subramanya Bhujagam*
by Adi Shankaracharya

ॐ *Sharavanabhava!*

ॐ
Dharmashastaaya Namaha!

BOOK THREE

Sarva dharmaan parityejya,
Maam-ekam sharanam vraja,
Aham twa sarva paapebhyo,
Mokshayishyami Ma shucha

Renouncing all other duties,
Have recourse to me alone,
I undertake to pardon all your sins
And give you total liberation

— *Srimad Bhagavad Gita*

Ayyappa as found in the idol of Sabarimala (Illus. done in ancient Kerala
mural style using only vegetable dyes by K. Suresh).

ॐ
Shivaputraya Namaha!

CHAPTER ONE

HARI HARA PUTRA

Story of Mahishi

Bhootanathaaya Vidhmahe
Bhava Nandanaaya Dheemahi
Tanno Shasta Prachodayaath!

I pray to Bhootanatha, the son of Shiva,
To enlighten me.

— *Dharma Shasta Gayatri*

As has already been discussed the Puranas abound in stories which outwardly seem incredible but are actually saturated with esoteric secrets, which are available to the sincere seeker. We all know that the Supreme can only be realised by our own individual effort. The Puranas are given to us in the form of stories to encourage us to search for this Truth. The lives of the gods and their devotees kindle the flame of spirituality in us and we get a burning desire to experience this Truth for ourselves. They are filled with the experiences of those who have known this Truth and are longing to share their knowledge with those who are on the same path. Most prophets and saints have communicated the nature of Ultimate Truth to the world at large, in a mysterious packing. Obviously these souls, who had attained this wisdom, were great individuals who had reached the highest stages of spiritual development. Their names are never mentioned. They were far above the vulgar desire to see their names associated with the knowledge that they passed on to others. They did it with the hope that there might be some soul somewhere who would understand their language and be tempted to follow their advice. Their stories speak to our innermost Self, which is the same in all human beings and that is the reason why they are still read and appreciated by all whether young or old, erudite or uneducated.

The lives of our saints and *siddhas* are all true accounts of those who have pierced the veil of *maya* that covers the ordinary human consciousness and emerged into the world of Ultimate Reality and become one with the universal consciousness.

"The world is like the impression left by the telling of a story," is what the sage Vasishta, told Sri Rama. Vyasa as we have seen was one of the greatest storytellers the world has ever seen. He is the author of all our Puranas. However it will be noticed that in all the books on the different deities that Vyasa wrote he extolled that particular deity above all others. This is because he knew that all of them stemmed from the same source. They take on all the aspects and powers of the Supreme Reality as and when they are invoked.

Dharma Shasta has an important place in the Hindu scriptures since he is supposed to be the last human *avatara* of the Lord in this *Kali Yuga* apart from that of Kalki. We have seen that both the sons of Shiva – Ganesha and Kartikeya had strange births. Similar is the case with Dharma Shasta. The story of his birth is told in many Puranas including the *Srimad Bhagavatam* and may appear bizarre to the modern mind.

The ancient story of the birth of the incredible son of Shiva and Vishnu starts with the story of Dattatreya who was the son of the sage Atri and his wife Anasuya who was noted for her great austerities and chastity. The couple had performed intense *tapasya* on the three gods, Brahma, Vishnu and Shiva in order to get a son and at last they had been blessed with a son who possessed all the glory of the Trinity. The consorts of the three gods now took birth as the daughter of the sage called Galava. She was named Lila. Dattatreya married Lila and they lived for many years very happily.

However a time came when Datta remembered his divine lineage and decided to retire to the forest to start his austerities to re-discover the Truth, which had faded from his mind due to the life of pleasure that he had been leading. He told his wife Lila about his decision. But unfortunately Lila was in the prime of youth and far from having exhausted her sexual desires. She begged her husband not to leave her since she could not bear to be separated from him. Datta advised her not to cling to youth, beauty and fortune which would all vanish with time but to cling instead to the Supreme which alone would bring her eternal happiness.

Lila was hardly convinced by his arguments and stuck to her opinion. The Sanskrit word *mahishi*, means both a female buffalo as well as consort.

Lila told Datta, "I'm your *mahishi* and I have every right to ask you to fulfil my desires. I will never let you go."

Datta tried his best to persuade Lila to change her mind and accompany him to the forest in order to get lasting benefits rather than effervescent pleasures. But she was bent upon getting her own will and refused to listen to his pleas. At last Datta's patience came to an end and he cursed her and said, "Since you are constantly referring to yourself as my *mahishi*, you will indeed be born as a *mahishi* (she-buffalo) and thus be enabled to slake your inexhaustible thirst for sexual pleasures!"

Not to be outdone, Lila cursed him back that when she was born as a *mahishi*, he would also be born as a *mahisha* or male buffalo and be her mate once again!

Many years passed and Lila was born as the daughter of the *asura*, Karamba. She had the face of a she-buffalo and was called Mahishi. In the meantime Karamba's brother Ramba had a son known as Mahishasura. He also had the face of a buffalo. His inequities were legion and the gods begged the Divine Mother to take an incarnation and kill him since he had got a boon from Brahma that only a woman could kill him! The Supreme Shakti took the form of Chandika and killed Mahishasura.

Mahishi was devastated to hear this and swore revenge on the gods. She went to the mountains and started rigorous austerities to invoke the blessings of Brahma. At last he appeared and told her to ask for anything except immortality.

She requested that she should have protection from all natural calamities. She then very craftily demanded that only the son of two male gods – Shiva and Vishnu should have the power to vanquish her. Moreover she insisted that he should also have spent twelve years of his life on earth as a human being before getting the power to kill her.

Brahma weakly agreed to all her demands. Having got all these boons, Mahishi became bloated with pride since she was sure that a son born out of two male gods would be an impossibility. So she set out to wreak her vengeance on the gods and created havoc in heaven. The gods approached Brahma who accompanied them to the abode of Vishnu and Shiva. When the three gods came together once more, the spirit of Datta, which had become absorbed in them, now took on the form of an exceedingly handsome male buffalo called Sundara Mahisha. This was in fulfilment of Lila's curse. Lord Vishnu blessed Mahisha and told him to go to the heavens where Mahishi had deposed the gods and was ruling in their stead. He was to cajole Mahishi and take her down to the earth and fulfil all her desires. Mahisha went to heaven. The moment she saw him, Mahishi became totally enamoured of Sundara Mahisha and followed him with great docility to the forests of South India and sported with him for many years. The gods joyfully returned to their kingdom. But this happy state of affairs was not to last long.

The defeated *asuras* went and complained to Mahishi about their sad state of affairs and begged her to stop her sport with Sundara Mahisha and help them in their distress.

"You are the sole support of the demon clan," they said, "and it ill behoves you to forget our miseries and carry on with your own blissful life. The gods have even cheated us of our rightful share of the nectar of immortality even though they made us work hard for it. Only you can help us!"

Hearing their plea, Mahishi assumed her original monstrous form and went back to the heavens and started wreaking vengeance on the gods. Once again the dejected gods went to Brahma, Vishnu and Shiva and begged them to help them.

Brahma told them not to worry since already plans were afoot to produce a child out of the union of Shiva and Vishnu, since Mahishi had got a boon from him that only such a child could kill her.

Loka Veeram Mahaa-Poojyam
Sarva Rakshakaram Vibhum
Parvati Hridayaanandam
Shastaram Pranamaamyaham

"I bow to Shasta, who is most worthy of being worshipped,
Who is the all-pervading, saviour of all,
And who is the delight of his mother Parvati."

— *Sri Dharma Shasta Pancharatnam*

Swamiye Sharanamayyappa!

Mahaatejase Namaha!

CHAPTER TWO

BHOOTANATHA

Churning of the Milky Ocean

Nakshatra naatha-vadanam,
Natham tribhuvanaavanam,
Nameetha-ashesha bhuvanam,
Shastaaram pranathosmyaham

I bow to Lord Dharma Shasta,
Who is as beautiful as the full moon,
Who is the Lord of the three worlds,
And is worshipped by the whole world.

— *Shasta Panchakshara Stotram*

A reason had to be created by which a child born out of two male gods could be born and hence we get the story of the churning of the milky ocean.

This story has been mentioned in almost every Purana and thus appears to have a very deep esoteric meaning, which only the mind that dives into the ocean of obscurity can understand and appreciate. Lord Vishnu reclines on his bed made of the curled up body of the snake known as Ananta on the milky ocean. Ananta actually signifies endless Time and the ocean of milk is the ocean of all possibilities (the zero point field of modern science), from which the whole world of infinite variety has appeared and into which it disappears at the end of one cycle of creation. In Hindu mythology creation is cyclical and a period of evolution is followed by another period of dissolution.

Once it happened that the sage Durvasa had visited Vishnu who had presented him with his Vanamala or garland of wild flowers. Durvasa took the garland and went to visit Indra, king of the gods. Indra was riding on his magnificent elephant when the sage came and ceremoniously offered the sacred garland to him. In his usual careless fashion, Indra threw the garland round the elephant's neck. Just then a bee came and poked the beast on its trunk. The elephant shook its head from side to side and chased off the bee. In the process the precious garland fell to the ground and was trampled by the animal, much to the watching sage's chagrin. He cursed Indra that he along with his retinue of gods would become old and decrepit and lose all his strength and beauty. Immediately all the gods became shrivelled and old and were hardly able to totter around. They hobbled off to the creator, Brahma and begged him to intervene on their behalf with Lord Vishnu.

The Lord appeared in all his glory and spoke to them.

"O gods!" He said, "Time is the master controller of all things. At the moment Time is favourable to the *asuras* who are your archenemies. The wheel of time turns slowly but one day it will turn in your favour. That will happen only if you churn the milky ocean and get *amrita*, the elixir of life, and drink it. Anyone who drinks it will get eternal youth and vigour."

The gods protested, "We are so weak that we can't even walk, how are we to undertake such an arduous task like the churning of the milky ocean. It is well beyond our capabilities!"

Vishnu said, "I realise that you will never be able to do it on your own, so you will have to beg the *asuras* to help you." The *devas* protested that it was beneath their dignity to ask for help from their enemies.

Vishnu said, "In desperate situations it may be necessary to eat one's pride and ask for help from one's enemies. After gaining your objective you may return to your original state of enmity! One who drinks *amrita* will become immortal so waste no time. Go to the *asuras* and solicit their help. Therein lies your salvation. It is possible that the ocean will throw up many precious objects as you start churning. Have no attraction or repulsion to whatever comes up and above all don't lose your temper and start quarrelling with your partners over the booty! Remember that you have no option but to agree to whatever terms they suggest."

The gods agreed to everything and went and solicited the help of the demons who were only too anxious to oblige them when they heard of the trophy in store for them. Immortality was one thing which they had always asked

Brahma to give them and which he had continuously denied them. They put up a show of hesitation and said that they would agree only if they were given their fair share of the *amrita*. Inwardly they exulted and thought to themselves, "These gods are too weak to fight, we will grab the nectar as soon as it appears and eat it all so that they will remain as they are now and we will become strong and youthful!"

Now the question arose as to what they should use for a churn. Vishnu suggested that he would uproot the Mandara Mountain and bring it on the back of his vehicle, the Garuda. He also offered his pet snake, Ananta to be used as a rope. Both parties were delighted at this suggestion. They wound the snake round the middle portion of the mountain and enthusiastically started to rotate the mountain this way and that. After some time the mountain started to sink and a big wail arouse from both sides. At this time Lord Vishnu took the form of an enormous tortoise and supported the mountain from beneath as if it were a mere pebble.

However, despite their best efforts the work was not progressing well so Vishnu took a gigantic form and stood in the middle on top of the mountain and maintained the balance. He held both sides of the snake with five hundred arms on either side and thus helped both parties. At last many things started to appear on the surface.

But the poor snake felt quite sick of the whole affair and started to throw up the dreaded poison known as *halahala*. Even one drop would be enough to destroy the earth if it fell on the ground, such was the potency of this poison. Both the gods and the demons cried to Vishnu who advised them to solicit Shiva. The Great God (Mahadeva) came along with Parvati and took the poison in his cupped palms before it could drop to the earth. He was prepared to sacrifice his own life in order to save the world from annihilation. Parvati was well aware of her husband's immeasurable power yet her love made her weak and she caught his neck and would not allow the poison to slip down to his stomach. The poison thus stuck in his throat so that it became blue in colour. All the gods extolled Shiva and gave him a new name, "Neelakanta" or the blue-necked one.

The ability to sacrifice one's own welfare for the sake of others is the highest form of the worship of the Supreme and all the *rishis* and great sages who had assembled at the banks of the ocean eulogised Lord Shiva. All of them passed the night in singing his glories since the belief is that one who has taken poison should not be allowed to sleep. This night is celebrated to this day in India and is known as *Maha Shivaratri* or the great night of Shiva.

The next day they resumed their churning and many fantastic things appeared from the ocean including Lakshmi, the goddess of auspiciousness.

Last to appear was the form of the Lord as Dhanwantari who is the father of the great science of healing known as Ayurveda. As soon as the *asuras* saw him they realised that the pot, which he was carrying in his hands, contained the nectar for which they had been waiting. Before the exhausted gods could make a move, they grabbed the immortal drink and ran off with it. The frustrated gods ran to their saviour, Vishnu and begged him to do something for them.

Vishnu said, "All those who worked for the accomplishment of this task should get their just rewards but since the *asuras* tried to appropriate the whole thing for themselves they deserve to be punished and will get nothing at all!"

Saying thus, he vanished from their view. In his stead there appeared a most captivating woman, lovely beyond description.

The *asuras* who had grabbed the pot of nectar had gone to a secret place and had started quarrelling amongst themselves as to how they should share the nectar and who should get the biggest portion. With undulating movements of her broad hips, the fascinating woman now glided into their midst. When they saw her they left the pot of nectar and rushed to her. They could hardly keep their hands off her.

"Who are you, O beauteous one?" They asked. "What is your name? Will you marry one of us? At least will you consent to distribute the nectar impartially to all of us and thus put an end to our quarrels."

She evaded their advances adroitly and said, "My name is Mohini and I am a woman of low morals, a harlot you might say. How can you possibly trust me?"

The *asuras* laughed merrily at her joke and swore that they trusted her implicitly.

Mohini gave them a sidelong glance from her mysterious eyes and said, "I shall divide the nectar amongst you only if you promise to abide by my decision whatever it might be and not start quarrelling afterwards."

They were so bemused by her appearance that they happily agreed to whatever she said. The maiden made them sit in a row. She then called the *devas* and made them sit opposite the *asuras*, facing each other. The *asuras* were a bit worried at this unexpected turn of events but did not dare to murmur since she had made them swear implicit obedience. When both parties had settled down and were meekly sitting in two neat rows, Mohini entered carrying the golden pot. All eyes were fixed on her as she appeared. They were so fascinated by her flirtatious glances and coquettish behaviour that they did not notice what she was doing. Mohini did not want to give the nectar of immortality to the *asuras* who were cruel by nature. To make them immortal would have been fatal since there would be no end to their wickedness. As she passed along the ranks of the *asuras*, all she gave them were loving glances. Of the nectar they got not even a drop. It was all given to the *devas*! The demons did not even notice what was happening since they were mesmerised by her armorous looks. Each one of them thought that she had fallen in love with him and would agree to marry him. At last when the whole of the nectar had been consumed by the *devas*, Mohini assumed her original form as Vishnu. It was only then that the *asuras* realised that they had been neatly tricked.

They were so angry that they immediately started to attack the gods. The latter had regained their youth and strength by now and they fought with redoubled vigour and eventually defeated the *asuras* who returned to the nether lands to lick their wounds and plot further ways to defeat their mortal enemies.

This story has a deep, esoteric meaning. The milky ocean is the human intellect, which is a field of all possibilities. There is nothing that the human intellect cannot devise. How else would be able to fly to the moon or delve into the depths of the ocean? The gods and demons are the positive and negative thoughts in our mind that churn it so forcefully. The Mandara Mountain is the load of abysmal nescience that we carry from life to life. It also stands for space. Ananta or the snake that is used as a rope is Time. "Ananta" means "endless", and Time is endless. The human being churns the intellect, which is the field of all possibilities, using the churn of space and the rope of Time. Each one brings out for himself many things. Sometimes what comes out may be sheer poison – the negative emotions like anger, greed, hatred, lust and so on. We have to ask for the help of the divine in order to get rid of these.

From this ocean of all possibilities, each one can draw out those things that she or he needs. Those who realise these material things to be worthless and keep trying to get something that will bring eternal joy will be able to get the precious nectar of immortality. Even at the moment of triumph this precious wisdom can be snatched away from us by our negative tendencies. The moment we start feeling proud of our capabilities and success, the pot of wisdom will vanish from our midst. Once again it's only the Lord who can save us and regain for us that which we lost through our pride.

Vipra Poojyam Visva vandyam
Vishnu Sambhu Priyam Sutham
Kshipra prasaadha Niradham
Saasthaaram Pranamaamyaham

I bow to Lord Shasta,
The son of Shiva and Vishnu,
Who is worshipped by all noble souls,
As well as revered by the whole world,
And who is easy to propitiate.

— *Dharma Shasta Pancharatnam*

Swamiye Sharanamayyappa!

"Unattached am I to the body, mind and intellect,
Alone and changeless am I, the form of consciousness and bliss,
Ever pure and free am I, without change of form or nature,
I alone exist – ever full and changeless."

CHAPTER THREE

VISHWAMOHANA

Mohini's Maya

Manmathaayuta-soundaryam,
Mahaabhutha-nishevitam,
Mrigayam rasikam shooram,
Shastaaram pranathosmyaham

I bow to Shasta, who is as beautiful as a thousand cupids,
Who is powerful and delightful,
And who is served by all the elements.

— *Shasta Panchakshara Stotram*   ॐ

The story of how two male gods produced a son is an incredible tale. But nothing is incredible to the Hindu mind. The Puranas are filled with such astonishing stories. The birth of Dharma Shasta belongs to this category of amazing tales.

Lord Shiva had been present at the churning of the ocean but after having saved the world by swallowing the poison, he had returned to Kailasa with Parvati. Ever engrossed in meditation, he never liked to waste his time in idle gossip with the other gods. However if there was anyone who needed his help he was ever ready to render it. He had not been present at the grand finale of the churning session when the *asuras* plundered the nectar, nor did he see the world-entrancing form of Mohini when he came to the rescue of the gods. Later on the sage Narada reported this spicy bit of news to him. When he heard about the bewitching figure of Vishnu as Mohini, a strong desire arose in him to witness this manifestation. Accompanied by Parvati and a host of goblins, he went to Vaikunta, the abode of Vishnu.

Shiva said, "I have seen many of your incarnations both as beast and human but I have never seen you in the form of a woman and I am most anxious to see it, so please show it to me."

Vishnu smiled and said, "Are you sure you want to see it? It is calculated to arouse passion in the heart of every male." Then with a sidelong glance out of his lotus eyes, Vishnu said, "But of course you being a perfect yogi, may not be beguiled by it!"

So saying Vishnu vanished from view. Suddenly Shiva felt that he was standing in an enchanted garden in which summer was at its height. There were cascades of sweet-smelling flowers and gushing brooks and bees buzzing around in delight, inebriated with the honey they had imbibed. There in the midst of those riotous blooms, he beheld an exquisite maiden playing with a golden ball. Her doe-like eyes fluttered hither and thither following the movements of the unpredictable ball that seemed to be eluding her grasp. At last it fell at the feet of Shiva who was standing, rooted to the spot. The maiden came near him in order to pick up her ball and just happened to glance up at him out of her mesmeric eyes. Shiva found himself drowning in her look and unable to tear his gaze away from her fascinating face. He seemed to be oblivious of everything, including Parvati who was standing beside him and watching in wonder. He bent down to help the maiden retrieve her ball but she eluded his grasp and jumped up clutching the ball and her clothes, which seemed to be in danger of falling off. She cast a bashful, sidelong glance at him as she darted off, trailing her transparent garments that seemed to be constantly slipping off her shoulders, giving him tantalising glimpses of her rounded breasts. With one last enticing look at him, she ran off into the woods. Even Shiva, the great yogi, the destroyer of Kama, the god of love, was swept away by Vishnu's *maya*, the illusory power of the Lord, so how can we mere mortals be blamed for succumbing!

Before the astonished gaze of Parvati, Shiva ran after Vishnu in his form as Mohini! At last after having led him a merry dance, Mohini allowed Shiva to catch her in a fierce embrace. This conjunction of Shiva Shakti and Vishnu Shakti resulted in the incarnation of Dharma Shasta, born to bring back *dharma,* the cosmic law of righteousness to the earth. He is the deity who is specific for this age of Kali and born to kill the ogress known as Mahishi.

As soon as he clasped Mohini in his arms, Shiva came to a realisation of his own inherent nature and dropped his hands. He also realised that he had been made to play this particular game in order to facilitate the birth of a baby who would incorporate within himself both his power as well as that of Vishnu. The Iron Age of Kali was fast approaching and the world was in urgent need of such an advent of the divine. Naturally Vishnu had also known of the divine plan and that is why he had agreed to play this particular role. The child had to be taken out of the right thigh of Vishnu, which is where Shiva's seed had fallen.

There is another interesting story describing the incarnation of Mohini and Shiva's infatuation with her. This is the story of Bhasmasura.

This demon had been born out of the ash, which had fallen under Shiva's feet and that is why he got the name Bhasmasura. *Bhasma* means ashes. This demon started doing *tapasya* to Shiva. After many years of intense austerities, Shiva appeared and told him to ask for a boon. Like all *asuras* he immediately asked for immortality, which of course was denied. Bhasmasura cogitated for a while and then came up with a most unusual request.

"Please give me the boon that any person on whose head I keep my hand, will turn to ashes!"

Shiva didn't think much of this boon and agreed without further ado.

Bhasmasura was filled with glee. Turning to Shiva, he said, "You have made me invincible by this wonderful boon. But how do I know that this really works? Let me try it first on your head!" So saying the ungrateful demon rushed at Shiva. Mahadeva did not stop to argue with him but took to his heels and fled to Vaikunta, Lord Vishnu's abode.

Vishnu told him not to worry and immediately took on his form as the beauteous Mohini and came and stood in Bhasmasura's path. Like all *asuras*, Bhasmasura could not resist a fascinating female. Mohini told him that she was a dancer so he begged her to teach him some dancing. Shiva was the sole audience at this extraordinary dance between the huge, ungainly *asura* and the divinely graceful Mohini. At last the *asura* could not contain himself any longer. He stopped his pretence of dancing and begged Mohini to accept him as her husband.

Mohini fluttered her eyelashes at him and declared, "I have heard that *asuras* are promiscuous by nature. Before I consent to marry you, you will have to agree never to take another wife!"

Bhasmasura agreed with alacrity.

Mohini said, "I can't really believe you. You will have to place your hand on your head and swear that you will never marry another woman."

Before the fascinated gaze of Shiva, the poor deluded *asura* unthinkingly placed his hand on his own head and was reduced to a heap of ashes.

The *asura* was not the only one to be fascinated by the divine grace and beauty of Mohini. Shiva, who was noted for being the slayer of Kama or Cupid, forgot all that had conspired up to this moment and came forward to take Mohini in his arms. This happened on the last Saturday of the month of *Margashirsha* (Nov/Dec) when the star *phalguni uttram* was in ascendancy. The birth of Sri Dharma Shasta took place on that day, hence this day is very important for all his devotees.

The baby was taken out of Mohini's right thigh since Shiva's seed had fallen there. As soon as he saw the baby, Shiva realised the necessity for his having been fooled by the deluding power of Vishnu's *maya*. The gods had been waiting for such an outcome when the combined power of Hara (Shiva) and Hari (Vishnu) would come together and produce the child who would be known as Hari-Hara Putra or the son of Hara and Hari. The gods rained flowers from the heavens on the heads of all three.

It would be absurd to suppose that Dharma Shasta was created out of the physical union between two male gods. He is the divine energy that was created out of the fusion of two divine forces, Shiva-shakti and Vishnu-shakti. He was a projection of their will. In the usual way of all puranic stories, the story of Mohini has been brought in to make it more credible as well as appealing. In fact the birth of all the three sons of Shiva are examples of the projection of the divine will. Ganesha was the projection of the will of the Divine Mother and Skanda of Shiva.

The parents put the baby on their laps and petted him. The sages and the other celestials came to pay their respects to the one who had been born to save them from the scourge of Mahishi. The goddess Saraswati came and blessed him with erudition and wisdom. The Creator Brahma took him on his lap and performed the naming ceremony. He named him Bhootanatha since he was the Lord of all creatures. He was also called Dharma Shasta, since he would be the upholder of *dharma* or righteousness.

Brahma told Bhootanatha that the purpose of his incarnation was to kill the demoness, Mahishi who was torturing the gods in a most cruel fashion.

"I myself have given her the boon that no one except the son of Hara and Hari will be able to kill her. Moreover I also gave into her request that if such a son was born out of their union, he would have to spend twelve years of his life on earth. This would be a sort of *tapasya* for him and would give him the power to kill Mahishi."

He told Shasta to go with his father Shiva to Kailasa where he would be given further instructions. Thus Dharma Shasta went to Kailasa where he spent some time playing with his brothers, Ganesha and Kartikeya. Shiva took on the task of teaching him all the sciences.

After he had learnt everything Shiva reminded him of the purpose of his manifestation.

"My child," he said, "the time is ripe for you to go to the earth and spend your allotted time of twelve years there as told by Brahma. Take on the form of a baby and lie on the banks of the Pampa River in the south of India. The King of Pandala has no heir and he is at the moment hunting at that place. You will have to go with him and spend twelve years as his son and servitor. I will tie a golden bell round your neck which will tinkle and attract the attention of the King who will be drawn to you."

Thus saying, Shiva blessed him and told him to proceed to the earth. Dharma Shasta went round his father three times and then vanished from view.

We know very little of the further history of Dharma Shasta since it is not elaborated in any of the Puranas. The only thing that we know is that he had two wives, Pushkala and Poorna and a son called, Satyakama.

However we do know a lot about his *avatara* as Ayyappa, the foster son of the King of Pandala. The killing of Mahishi is actually woven into the story of Ayyappa. This is what we shall elaborate now.

Matthamaadhanga gamanam,
Kaarunyaamritha Pooritham
Sarva Vignaharam De'vam
Shaastaaram Pranamaam Yaham

I bow to Shasta, who has the gait of a majestic elephant,
Who is filled with compassion,
And who is capable of removing all obstacles.

— *Sri Dharma Shaasta Pancharatnam*

Swamiye Sharanamayyappa!

"I am eternal and boundless,
Immutable and unshakeable,
I alone exist, in the form of consciousness and bliss."

ॐ

Shivapradaaya Namaha!

CHAPTER FOUR

AYYAN

Previous History of the King

Shiva-pradaayinam bhakta-daivatam,
Paandyabaalakam,
Shardula-dugddaharatharam
Shastaaram pranathosmyaham

I bow to Lord Shasta,
Prince of Pandya,
Who is loved by all Shiva bhaktas.

— *Shasta Panchakshara Stotram*   ॐ

The small and insignificant kingdom of Pandala in the South Indian state of
Kerala was the blessed place where Dharma Shasta chose to reveal himself.
This is also the land, which had the good fortune to be blessed by his footprints
for the duration of twelve years. How the king of this small kingdom had
the good fortune of getting the son of Hara and Hari as his adopted son
is a question that might occur to those who are interested in stories of previous
births. India is a land, which abounds in such stories. The previous history of
the king is thus given here.

During the time of the *Ramayana* there was an old tribal woman called
Sabari who was noted for her great austerities. Her *guru* had told her that she
would not get liberation in that birth and she would have to wait till the advent
of Lord Rama who would give her salvation. From that time onwards she
had started collecting wild berries and fruits for Rama. She would taste a small
bit and if they were sweet she would keep them aside. The sour ones she
would throw away. Thus many years passed while she prayed and waited for

the Lord to come. When Lord Rama came she presented the fruits that she had hoarded for him so lovingly and strangely enough due to the power of her love they were as fresh and juicy as when she had picked them. Rama blessed her but told her that she would have to await the coming of Dharma Shasta who was the one ordained to give her final liberation.

Many, many years passed while Sabari waited for the arrival of the Lord who would ultimately liberate her. At that time in the kingdom known as Pandya, in the south of India there lived a very rich Brahmin who was childless. He was very unhappy about this and didn't know what to do. One day a sage came to his house and advised him to go to Sabari and take her advice. He also told him to pray to Dharma Shasta.

The Brahmin went to Sabari who advised him to go northwards until he reached a waterfall, which was cascading from a very high peak.

"Go and immerse yourself in that water and you will be totally cleansed of all your sins and your desires will be fulfilled."

So saying she blessed him and gave him a mud pot to collect the water. The Brahmin went immediately to the spot directed by her and held the pot under the waterfall. As soon as he did this, the pot came apart in his hands. He was quite disconcerted and didn't know what to do. To his surprise a huge lotus started to bloom at the exact spot where the pot had fallen. It rapidly filled with the water from the waterfall. He immersed himself in this water and his sins flew away from him in the form of a black bird. The bird flew off to a little distance and then dropped down dead. The poor man didn't know what was happening and closed his eyes in silent prayer to Dharma Shasta as the sage had advised him. When he opened his eyes he saw a beautiful young boy standing in front of him. He realised that this must be Dharma Shasta. He prayed to him to grant his wish for a son.

Shasta said, "Your sins have vanished by taking a bath in this holy water as foretold by Sabari. In this birth you will have many sons and in your next birth I myself will come and live with you as your son and your servitor for twelve years."

The Brahmin was delighted and prostrated to the Lord. He then asked him to tell him what the sins of his past birth were.

The Lord replied, "Murder, robbery, debauchery and betrayal of trust. These were the sins of your past life for which you have now paid the price. You will have only one more birth and that will be as the King of the Kingdom of Pandala!"

The Brahmin then begged the Lord to reveal his Vishwarupa or universal form. However, when the Lord showed his Vishwarupa, the Brahmin, like Arjuna in the *Mahabharata*, could not bear to see it. He closed his eyes and begged him to return to his charming form as a young boy. When he opened his eyes he saw the vision of Dharma Shasta in his *balarupa* or the form of a young boy. He bowed low before him and when he looked up, the Lord had disappeared. He spent the remaining years of his life contemplating on Shasta and chanting his *mantra*s. This was the Brahmin who many years later took birth as King Rajashekara in the Kingdom of Pandala.

The Pandyas were a famous royal family of South India. Unfortunately, the *Diwan* (minister) of the Raja of Vijayanagar overthrew the royal family and started ruling the Pandya Kingdom. The royal family was forced to flee from Madura due to threats from their own ministers. One branch of the family kept moving westwards, staying briefly at various places until they reached Pandala in AD 903. They decided to remain there and build a palace and establish their overlord-ship over the people. It was only around the year AD 1194 that all the members of the family managed to reach there and a full-fledged kingdom came to be established. Their territories extended eastwards and covered the mountain ranges, consisting of eighteen holy hills including Sabarimala. King Rajashekara was the direct descendent of this dynasty. He was very talented, courageous and just. Even in those days, the royal family practised secularism and there was peaceful co-existence amongst the different religions groups. It was in this royal household that Dharma Shasta chose to spend his earthly career. The family still exists and they have records of the miraculous happenings that took place while Dharma Shasta lived with them.

The name given to him while he lived there was Manikandan. Later he came to be known as Ayyappan. The word "Ayyappan" is a union of the two names Ayya and Appan. Both mean father though Ayya also means Lord. Ayyan is actually a corruption of *Aryan*, which means "worthy of reverence". He used to be called Arya Appa or Arya Thata. Tatha and Appa both mean

father. Arya-Appa soon came to be modified to Ayyappa. Ayyappan's life is
not mentioned in the Puranas since it is a recent advent. However, an account
of his life is found in the records of the history of the kingdom of Pandala
in Kerala as well as in many Malayalam ballads. The amazing story of his life
is kept alive by the bards who sing it to this very day. The temple of Ayyappan
at Sabarimala is a very special one as we can see from the stories of the various
miracles that take place there every year.

Asmath kulesvaram devam,
Asmath Shathru Vinasanam,
Asmath Ishta pradhaadharam,
Shaastaaram Pranamaamyaham

I bow to Lord Shasta,
Who is our family deity,
Who vanquishes our foes,
And fulfils all our desires.

— *Sri Dharma Shasta Pancharatnam*

Swamiye Sharanamayyappa!

"Effulgence am I both inside and outside,
That light which is both apparent and transcendent,
Light of all light, light of the ATMAN, self-effulgent,
Filled with auspiciousness, am I."

— Adi Shankaracharya

CHAPTER FIVE

MANIKANDAN

Prince of Pandala

Maam hi Partha vyapashrithya,
Yepi syu paapayonayaha,
Sthriyo vaishya sthada shudra,
Sthepi yanti paraam jatim

Those who take refuge in Me O Arjuna,
Will attain the supreme goal,
Even though they are outcastes, women, merchants or menials.

— *Srimad Bhagavad Gita*

Brahma had granted Mahishi the boon that in the unlikely event of a son being born to Shiva and Vishnu, he would still have to spend twelve years of his life on earth before he attained the power to kill her. Bhootanatha (Dharma Shasta) was forced to go to the earth to comply with the final part of this boon.

His father had commanded him to proceed to the banks of the Pampa River and this is what he proceeded to do. In fact it is said that the anxious parents, (Shiva and Vishnu) both accompanied Dharma Shasta and took him to the banks of the Pampa River where the king of the country was soon to come.

The rich Brahmin of the Pandya Kingdom had been born, as king Rajashekara of Pandala. He lacked for nothing except an heir to the throne. The King and the Queen as well as his subjects were very depressed over this. They were great devotees of Lord Shiva and had been requesting him constantly to bless them with a son. One day the king along with his retinue went hunting in the forest adjoining the banks of the Pampa River. At the end of the day he was very tired and wandered off by himself. He was resting with his back against a tree when he heard the musical tinkle of a bell. This was followed by the sound of a baby's cry. The king was startled at this unexpected sound coming from this dense forest. He followed the sound of the tinkling bell and came to the banks of the river. It was there that he had the beautiful vision of a lovely baby kicking its legs in the air and gurgling with joy. As it turned its head hither and thither, the little golden bell that had been tied round its neck would tinkle merrily. The king was fascinated by this sight and ran forward and picked up the baby who immediately stopped crying and started to smile at him. Even though the baby enchanted him, he wasn't sure whether to take it with him or just leave it there for his actual parents to come and find him.

The *Diwan*, who had been hoping to inherit the throne after the king's demise came after the king and was shocked to see the baby in his arms. He strongly urged the king not to take the child since they did not know his parentage. He might even be the child of an outcaste for all they knew. The king was perplexed and didn't know what to do. Just then an old *sanyasi* approached him and said.

"O King! Don't hesitate to take this child. He is a Kshatriya and will bring great good fortune to your family. Bring him up, as your own son and your whole kingdom will prosper. You may call him "Manikandan" since he has a golden bell round his neck. When he becomes twelve years old, he will reveal to you the secret of his birth". So saying the *sanyasi* disappeared. The king was not to know that the sage was none other than Lord Shiva.

Rajashekara was thrilled to hear this. Hugging the divine baby close to his heart he brought it back to the palace. The queen was also delighted to see the wonderful baby boy who shone with a heavenly lustre. They had been praying to Lord Shiva for a son and they were sure that Manikandan was the fruit of their penance. All the citizens were also overjoyed at seeing the child. The only one who was unhappy was the *Diwan* (prime minister) who had hoped to inherit the kingdom.

Needless to say, the kingdom of Pandala became extremely prosperous after the advent of Manikandan.

When the child reached the age when he needed a tutor, his father sent him to a *guru*. The king was not happy about being separated from his son even for a minute but since the boy was a prince it was most necessary to give him a proper education.

The *guru* was amazed at the boy's precocity. He mastered all the Vedas as well as the art of warfare and administration in a very short time. The *guru* was convinced that the child was divine.

At the end of his studies when the time came for him to depart, Manikandan approached the *guru* and asked him respectfully what he could give him as *guru dakshina* or the fee to be paid to a preceptor. All through his discipleship, Manikandan had guessed that the *guru* was a most unhappy man. The reason was easy to find. His only son was both blind and dumb. When Manikandan asked the *guru* to name his spiritual fee, the *guru*, who suspected his divine origin, begged him to restore his sight and speech to his son. Manikandan called the boy to him and put his hands on his head and told the boy to open his eyes and speak. To the great wonder of the parents, the child immediately did as he was told. Their joy could well be imagined. However, Manikandan warned them not to reveal this miracle to anyone since the time was not yet ripe for him to reveal his divinity. He had to accomplish the purpose of his incarnation first, which was to kill Mahishi.

While Manikandan was in the *gurukula* (institute of learning), the queen conceived and delivered a baby boy much to everyone's delight. The child was named Rajaraja. Even though he had a son of his own flesh and blood, the king's affection for Manikandan was undiminished. He treated him as his eldest son and was determined to crown him as heir apparent.

It was at this time that the notorious bandit and pirate known as Vavar started looting and plundering the neighbouring states. He had a ship, which he anchored off the coast of any port he wanted to plunder. He would then swoop down on the unwary citizens and ransack and kill if necessary. News of his approach was brought to King Rajashekara. He was very worried since he did not have a sufficient army to wage war against such an accomplished warrior like Vavar who had skilled fighters with him. All the same he decided that it was better to face the enemy with courage and die like a hero than remain at home with fear constantly lurking in his heart.

Just as the king was planning his next move, Manikandan came and asked him the reason for his despondency. When he heard the news, the young boy said.

"Father why do you fear when I am here. I will go and fight with this enemy myself."

The king was shocked when he heard this. "Do you realise what sort of a person you will have to confront. He is a notorious bandit and murderer of innocents. You are only a young boy. How can I possibly send you to fight with him?"

Manikandan was undaunted and replied, "Have no fear Sire! It is the duty of a prince to settle such matters. I will deal with this man in a fitting manner. Please give me leave to go."

When he realised that it was impossible to deter him, the king, most reluctantly, agreed to let Manikandan lead the army and face Vavar.

Manikandan took the army to the seashore where he spied the vessel in which Vavar had come. It was his practice to sail to a port and pounce on the unwary populace from there. Manikandan immediately shot an arrow and brought down the mast along with the pennant of the pirate vessel. Vavar was startled to see this. He fully expected a big army to be arrayed on the shore but all he saw was a handsome young boy standing proudly with his head thrown back without the slightest trace of fear.

For some reason the hardened heart of Vavar melted at this sight and he shouted out to the boy.

"Who is the fool who has sent a small boy like you to fight with a practised warrior like me? I can make mincemeat of you but I'm not in the habit of fighting with infants. So go quickly before I change my mind!"

Manikandan smiled when he heard this and replied, "O Vavar! Actually I'm against any form of violence. I will be glad to avoid this war if I can. So if you agree to surrender to me we can avert a lot of unnecessary bloodshed."

Vavar laughed in scorn and said, "Don't talk nonsense. There is no question of my surrendering to you. But I'll give you one more chance to get out of my sight before I change my mind. I don't know why I even waste my time in talking to you but somehow you have touched something in me!"

Manikandan then said, "All right, if that's what you wish, let us at least spare the lives of our innocent soldiers. Let us have a duel which will decide the outcome of the battle."

Vavar was amazed at the boy's courage and said, "O boy! Even if you fight with your entire army, your end is certain. What foolishness to think that a young boy like you can fight a duel with warrior like me!"

However, Manikandan refused to budge from his resolve. At last Vavar was forced to ask his army to stand aside and confront the boy himself. A fierce battle ensued in which Vavar used every trick at his command but all his weapons were of no avail against the young boy. Then he tried some of his magic tricks but nothing was of any use. Manikandan stood there with a smile on his lips and parried every weapon with one of his own. At last, Vavar tried and trained warrior though he was, was forced to admit defeat. He stood with folded palms in front of Manikandan and said,

"I have never been defeated by the greatest kings of this land. How is it that a mere boy like you has brought me to heel! Surely you are not an ordinary child but a divine personage. Please tell me who you are."

Manikandan replied, "Before I tell you who I am, you have to promise me something. From this day onwards you have to give up your terrible life of plunder and pillage. What dreadful sins have you committed? You believe you are doing this at the dictates of God and your prophet but please understand that this is not true. Please understand that you will be punished for your atrocious acts."

Vavar was overwhelmed by Manikandan's kindness and advice. He realised the extent of his crimes and was anxious to make amends. He begged Manikandan to keep him as his servitor always.

Manikandan smiled and said, "The time for this has not yet come. It will come soon and I will send word for you and then you can come and be with me always. I will ensure that you will always be a part of me."

When the king and the citizens heard of this remarkable feat of their beloved prince they were wonderstruck and the king's love for him grew with every passing day. Neither he nor the citizens could believe that a young boy of twelve could have accomplished something that the greatest rulers of Kerala had not been able to achieve. It was not an easy joke to have subdued a notorious

pirate of Vavar's reputation and brought him to heel without killing him!
Manikandan had subdued him with the power of love and not with the might
of his arms.

Pandyesavamsathilakam
Ke'rale'Ke'li-Vigraham
Aartha Thraana Param De'vam
Shaastaaram Pranamaamyaham

"I bow to Lord Shasta,
Who is the star of the race of Pandya,
Who is the idol of the people of Kerala,
And who saves all those in distress."

— *Sri Dharma Shasta Pancharatnam*

Swamiye Sharanamayyappa!

"O foolish mind! Meditate on God,
At the time of death, all your erudition will be of no avail."

— Adi Shankaracharya

ॐ

Tejase Namaha!

CHAPTER SIX

MAHISHI-MARDAKA

The Killing of Mahishi

Yakshinyabhimatam,
Poorna-Pushkala parisevitam,
Kshipra-prasaadakam nityam
Shastaaram pranathosmyaham

I bow to Lord Shasta,
Who is waited upon by Poorna and Pushkala,
And who is easily pleased.

— *Shasta Panchakshara Stotram*

ॐ

Soon after this incident, the king called his minister and told him to make all preparations for the coronation of Manikandan as the Crown Prince. The minister as we know had been against the boy from the time he had been brought to the palace. He could not bear to think of the throne of the kings of the Pandya dynasty to be taken over by a boy who might well be a tribal or even an untouchable. So he asked for at least two weeks in order to make all the necessary preparations.

Actually he had made quite a few attempts on the boy's life but all of them had failed. Once he had given him poisoned milk and Manikandan had become seriously ill with violent stomach pains. At that time Shiva had come to the court disguised as a physician and told the king that he would cure the boy. The desperate monarch agreed and Shiva went to the boy's room and locked the door from inside. Then he rubbed the boy's body with the snake round his neck. The snake sucked the poison from his system and Manikandan was cured. Another time the minister invited Manikandan for his son's birthday and gave him poisoned food but somehow this also had no effect on the boy since he had become immune to all poisons after having been rubbed with the snake. The minister began to get desperate and started to think that the boy was having some sort of charmed life.

At last he came up with a brilliant idea by which he hoped to get rid of the little upstart, once and for all. He decided to enlist the queen's support for this. He played the role of Manthara, the servant of Kaikeyi in the Ramayana. In just the same manner he kept poisoning the queen with stories of how the king was doing her a great injustice by placing an unknown vagabond on the throne and denying this privilege to her son who was his own flesh and blood. Unless she acted immediately, he said, her son would undoubtedly be banished and this clever nonentity, who had wormed his way into the king's heart would become ruler of Pandala.

The queen was actually very fond of Manikandan and refused to listen to his evil counsel but he wore her resistance down by constant insinuations. At last she agreed to comply with his plan. He told her to feign a terrible headache that even the court physician was unable to cure. He instructed the physician to say that she could be cured only if the herbal powder he gave her could be mixed with some tigress's milk and applied to her forehead for some days. He felt sure that Manikandan would offer to go to the forest and get the milk.

Everything happened exactly as he had foreseen. The queen feigned a severe headache and the court physician prescribed tigress's milk as prompted by the minister. As expected, without the slightest hesitation Manikandan offered to go for the milk since it fitted in with his own divine plans. At first the king refused to let him go but on seeing the desperate condition of the queen, he was forced to give into Manikandan's persuasions. Mothers with young cubs are most ferocious and protective and the king shuddered to think of his beloved son going to the forest to milk a tigress.

As usual Manikandan was calm and composed and told his father not to worry. He started to prepare himself for the journey. The king gave him a coconut with three eyes representing the three-eyed Shiva, their family deity. He hoped that this would be a talisman to guard him from all danger. Manikandan put the coconut and some food in a bundle and carried it on his head. Even today all devotees to Sabarimala carry something called the *Irumudi* which is a bundle containing a coconut and some offerings for the I ord. The king was all set to send his army with him but the boy refused and said that he preferred to go alone. He knew that the last lap of his earthly sojourn was coming to a close and he had to fulfil the appeal of the *devas* before he left. He had to a make an end of Mahishi since this was the reason for his advent and he certainly did not want any witnesses to this scene. After Manikandan left, the unhappy king spent his time in praying to his favourite deity Shiva, begging him to save his beloved son from all dangers. It was indeed strange that his earthly father was praying to his heavenly father to save him!

After traversing through the thick forest for some time Manikandan came to the hut of an old woman. He stepped in for a while. The old lady told him that the whole forest was the stamping ground of a terrible she-buffalo. The forest dwellers went in dire fear of her. She warned him not to venture further into the terrible forest. He agreed, but hardly had he gone a few yards from the hut, when an enormous buffalo came charging at him with full intent to kill him. Manikandan calmly stood his ground and shot her dead with just one arrow. This place came to be known as "Erumakolli" (the place where the she-buffalo was killed). The word *eruma* actually means she-buffalo in Malayalam, the language of Kerala. With the passage of time this was shortened to "Erumeli". The hazardous trek to the temple of Sabarimala starts from this place.

In the morning he lifted the buffalo on a pole and took it for the old woman to see. She was amazed that such a young boy could have actually killed this monstrous buffalo. She begged him not to leave her. Due to her pleas he made a small temple to Dharma Shasta at that place and told her that he would guard over her. This temple is the first place that devotees have to pray before proceeding up the hill to the Ayyappa temple at Sabarimala.

Manikandan left the hut and walked into the thick forest. Lord Shiva sent his four main *gana*s (attendants) to escort him. They halted at many places during their journey into the forest and even today pilgrims follow the same path which had been trodden by his holy feet and take rest at those very places where he had rested. At last when they reached the Pampa River he saw that all the seven sages were there ready to welcome him. They had prepared a

repast for him and at that holy spot the sages and other *siddhas* who had come
to meet him, spent the night in his divine company. Even today, pilgrims are
supposed to prepare a feast and offer it to Dharma Shasta and then partake
of the *prasadam* (offerings), before beginning their climb.

After this the sages invited Shasta to accompany them to the hill some miles
away. They had constructed a beautiful temple of gold and jewels, which is
known as Ponnambalam (temple of gold). Here they performed the first *puja*
to him in a most elaborate fashion and it is said that he still resides there. This
place is known as "Poonambalamedu" (hill of the temple of gold). No one
has been able to go there but it faces the present temple of Sabarimala and
it is from there the bonfire is seen on the day known as "Makarasankranti".

In was at this time that the gods approached Shiva and Vishnu and begged
them to deliver them from the scourge of Mahishi who had returned to heaven
at the bequest of the *asuras* and was bent on torturing them. Shiva and Vishnu
told them to proceed to Ponnambalam where Dharma Shasta was residing. He
was born to kill Mahishi and deliver them from her scourge. The *devas* rushed
to Ponnambalam and begged Shasta to help them. He assured them that he
had taken an incarnation just for this and accompanied them to Indra's heaven
where Mahishi was reigning as queen in lieu of Indra, King of the gods.

When he approached the golden throne on which she was seated, she asked
him scornfully, "Who are you and why have you come here?"

"I am the personification of your death O Mahishi!" said Shasta. "It would
be better for you to give back this heaven immediately to Indra and the *devas*.
If you don't do so I shall kill you!"

Mahishi roared with laughter when she heard this. "Insolent boy!" She said.
"Even the trinity are unable to kill me and you dare to say that you are my
slayer! Let us see you put your words into actions!"

Once again Shasta warned her not to play with him but to surrender if
she valued her life.

She was enraged at this and rushed at him with upraised arms determined
to crush him to death. Without the slightest difficulty he lifted her bodily above
his head and hurled her to the earth. She fell near a river called Azhutha that
lies to the west of the Pampa. Shasta jumped down after her and started to
dance on her huge body. At the touch of his divine feet, she was delivered

from her curse and she reverted to her personality as Lila, the daughter of the sage, Galava.

Shasta got off her chest and lo and behold! Out of the body of the enormous demoness there appeared a most beautiful woman. She recognised her deliverer to be none other than Dharma Shasta or Bhootanatha. She started to extol him with the hymns she had chanted a long time ago. She bent low before the Lord and begged him to accept her as his wife. Manikandan told her that in this incarnation he was a pure *brahmachari* (celibate) and would never marry. However, to appease her, he promised to marry her in the year when not even one new devotee came to visit him in the temple which would soon be built for him! This has never happened so far. In fact every year more and more people throng to the temple of Ayyappan at Sabarimala. Mahishi was so grief-stricken at this that he felt sorry for her and gave her a place on the left side of his temple. This is the shrine for "Maallikapurathamma" which is seen today just below the main temple.

It is said that Shiva himself accompanied by all the gods had come to witness the destruction of Mahishi. The place where Shiva tethered his bull is known as "Kalaketti Ashrama". In Malayalam this means exactly this, "*ashrama* where the bull was tethered".

Shiva now spoke to him thus, "My beloved son, you have successfully accomplished the reason for your incarnation. But there are still a few more things to be tied up. You have a duty to your earthly father who loves you very much and is frantic about your whereabouts. Go to him without delay and comfort him. You may now reveal the secret of your birth. He will agree to make a temple for you. To the north-east of the Pampa River there is a hill called Neeli. A very old *tapaswini* called, Sabari resides there. Even though Rama has given her liberation she is still waiting to have a glimpse of you. It is your duty to go to her and give her final release. From this time onwards that hill will be known as Sabari hill (Sabarimala), in her memory and you can ask the king to make your temple at that place." Thus saying Shiva and Vishnu blessed their son and left.

Brahma now told him, "My child it is not right that you should leave this carcass of Mahishi over here. It will grow in height and eventually try to surpass

the Vindhya Mountain so you must immediately take it to the north of the
Azhutha River and cover it with stones."

In obedience to Brahma's orders, Manikandan removed Mahishi's carcass
to the north of the river. He dug a pit and put the carcass into it and covered
it with a big mound of stones. This place to this day is known as "Kallidum-
Kunnu". In Malayalam, this means "the hill where stones are dumped". In
memory of this event, today when devotees go for a bath in this river, it is
customary for them to climb this hillock and place a stone from the river on
top of the mound.

Before Ayyappan left the forest he ordered one of Shiva's *gana*s called Vapara
to guard the forest and the tribals who lived there as well as all the devotees
who would soon start to come. He also went to the *ashrama* of Sabari who
had been patiently waiting for him for thousands of years. He blessed her and
gave her final liberation.

Now it was time for him to go and comfort his earthly father who was
in agony at the non-appearance of his beloved son. He had not touched food
since the departure of his son.

Manikandan made a spectacular entry into the capital city of Pandala. Indra
had ordered all the goddesses to take the form of tigresses and accompany
him while the gods took the form of their cubs and followed them. Indra
turned himself into a magnificent leopard, seated on which Manikandan rode
in all splendour to the state capital.

Seeing this extraordinary contingent riding into their city, the citizens were
in a panic and started rushing hither and thither. They couldn't believe that their
prince was actually riding a leopard and being followed by so many nursing
tigresses and their cubs! The news was flashed to the king. When he came to
the gate of the palace, he was truly amazed. There was his beloved son seated
on a leopard, followed by a family of tigresses! He couldn't believe his eyes.

Manikandan came right up to where the king was standing and said,"Sire!
I have brought the tigresses as I promised. You may now milk them and take
as much as you need for the queen."

The unhappy king now begged Manikandan to forgive him and his foolish
queen. The moment Manikandan left the gates of the city, the queen's ailment
had vanished! What could the poor king say? He fell at Manikandan's feet and

begged him to forgive him. He also begged him to send the wild animals back to their habitat. Hardly had he said this when all the animals vanished from view and people slowly started to creep out of their houses and prostrate to their young prince whom they now realised to be a divine personage.

Manikandan lifted up his father who had thrown himself at his feet and hugged him close to his chest. The time had come to reveal the secret of his birth.

"Father!" He said, "It is now time for me to tell you who I am. I am Dharma Shasta, the son of Hari and Hara. I was born to kill Mahishi and free the *devas*. I have already accomplished this task so it is time for me to return home. I stayed twelve years in your palace masquerading as your son only to fulfil the divine purpose. Please don't punish the minister or the queen for what they tried to do to me. They were only playing their part in the celestial drama. They were quite helpless. Now you may ask for any boon you like and I shall grant it to you."

"O Lord!" said the king, "You have blessed me beyond all belief. What more can I ask for except that you should always stay with me in this place."

"O Father!" said Manikandan, "I can never be parted from you. I am ever residing in your heart and in the hearts of all my devotees all over the world. However if you wish, you may build a temple for me in which I shall reside for the sake of all the people who will come in the future."

By this time both the queen and the minister fully realised their folly and also the fact that they were dealing with a divine personage. They rushed and fell at his feet and begged him to forgive them for their transgressions. Manikandan was the soul of compassion. He hugged them to his breast and told them that far from punishing them, he would bless them for they were the unwitting instruments to carry out the divine plan!

After this he gave his supreme advice to the king by which he could liberate himself from all earthly bonds. This discourse is known as "The Bhootanatha Gita" and contains many words of counsel but the main theme was that *bhakti* or devotion to God was the best method of liberation from earthly coils, especially in this Age of Kali.

He knew of his father's deep desire to keep him by his side forever. So he told him, "Father! In accordance with your wish I will always stay in this place. There is a hill called Neeli to the north-east of the Pampa River where the great *tapaswini*, Sabari had been awaiting liberation at my hands. You may make a temple for me there and I will reside there in my subtle form to bless you and all those who come there. The temple should face the east. There should be eighteen steps leading to the boundary of the temple. These steps will stand for the five senses, the eight *ragas* (emotions), the three *gunas (sattva, rajas* and *tamas)*, and wisdom and ignorance (*vidya* and *avidya*). At a little distance on the left side of my temple, you must build a shrine for my *Shakti* – Mallikapurathamma. Two other shrines are to be built close by for my lieutenant, Katuvara and the *gana* known as Pavara and one for Vavar as well as for those who will soon be coming to help me. Now I will shoot an arrow. Watch carefully where it falls for that is the spot where you should build my temple. This place will be known as Sabarimala in future – the hill of Sabari. In time to come it will equal the city of Varanasi in sanctity and the Pampa will be equal to the holy Ganga! O King, I will now give you divine eyesight so that you can watch the flight of the arrow and note where it falls."

So saying Manikandan shot an arrow into the air and the king watched the progress of the arrow with fascination and noted the exact spot where it fell and recorded it in his memory.

After this Manikandan instructed Rajashekaran about the exact method of worship in this temple. He told him what austerities had to be practised, the route that the pilgrims had to take and all details of the other formalities to be followed.

"Devotees should observe certain austerities for a period of forty-one days if they want to derive maximum benefit from the pilgrimage. They should carry a cotton bag with two compartments on their heads and a staff in their hand. Their first stop should be at Erumeli and then Kalaketti Ashrama where Shiva tethered his bull while he watched me kill Mahishi. After this they should cross the Azhutha River and climb the hillock known as "Kallidum -kunnu" and place a stone there in memory of this event. From there they should proceed to the Pampa River and take a bath in its purifying waters. Then they should climb the Neeli hills and visit Sabari's *ashrama*. After this, the pilgrims can ascend the eighteen steps leading to my temple. Only those who can overcome these eighteen *tattvas* (mentioned above), can reach me. The great sage, Agastya will come to you and direct you about the type of *pujas* to be conducted there and also advise you on the construction of the temple and the installation of my idol."

Having said this much, Manikandan placed his sacred hands on his father's bowed head and blessed him. Realising that his son was going to leave him, the heart-broken father begged him to allow him to have the pleasure of adorning him with the crown and jewels he had kept in store for the Crown Prince and installing him on the throne just once with all due formalities. Manikandan was touched by his father's love and gave in to his request.

Immediately all preparations were made, the priests were called and Manikandan was formally crowned as the Crown Prince of the kingdom of Pandala. The king could not take his eyes off his beautiful form. He gazed and gazed at his beloved son and started to sob when he realised that he would never see him like this again.

Knowing his agony, Manikandan said, "Dear Father! Don't worry. You may keep these ornaments with you safely. Every year on the 1st day of the month of *Makara* (December/January) you may bring all these jewels and see me adorned with them. For seven days I shall wear them. After that you can bring them back and keep them safely in the royal treasury."

Saying this Manikandan took off the crown and removed all the accoutrements of a prince and gave them back to the king.

Then in front of the astonished gaze of all those who had assembled there, he vanished from view. From then on Manikandan came to be known as Ayyappan.

Manmana bhava madbhakto,
Mad yaaji mam namaskuru.
Mamevyshashi yuktvaivam,
Atmaanam matparayanaha!

"Be devoted to Me; fill your mind with Me,
Worship Me and make obeisance to Me.
Consider Me to be the supreme goal,
Be in constant union with Me
Then you will undoubtedly come to Me."

— *Srimad Bhagavad Gita*

Swamiye Sharanamayyappa!

CHAPTER SEVEN

TARAKA BRAHMAN

Agastya's Advice

Manaprasada saumyatwam,
Mounam-atmavinigrahaha:
Bhavasam-shuddhirityetat,
Tapo maanasamuchyate

Serenity, gentleness, silence, self-control and purity of motive,
These constitute the austerity of the mind.

— *Sriemad Bhagavad Gita*

After Manikandan's disappearance, the king fell into a deep depression from which it was impossible to shake him out. Nothing seemed to interest him any more. He spent his time thinking of all Manikandan's antics when he was a small child and of the various miracles he had performed as a young boy. He lost interest in all state affairs and left everything in the hands of his minister. He didn't even seem to remember that Manikandan had put him in charge of the construction of the temple.

The Lord knew of the pathetic condition of his father and instigated the ancient sage, Agastya to go and comfort him. The sage went to him in the guise of an old Brahmin and was given all due honours by the king.

"O Auspicious One! Looking at your shining countenance I feel sure that you are no ordinary Brahmin. Please tell me who you are," said the king.

The Brahmin replied, "You are right. I am Agastya and I have been sent by Dharma Shasta to shake you out of your mental depression and get you started on this great work, which you have undertaken. You are indeed truly blessed. Bhootanatha who is the Lord of all creatures has come and resided at your palace for twelve years and pretended to be your son. Now stop thinking of the past and start the work which he has entrusted you with."

"O Great Maharishi! Please tell me where my son is? Who is he? Where is he? I keep thinking of all his wonderful exploits. I cannot think of anything else. I realise that he is a god but I cannot live without him!"

Sympathising with the king's anguish, the sage spoke thus. "O King!" He exclaimed, "First of all you have to accept the fact that the boy who you thought to be your son is actually the Taraka Brahman. He has no form or name and is beyond the three bondages of space, time and causality. He exists, pervading everything. He has taken a form only for a specific purpose. That purpose has been accomplished and he has returned to his original state. Traces of your previous life's sins are still accruing to you. Hence it is that despite the advice given by him, you are unable to overcome your emotions. The only way to get rid of them is to contemplate on Dharma Shasta, who has come to give release to millions of people from the travails of their earthly lives. He has come to establish the law of righteousness once again in this yuga known as Kali. In the previous yuga of Dwapara, he incarnated himself as Lord Krishna, the son of Devaki and Vasudeva in order to establish dharma on this earth. With the passage of time, this eternal dharma starts to wane and recede from the earth and thus in this yuga, Dharma Shasta has come to revive it. An avatara is the expression of the redeeming love of the Supreme for the human being, which manifests itself in different ages and in different lands, bringing spiritual enlightenment and bliss into the otherwise dreary life of humanity."

The king eagerly questioned the sage. "If, as you say Manikandan is the timeless 'Taraka Brahman' how is it that I did not get rid of all my sins merely by his vision?"

The sage replied, "O King! Even though he lived with you for twelve years, you did not look upon him as God but only as your son. Even when you saw him riding on a leopard, you did not believe that he could be God incarnate. Nor did the citizens who saw him believe this. You are still entangled in the bondage of maya and have to atone for your past karmas. In your case, this can easily be done by meditating on Manikandan as the Taraka Brahman. Now that your doubts have been cleared you should not waste any more time in idle talk but should immediately set about the task he has entrusted you with. Call the best architect and temple planner in the land and get started on the construction."

With this instruction, the sage left in the same manner in which he had appeared.

The king realised the truth of all that the *rishi* had said. Shaking himself out of his despondency, he called his ministers and experts in temple architecture, priests and other artisans and set forth to the place that had been pointed out to him by Manikandan. The gods rained flowers on him as he started.

At Erumeli, as instructed by Manikandan, the king erected a shrine for the *gana*, known as Vapara. Then they crossed the Azhutha River and entered an impenetrable forest. They continued along their way till they reached the Pampa River where they took a ceremonial bath. They felt refreshed after this and climbed the hill to Sabari's *ashrama* where they rested for the night. After this, they proceeded to the spot that had been chosen by Manikandan for the construction of the temple. Here his men fell asleep but the king could not sleep.

At that time Vapara approached Rajashekaran and told him that he had been sent by Dharma Shasta to take him to the place known as Ponnambalam, which was his permanent abode that the gods had built for him when he first went to the forest.

The king was thrilled at the prospect of meeting his son again. Without waking his sleeping attendants, he went with Vapara to Ponnambalam, the mystic golden temple studded with gems, built by the power of the *rishi*s for Shasta. The king was dazzled to see Dharma Shasta sitting on a golden throne surrounded by gods and sages. He prostrated fully before him but was overwhelmed by Shasta's grace for he jumped up from his throne and gathered him into his arms.

"When I was with my *guru*, I was blessed by him that I would become the King of Kings. I wanted you to have a vision of this state of mine. I know your feelings and your deep longing to see me once again. That is why I brought you here. Do not grieve O Father! Consider the body to be the world, the heart as my temple and the *atman* inside as myself. Contemplating on the truths which I have given you, you will be able to cross over this crocodile infested waters of the ocean of life and attain the bliss of union with the Paramatman."

With tears streaming from his eyes and his voice choked with emotion, Rajashekaran prostrated before that Supreme Being who for some mysterious purpose of his own had deigned to play the role of a human infant. He begged Ayyappan to deliver him from this sorrow that was threatening to overwhelm him and give him the strength to carry out the instructions, which he had given him regarding the construction of the temple and installation of the idol.

Ayyappan cast his benign look on his father and immediately the monarch felt a deep relief. Sorrow gave place to a deep peace and a determination to do the work, which had been entrusted to him by his beloved son, god and *guru*.

"Do not fear, O Father! At the appointed time one of the greatest sculptures in the art of idol making as well as the layout of temples will come to you. Follow his instructions and you will not go wrong. As for my idol, he will make it with the stone known as *anjana*. The pose should be in *pattabandha asana* (a particular posture of sitting which can be seen from the painting). My right hand will have the *chinmudra* or the mystic sign giving all knowledge. My left hand will be supported on my left knee. Now don't delay any more. The faster you get the construction started the better it will be for everybody."

Having said this much to his father, Manikandan presented him with a sword and told him, "This will be of use to you in times of danger."

So saying he vanished from view. The temple and everything vanished along with him and the king was left alone and desolate on the lonely hillside with Vapara who escorted him back to his sleeping attendants, just as the eastern sky began to brighten with the coming of dawn. Sunrise over the Pampa River was an incredibly beautiful sight and as the sun rose in the east, the sorrowing mind of the monarch also slowly started to fill with light.

King Rajashekaran and his retinue started their trek up the Neeli hill. On the way they were accosted by a hunter who accused the king of trespassing his territory and challenged him to a fight. The hunter was none other than Indra, king of gods who was filled with doubt. He thought that perhaps Shasta wanted to depose him and put his father Rajashekharan in his stead.

The king retorted, "I am the monarch of this land and all this belongs to me! How dare you accost me like this?"

Indra took his weapon and threw it at him. However, the king immediately defended himself with the sword that Shasta had given him. Indra's weapon was no match for this. He ran to Dharma Shasta and begged him to rescue him from the sword that was following him with a vengeance.

Shasta said, "The sword doesn't belong to me any more. I have given it to my father. You will have to go and fall at his feet if you want to be saved."

Thus Indra's pride was totally humbled and he fell at the king's feet and begged him to forgive him. In reparation he sent Visvakarma, the architect of the gods to construct the temple.

Construction work on the temple started immediately. All the gods and *rishi*s came to watch the construction. The king installed the sword given by Manikandan at the place where the arrow shot by him had fallen. When he saw this, the face of the preceptor became grim. The king asked him the reason for his gloom.

The *guru* replied, "You have placed it facing south-east and this portents fire hazards to this temple."

The poor king was sorely troubled and didn't know what to do.

At that time they heard Ayyappan's voice proclaim, "O Father! Don't be afraid. Fires will occur in the temple from time to time but consider it to be my will for the temple precincts will need to be purified now and again. You may disregard this omen and continue with the construction."

This has come to pass and many times there have been outbreaks of fire in the temple!

After the construction was over, the next question was about the making of the idol. Just at that moment as predicted by Ayyappan, a sculptor presented himself. He proclaimed himself to be a master in the art of idol making and showed Rajashekharan many sketches of Shasta, which he had made and asked him to choose which he wanted. The poor king was bewildered and asked the master craftsman himself to choose. He chose the one with Shasta sitting on his haunches with a scarf tied round his knees (*pattabandha*). His right hand displayed the *chinmudra* and his left was hanging over his left knee. Now the king remembered that this was exactly what was told to him by Manikandan, so he was very happy.

But he still had a doubt. "Please tell me who you are and how is it that you appeared here at the right time. I feel that you are not an ordinary sculptor?"

The man smiled and said, "You are right. I am not an ordinary sculptor. I am Parashurama (the 6th incarnation of Lord Vishnu) and I have come here to carry out the instructions of Dharma Shasta."

The king was overwhelmed by the Lord's grace in sending him the correct people at the correct time as he had ordained. He fell at Parashurama's feet and got his blessings. It is said that Parashurama himself carved the idol of Ayyappan.

Parashurama as well as Agastya came on the day on which the idol was to be installed. Parashurama installed it according to all the Vedic rites. Immediately after the installation, Manikandan arrived on the scene. He blessed his father once more and entered the sanctum sanctorum and merged into the idol. Tears streamed down the eyes of his father as he realised that he would never see his son in human form again. Gods and other celestial beings thronged the sky to watch this unique installation. The idols of Vapara and Maallikapurathamma were also installed by the *guru* as ordained by Manikandan.

Due to the harshness and inaccessibility of the place, Parashurama told the king that the temple was to be opened only on the first day of each Malayalam month. He also declared that a seven-day festival should be conducted with all due rites and chanting of the Vedas. This was to be concluded on January 14th, the first day of the Winter solstice in the month of *Makara*. This is the most important festival in Sabarimala.

After this, as advised by the *guru,* the king and his retinue returned to Pandala where the queen and her son were anxiously awaiting his arrival. Everyone was astounded to hear about the miraculous events, which the king reported. However, Rajashekharan was no longer in a mood to rule the country. He made all arrangements for the monthly *puja* of the Ayyappa temple in Sabarimala to be conducted as well as all the other festivals that Parashurama had decreed. He then placed his son on the throne and retired along with his *guru* to the banks of the Pampa River where he had first seen the baby, Manikandan. He gave up all material comforts and lived in a wattle hut and spent his time in meditating on Lord Bhootanatha. As predicted by Manikandan, this was his last birth and it was not long before he gained liberation from his earthly coils.

SivaVeerya Samuthbootham,
Srinivaasa-Thanuthbhavam
Sikivaahaanujam Vandhe',
Saasthaaram Pranamaamy-aham

I bow to Lord Shasta,
Who was born of Shiva and Vishnu,
And is the younger brother of Kartikeya.

— *Shasta Panchakshara Stotram*

Swamiye Sharanamayyappa!

"Day and night, dusk and dawn,
Winter and spring come and go,
But the foolish man keeps lusting and thirsting for material pleasures."

— Adi Shankaracharya

ॐ

ॐ

Karunabdaye Namaha!

CHAPTER EIGHT

AYYAPPAN

Dangerous Dacoit

Daadavyamiti yaddaanam,
Deeyate-anupakaarine,
Deshe kale cha patre cha,
Taddaanam satvikam smritam

That gift which is made to a worthy person,
From whom nothing is expected in return,
Which is given with love,
And with regard to the proper time and place,
Is said to be sattvic.

— *Srimad Bhagavad Gita*

Out of the cloudy mists of time another interesting story about Ayyappan has
come down to us through the mouths of the bards. In the previous account
of his life, mystery and myth supersede facts and figures. This account seems
to be more factual and perhaps more credible to the modern mind. It is
connected with a dangerous dacoit called Udayan. There are no written historical
accounts connected with this. The only records are the songs that are still being
sung and have floated down the river of time and the memory of a race.
Who is to say what is true and what false? But we have every reason to believe
that the songs were based on actual facts. Ayyappan had become a hero and
a champion of the downtrodden even during his lifetime. In Kerala there is
a tradition by which the lives of such noble souls are written and set to music
and sung by minstrels who wander from place to place. There are a number
of such ballads in Kerala describing Ayyappan's incredible exploits and the defeat
of Udayan. The bards sing them to this very day.

An ancient temple to Dharma Shasta had always existed on Neeli hill and was looked after by the villages around the place. At this time, King Rajashekharan who was noted for his wisdom and sagacity ruled the kingdom of Pandala. We have already read the previous history of the king. However, the rest of the country was divided into small principalities and there was a lot of bickering and internal fighting amongst the rulers. When the country is divided within itself, law and order will be disrupted. Many bandits and thieves started to exploit the situation and loot the land. Villages were pillaged and plundered and people went in fear of their lives. The leader of the band of robbers was a famous dacoit called Udayan who was the virtual ruler of the land.

Even in those days many pilgrims used to go to the temple of Dharma Shasta. Udayan's strongest fortress was at Karimala, which was on one of the hills by which the pilgrims had to pass. Udayan used to waylay them and rob and kill them. One day Udayan decided to attack the temple itself. When the chief priest tried to stop him, he had no compunction about killing him. However, the priest's son had escaped and was hiding in the bushes and was a witness to the gory end of his beloved father. The boy crept away unnoticed by the brigands and swore vengeance. Udayan destroyed the temple and callously threw away the idol.

The village just beneath the temple was known as Nilakkal and had been a very prosperous and contented village. But after the desecration of the temple, the village fell into ruin and the villagers were bereft and unable to eke out a livelihood for themselves. They migrated en masse to Pandala and to some of the neighbouring villages.

The king of Pandala found himself helpless to stop Udayan's atrocities. His army was powerless to capture this notorious bandit who had established three impregnable fortresses in the Neeli hills. The people lived in fear. Famine stalked the country since no one dared to go outside even to till the land.

Now that he was the virtual ruler of the land, Udayan was filled with a desire to form a marital alliance with a girl from one of the royal households. He was determined to marry a woman from a noble family so that he could establish a royal lineage for himself. Due to fear, some of the neighbouring kings pretended to be his friends. Udayan knew that this was only through fear. But of course even those who pretended friendship were reluctant to give their daughters in marriage to him.

He thought of a master plan to ingratiate himself into the Pandala king's favour. As the princesses of the royal household were going to the temple he got his henchmen to attack them. He then posed as their saviour and rushed into the fray and rescued them with a great show of bravado. Nobody knew who the hero was since Udayan had come disguised as one of the Lords. Moreover very few people knew what he actually looked like since hardly anyone had seen him. Naturally the king was very grateful. He invited him to the palace and presented him with a golden chain. Udayan refused to accept this. The king was surprised and wanted to know who he was. After much persuasion he declared his real identity and told the king that all he wanted was to make friends with him since he deeply repented all his previous acts of atrocity. The king was astonished when he heard this but still he was willing to give him a chance and declared himself willing to make friends. Just at that moment a young man entered the room and asked the king for a private audience. He insisted that it was a matter of extreme importance. So the king took him aside and asked him to explain himself.

The boy warned the monarch to beware of making friends with Udayan since he was only pretending to be a friend and was actually plotting to abduct one of the princesses. He begged permission to deal with the matter and advised him to go inside.

The young man took Udayan outside and challenged him. Knowing that the game was up, Udayan rushed at the boy with upraised sword. The young man parried the lunge and whipped out his own sword. A fierce fight followed much to the amazement of the onlookers who had gathered. Very soon Udayan realised that he had underestimated his opponent and would not be able to kill him as easily as he had expected. He decided that discretion was the better part of valour and ran off before people came to the boy's aid. The whole matter was reported to the king who was really perplexed as to the identity of the young man who had saved him from a dangerous alliance. He asked the guards to search for the boy but no trace was found of either the young man or Udayan.

Later it was discovered that while Udayan was keeping the king engaged with his overtures of friendship, his men had orders to abduct Maya Devi, the king's younger sister with the intention of forcibly getting her married to Udayan, since he realised that the king would never give his consent willingly.

When Udayan returned to his fortress he learnt that his plans to abduct the princess had misfired thanks to the youth who had challenged him to a duel. His men had found out that the young man was actually the son of the chief priest of the temple of Dharma Shasta whom he had murdered long ago. After his fight with Udayan, the young man had intercepted the men who were abducting the princess and rescued her and taken her to safety. Udayan immediately issued a declaration that the couple should be brought before him within forty-one days. If not the general's head would be forfeit.

Though they searched high and low, Udayan's spies could not find the pair. They seemed to have disappeared into thin air. But as per the decree of fate, the young man who was the son of the murdered priest married the princess, Maya Devi. Fearing discovery, they took refuge in the thick forest in the vicinity of Ponnambalam where the *devas* were supposed to have installed a temple to Dharma Shasta. Here they lived in great secrecy, leading a most austere life, eating very little and practising meditation. They begged Lord Dharma Shasta to incarnate himself as their son and kill Udayan and free the land from his atrocities. Pleased with their *tapasya,* Dharma Shasta was born as their child. The baby was born on the eve of the 1st of the Malayalam month of Makara. This is the auspicious time of *Makara Sankranti.* He was a wondrous child with all marks of divinity. The delighted parents tied a small golden bell round his neck and named him Manikandan. They made an elaborate plan by which their child would be taken to the palace and adopted by the king. When the baby was about three months old they heard that King Rajashekharan who was actually Maya Devi's brother had come to the forest near the Pampa River for hunting. Now was the time to put their plan to execution and ensure that their son would become the saviour of the country.

Suppressing the tears, which were threatening to overwhelm her, she hugged the infant to her breast and followed her husband into the dim light of the early hours of the morn. Pearly tendrils of mist were still curling over the hills and the river when the parents reached the banks. They had come prepared to make the greatest sacrifice any parent can make, for the sake of their country. Lovingly they kept the baby on the ground near the king's camp. Her tears were flowing over the baby's face as she kissed him for the last time. She knew that this sacrifice had to be made for the sake of her son and for the sake of the country. They knew that the king had no heir and they prayed that he would adopt their son. The baby started to cry as soon as he was kept down and Maya Devi had to be forcibly dragged from the spot by her husband. If they were discovered, their plan would come to naught and even though the poor mother could not bear to hear her baby cry, she knew that she had to leave him and go away. She stifled her sobs as they hid in the bushes and watched anxiously to find out if their plan was working.

The little bell round the baby's neck kept tinkling delightfully as he turned his head from side to side. As described in the previous story, the king heard the cries and came to investigate and was delighted to find such a lovely baby. He picked him up despite the minister's warning and took him back to the palace where he was brought up as his own son. The rest of the story is the same until the time came for Manikandan to return to the palace after his stay at the *gurukulam* where he had been sent to study all the arts as befitting a prince of the royal blood.

The king was greatly interested in the martial arts and had established many schools all over the country. These schools were known as "Kalaris". The Kerala art of self-defence is known as *kalaripayattu*. The Kalari was actually a pit in which classes and competitions were held. In India everything has a spiritual foundation so at one corner of the pit the idol of a goddess was installed so that the pupils could pray to her before commencing their training. It is said that one of the great exponents of this art had gone to Japan a long time ago and taught it to the people there and that was the origin of the Japanese martial art called jujutsu. Later it came to be known as Karate. The word "Karate" is a distorted Japanese version of *kalari*.

The head of all these schools was an expert known as Kadutha Asan. Every year the king held a competition where boys from all the schools all over the country came to participate. In that particular year the king proclaimed that the winner would be appointed as the general of his army. There were a series of matches and eventually on the final day only six boys remained. Out of these six the winner was a boy called Rama. He was given the honorary name of Kochu Kadutha and was to become one of Ayyapan's most trusted lieutenants. The king declared that Kochu Kadutha would become the general of his army.

Just then a young man came out of the crowd of spectators and requested that he be allowed to fight with all the six as well as with the master. The young man defeated the boys easily and started to fight with the master. At first the master found himself helpless against the brilliance of the boy but at last with a superhuman effort he overthrew the boy and wrenched his sword and shield from him and threw it into the *kalari* where it fell at the feet of the idol of the goddess, which was always kept at the corner of every *kalari*. Immediately the master, Kadutha Asan found that his own sword and shield came apart in his hands and he himself fell helplessly to the ground. His young opponent now came and stood over him. The master as well as all those who were present realised that this was not an ordinary boy but someone with a touch of divinity. The king jumped up for he had recognised the boy to be none other than his son, Manikandan who had been sent to the *gurukulam* for completing his studies. He was thrilled to see that the boy was an expert in the martial arts. Manikandan went up to him, kneeled before him and said, "Sire, I was told to give you this." He handed over a Palmyra leaf with a written message. The king read the message and turned pale. He cupped the boy's face in his palms and scrutinised him carefully as if searching for some resemblance. Tears came into his eyes. In a trembling voice he said, "O Manikandan! I see that you are indeed the heir to my throne. You are the one who should rule this country after me."

Everyone assembled there was amazed by this pronouncement.

Naturally everybody was agog to know what was written in the palm leaf that had made the king declare such a thing. The queen kept pestering him to tell her but Rajashekharan was strangely reluctant to do so since he had been told not to divulge the contents of the leaf till the appropritate time.

Since he had finished his studies, Manikandan came to live in the palace and was officially declared as the heir apparent much to the chagrin of the minister who had hoped to appropriate the throne for himself.

One day a Namboodiri (Kerala Brahmin) from a well-known family came to see the king. He complained about Manikandan's behaviour and said that he was always consorting with the lower classes. He demanded to know his caste and lineage and what had prompted the king to declare him as heir apparent.

The king replied, "Whatever Manikandan does has my full support. As for his birth and lineage, you may question him yourself!"

Just then Manikandan came in and said to the Namboodir. "People think that the lower castes are unclean and those who consort with them should take a bath and purify themselves. But as far as I'm concerned I feel that a pure mind is as important as a clean body. A person with negative thoughts is far more unclean than an outcaste."

Looking sternly at the Namboodiri, he said, "As for you, though you profess to belong to the highest caste, I know that you are unclean both in body and mind. You are suffering from the dreaded disease called leprosy. As for your mind it is filled with impure thoughts. If people find this out you will be shunned like an outcaste. No one will come near you. This being the case, how dare you call yourself clean and the so-called lower castes unclean!"

The Namboodiri couldn't believe his ears. He confessed that he was indeed suffering from leprosy. He fell at Manikandan's feet and begged him to cure him of this fatal ailment that he had managed to conceal from everyone else so far and would be difficult to conceal in the future. Manikandan took pity on him and blessed him and he was cured of his dreadful disease. He then sent the Namboodiri away after exhorting him to stop thinking ill of others.

The queen had conceived and delivered a baby boy during the two years that Manikandan had spent at the *gurukulam*. The rest of the story is similar to the one narrated in chapter five. The minister contrived with the queen to send Manikandan to the forest to get tigress's milk and so on. After killing Mahishi he returned in state to the city, riding on a leopard and followed by the tigresses.

After his triumphant return Manikandan asked permission from his father to go on a mission to quell the might of the pirate – Vavar. The king was most reluctant to let him out of his sight but Manikandan prevailed upon him.

The King made him take his two best generals with him. Their names were Kochu Kadutha and Valiya Kadutha.

Vavar was a Muslim who had been lame at birth and that is why he got the name Vavar. He was an expert in the martial arts as well as in magic and Ayurveda. He became a pirate and used to go round the ports in his ship looting the rich. But he was also a sort of Robin Hood since he gave lavishly to the poor. By the time Manikandan came into the picture, Vavar was a notorious brigand and bandit. News of his approach was brought to the palace and the king was in a dilemma as to what he should do. He knew that his army was incapable of defeating Vavar. Manikandan found that the dreaded pirate had devastated many places along the seashore but of him there was no sign. He had returned to his ship, which had been anchored in the harbour. Manikandan went to the beach and saw the mast of Vavar's ship. He shot four arrows and brought the mast down. Vavar charged out angrily and demanded to know who had the temerity to bring his mast down. He laughed in scorn when he saw the young boy, and told him that he wasn't in the habit of fighting with infants!

Manikandan ignored this insult and challenged him to a duel which would conclusively decide who was the victor. In this way the rest of the army would not be hurt. At last Vavar agreed but to his astonishment, he found that expert though he was, this young boy was able to beat him in everything. At last they fought with daggers and Manikandan brought him to his knees. He jumped on his chest with the dagger poised above his throat. Vavar closed his eyes expecting to feel the cold blade penetrating his throat at any moment. When nothing happened, he opened his eyes to see that the dreaded dagger had been removed and the beautiful eyes of the young boy were gazing into his own with great love! For a long time they looked at each other and Vavar felt as if his soul had been washed clean of all the sins he had committed. At last Manikandan released him and told him that he would spare him if he promised to stop his nefarious activities and help him in his endeavour to rid the land of dacoits and thieves! Vavar realised that he was dealing with a divine personage. He rose up and bowed low to him and promised to stop all his atrocities and help him. Thus Manikandan subdued this famous pirate through the power of his love and not the strength of his muscles. He made him his trusted general and forged a pact with him to help him in capturing Udayan. He told him to collect his troops and assemble at the place known as Erumeli.

All the petty chieftains of the land now decided to unite and rout out Udayan. They assembled at the place called Alangad. All the Lords who were known for their expertise in the martial arts had joined together. The king was also present. Just then Manikandan entered the arena looking like a veritable Prince of peace. The king embraced him and congratulated him on having suppressed the famous pirate, Vavar and made him into an ally.

Manikandan now made his famous speech to the assembled elite that showed the greatness of his nature and the depth of his compassion for humanity.

"My friends!" He said, "Our brigade stands for *dharma*. Lord Krishna has declared that whenever *dharma* declines, he will incarnate himself to uphold it. Such an occasion has risen now when the ruthless Udayan has violated our ancient *dharma*. This is our holy land. Dharma Shasta is our Lord and protector. Udayan has desecrated this land and destroyed the temple and idol of our God. It is our duty to re-build the temple and install the idol of Dharma Shasta. Today is the first day of the auspicious forty-one days known as Mandala. Let us take an oath on this day that we will fight injustice and *adharma* and restore the temple and re-instate the idol of Shasta. We will purge this land of negative elements and exterminate all antisocial and cruel wrong doers. Shasta does not differentiate between caste and creed. He belongs to all races and all castes and all religions. Hence he is known as the son of Shiva as well as the son of Vishnu. He is even taken to be an incarnation of Buddha and the Jain prophets. So let us forget the differences in our castes and religions and remember that we stand united as citizens of this holy land. Let us join together in harmony to bring peace to this bleeding country. Any noble enterprise has to be preceded by *tapasya*. First of all we will have to lead a strictly disciplined life. We have to regulate our own thoughts and actions before we become fit to change others. So let us observe a strict vow for forty-one days starting from today so that we can become worthy of installing the idol in the temple of Dharma Shasta at the place which will henceforth be known as Sabarimala."

Everyone cheered when they heard his speech and all agreed to abide by his decision in everything. Henceforth people started calling him Ayyappan. "Ayya" and "Appan" both mean "father" as well as "god". Such was the respect that he commanded from the people. He now asked the troops to proceed to Erumeli by different routes. The army had to be given a special training before they could proceed to Sabarimala.

While they were stationed at Erumeli, Ayyappan made a mosque for the Muslim followers of Vavar. Even today pilgrims to Sabarimala pray at this mosque where Vavar's idol has been installed, before proceeding to the temple. There is also a temple to Vavar at Sabarimala at the bottom of the eighteen steps on the eastern side. Pilgrims pay their respects to him before proceeding to the main sanctorum. Ayyappan's two other trusted generals were known as Kochu Kadutha and Valiya Kadutha. Even they have their own shrines at Sabarimala. Ayyappan demonstrated in his own life the principle of unity that he always preached. All are children of God and all have to be treated equally. Hence we find that Sabarimala temple is unique in India since everyone regardless of his caste or creed is allowed to worship in the temple unlike other Hindu temples.

The perception of an underlying unity is what causes Hinduism to adhere to the fixed principle that their faith is part and parcel of the unity of the universe and therefore all other faiths are also part of that universal whole. To make demarcations between different religions would be tantamount to blasphemy for it would be going against the universal law of nature and of the cosmos. All religions are part of the process of discovering this unity between human beings, nature and God! This was one of the great principles that Ayyappan taught to all his devotees and this is what the devotees who go to Sabarimala are practising even today. Because of the rigid discipline he imposed on all those who wanted to worship him, many of them were able to keep up these ideals even after the pilgrimage was over.

Thousands of men joined Ayyappan's army as he marched forward. There were many women also. The bards also sing the glory of the woman called Lila who was an expert in the martial arts. She was one of the greatest of Ayyappan's devotees and she was in charge of feeding all the people who had followed him to Erumeli. Ayyappan trained all of them at Erumeli before proceeding to Sabarimala. Udayan had established his fortresses in three places, Karimala, Injipara and Talapara. His stronghold however was the Karimala fortress and that was the target for Ayyappan's army.

Aumkaara-murtim-aartignam,
Devam Hariharatmajam,
Shabari-peeda-nilayam,
Shastaaram pranatosmyaham.

"I bow to Lord Shasta,
Who is the essence of Aum,
Born of the union between Hari and Hara,
Who resides in Sabari."

— Shasta Panchahshara Stotram

Swamiye Sharanamayyappa!

"Again and again we are born and again and again we die
Repeatedly we are thrown into some womb or other,
This transmigratory existence, is impossible to overcome,
O compassionate one, you alone can save me from this."

— Adi Shankaracharya

ॐ

Komalangaaya Namaha!

CHAPTER NINE

AYYANAR

The Crusaders

Sarvabhuteshu yenaikam
Bhavamavyayam-iksha te,
Avibhaktam vivhakteshu,
Tat jnanam viddhi satvikam.

Sattvic knowledge is that which sees the One immutable Being,
In all becomings,
The One indivisible whole in all divisions.

— Srimad Bhagavad Gita

Ayyappan's army was a brigade of love. They followed him because they loved
him and as for him, he considered them as his very own even though they
were a motley crew. However this did not mean that he was lenient with them.
They were all given strict instructions as to how they should behave, what they
should wear, and what they should eat. They were all dressed in black or dark
blue to show the power of their renunciation. Ayyappan had told them that
the body itself was the temple of God. Thus it had to be kept immaculate.
It was not caste or creed that made a person an outcaste but the mind. If
the mind and body were kept pure, then the light of the divine within would
shine forth in all splendour whatever the caste. The only armour they needed
was their purity. That alone would protect them and give them success in all
endeavours. Over and over again he exhorted them to remember that they
were divine, everything in the universe was divine and thus they should love
everyone as they would love God. However they had a duty to chastise wrong-
doers who hated others and tortured them. But even this chastisement was

to be done with love and not hate. This is exactly what Lord Krishna had advised Arjuna in the *Srimad Bhagavad Gita*. Thus, we find a startling similarity between the teachings of these two great *avatara*s for both had incarnated in order to protect *dharma*.

All the crusaders carried a bundle on their heads in which they kept the things they might need. This was the forerunner of the present *irumudi* which all pilgrims to Sabarimala carry on their heads. Every bundle contained a coconut filled with ghee. The coconut was a symbol of the body and the ghee was the love in their hearts, which alone was the fitting offering to be given to the Lord. Ayyappan was the officiating priest for the first *kettunira* or tying of the bundle. This is a ritual that has to be done even today by anyone who wants to go to Sabarimala. Ayyappan placed the first *irumudi* on the head of Kochu Kadutha and then on Lila's head. One by one all of them came to have their bundles kept on their heads. The last to come was Vavar. When Ayyappan had anointed everyone a big shout of glory went up into the pellucid air. The Brahminy kite (vehicle of Vishnu) was seen to be slowly circling the army of the Lord from above. The star called (*uttram*) on which star Ayyappan was born slowly became clearer on the horizon as darkness set in.

The army was well aware of the fact that theirs was a crusade against *adharma* and God himself was leading them. Thus they marched to the chanting of *mantra*s. Kochu Kadutha was in the vanguard of the army and Vavar at the rear. Ayyappan himself was everywhere. Wherever people looked they saw his charming face with a smile meant just for them. Seeing his delightful form they forgot their fatigue and their fears. At night they would sleep in small huts made of leaves. With his usual foresight, Vavar had arranged for rations for the army to be delivered to their camping sites by his henchmen. He had stocked a lot of food in his ships for any unforeseen contingency. This came to good use now and his men brought the food in relays from various parts of the land. When night fell everyone huddled together in front of the blazing fire. All around could be heard the menacing growls and howls of wild beasts. Yet no one felt afraid when they looked at the blissful countenance of their dear Lord. At sunset he could be seen meditating in one of the huts with a tiny lamp before him and a divine radiance emanating from him. As long as they could have at least a passing glimpse of this celestial being, no one felt really frightened. Again and again he exhorted them not to lose heart. This was a journey through the jungle of life, he said, and they were the soldiers of the Lord. They were the chosen ones. They were the forerunners of many who would follow in their footsteps. These were prophetic words that he uttered. Millions of pilgrims have trodden the route that they cut out.

Kochu Kadutha would always go ahead and hack the jungle and make a track for the rest to follow.

They camped on the banks of the Pampa River where Vavar had arranged a big feast for them. This is the custom even today. It's only after the feast at Pampa that pilgrims start the climb to Sabarimala. From Pampa, the army marched to the banks of the Azhutha River. To an onlooker the army might have looked like a motley rabble but they were held together by their love for Ayyappan and their implicit faith in his words. Time and time again he had dinned into them these divine thoughts.

"God is Love! Devotion is Love! The power of love can overcome the greatest obstacles and conquer the strongest fortresses. Fear not. The power of love supports you from all sides. It is your invincible armour!"

Ayyappan's words reverberated in their hearts and minds and they were totally unafraid. The path was cleared diligently by Kochu Kadutha who hacked a way through the formidable forest until they reached the Azhutha River which was their next halting place. Again Ayyappan spoke to them.

"Remember the path may be difficult at first but continue to persevere. The end is worth any effort. You will surely reach the further shore of bliss."

Thus they trudged on – young and old, women and children, drawn like magnets by his divinity. They cared not for the discomforts of the journey. They sang this ditty – *kallum mullum, kaalukku methai*! The literal translation is this, "these stones and thorns are a carpet under our feet!" Many such ditties were sung by them to encourage themselves to march on without fatigue. The pilgrims sing these even today.

The forces sent by the king, met Ayyappan at Azhutha. Even they were made to carry the *irumudi*. They were also enfolded in the light of universal love that was emanating from Ayyappan. They were transformed from mere soldiers who fought for money to crusaders who fought for God. Many tribals who lived in these dense forests now came and bowed before Ayyappan. They begged to join his army and he acceded to their request. They picked the sharpest stones they could get from the river and carried them on their heads in lieu of other weapons.

News of the approaching army was brought to Udayan in his fortress in Karimala. A quiver of fear shot through him. Who was this Ayyappan? Was it true that he was really an incarnation of Dharma Shasta as people were whispering? Would he be able to conquer him? Could a boy of twelve conquer an expert warrior like him? These and many other doubts were torturing Udayan's mind.

Injipara was the first fortress on the route of the advancing army. The person in charge was his trusted general, Puthusheri Mundan. Beads of perspiration broke out on Mundan's forehead when he heard the sounds of the approaching army. Udayan was in the Karimala fortress and he immediately sent a messenger to Mundan to prepare a fitting reception for Ayyappan's army. He ordered him to decapitate a few of the poor women whom he had incarcerated in his dungeon and throw their carcasses outside the gates. The stench of blood attracted many wild beasts that rushed to the gates and started eating the corpses, thus forming another fearsome barrier to the fort.

When the army saw the gruesome sight that had been prepared for them at Injipara, they flinched and drew back a little. Tears came to Ayyappan's eyes when he saw the dismembered bodies. He shrugged them off and spoke to the people.

"This body is only a house for the soul. When one house is vacated another will take its place. The *atman* has no birth and therefore no death. Remember this and be not afraid."

Comforted by his words and his loving looks, they pushed on, only to be met with a shower of arrows from inside the fort. Many fell back wounded. Those who were pierced by poisoned arrows fell dead. Kochu Kadutha charged forward and broke open the gates of the fort. The rest of the *dharmic* army surged after him. Lila was one of the first to enter. She found that many women and children had been incarcerated in dungeons and windowless rooms. They had lost all hope of being saved. She threw open the doors and gave them hope and courage. The sight of her shining face and her loving words filled them with optimism. Hope brimmed in their hearts once again when they heard that succour was at hand.

Those standing outside threw lighted firebrands into the fort forcing the soldiers to come charging out. They stopped short when they saw the divine form of the young boy standing fearlessly in front, looking at them with love in his eyes. All of them fell under the mysterious mantle of love that Ayyappan threw over them and refused to fight any more. Seeing this inexplicable alchemy wrought by Ayyappan's look, Mundan did not wait to face him. Though Vavar and Kochu Kadutha combed the fortress they were unable to find the general, who had escaped through a tunnel. The opening to this tunnel was a pit that contained Udayan's collection of weapons.

Vavar and Kochu Kadutha did not waste any more time there. The crusaders pushed onwards to the next fort, known as Thalapara. Mundan had escaped through the secret tunnel to the Thalapara fort. He was really amazed. He had expected to overcome Ayyappan's army without any trouble and now it looked as if he had failed. How was it possible for this motley crew to have conquered his stronghold? Was Ayyappan indeed an *avatara*? Had he mesmerised them? Udayan had ordered all the weapons that had been kept in Injipara to be taken to the next fort but even this could not be done. Instead the weapons had fallen into the hands of Ayyappan's army.

Udayan soon received the news that Mundan had fled to Thalapara and was fighting a grim duel with Vavar. At last Vavar killed him. The rest of the army immediately gave up. After the conquest of Thalappara, Ayyappan ordered the women, children and old people to return to Azhutha with Lila in charge. The rest of the army started to march towards the dreaded Karimala fortress.

Mundan's body was wrapped in silk and sent to Karimala as an offering to Udayan! This was followed by a request that he should surrender to Ayyappan and thus put a stop to any further bloodshed.

Udayan was shaken to see the dead body of his dear friend. However, he scorned to accept Ayyappan's offer of a truce. By now Ayyappan's army had surrounded Karimala fortress. The tribals joined the fray enthusiastically and started throwing huge stones into the fort from vantage points on the rocks. Udayan could see firebrands falling like meteors into his impregnable

Karimala fortress and hear the sound of weapons clashing and the shouts of the excited men. Even though he was no coward, he felt that he was incapable of facing Ayyappan. In the middle of the night he took a lighted torch and escaped into the forest through a concealed gate. Wild animals were growling all round him. He realized that he didn't stand a chance of escaping. He decided that it would be better to be killed by Ayyappan than to be eaten alive by the beasts. He returned to the fortress and ordered the men to throw the bodies of the dead who had fallen under the onslaught of rocks and firebrands, out to the animals that were prowling outside the fortress walls.

Suddenly in and through the clash and clang of weapons outside the gates, Udayan heard the sound of temple bells. It was a strange sound to hear in the midst of a battle. He had no idea from where it came. Whatever courage he had mustered up was lost at the sound of the bells. He knew the time of reckoning had come. He girded up his loins and went out of the fortress to face the attacking army. Vavar came forward unarmed and requested him to surrender. Udayan scorned to reply and drew his sword out of its scabbard and lunged at Vavar. Kochu Kadutha immediately jumped in front of Vavar and parried the stroke with his shield and thus saved Vavar's life. The tribals were hiding in the tops of trees and peaks and throwing huge boulders into the fort with deadly accuracy. Udayan ran back into the fortress and once again tried to escape through a secret doorway. Ayyappan's army, which had surrounded the fortress, now forced their way in. Udayan found his exit barred from all sides. Like a tiger at bay, he faced the two captains of the opposing army. But they were no match for him. Before he could kill them Kochu Kadutha jumped into the fray and challenged Udayan to fight with him. Udayan fought like a man possessed. Both were well matched. At last Kadutha used the famous snake sword called *urumi* which neatly wound round Udayan's waist and sliced him in two. As the sword snaked round his belly, he thought he saw Ayyappan's compassionate face looking lovingly at him. Before he could rejoice in the sight, Kadutha's sword had sliced him in two.

It was a fitting end to one who had dared to desecrate the holy land of Sabarimala and destroy the temple.

Ayyappan ordered all the corpses to be given a proper cremation. A huge bonfire was lit and the fortress became a burning *ghat* for all those who had fallen. Ayyappan himself carried out the last rites for all the dead, without discrimination of caste or creed.

The victorious army now proceeded to Sabarimala in order to construct the temple. The construction work was entrusted to his trusted generals, Vavar and Kochu Kadutha. Udayan's ill-gotten gains were utilized for the purpose of temple construction.

While the construction was going on, Ayyappan returned to Pandala where he found the king anxiously awaiting his arrival. He assured him that everything was under control and the temple would be finished soon. The king informed him that he had some guests who were anxious to meet him. He took him to the audience chamber where an ascetic couple was waiting. As soon as he saw them, Ayyappan ran forward and prostrated at their feet. The king naturally wanted to know who they were. Ayyappan confessed that these people were his real parents. The lady was Maya Devi, the king's sister whom Udayan had tried to abduct long ago. The man was the son of the chief priest of the Dharma Shasta temple who had been brutally murdered by Udayan. He had rescued the princess and married her. They had gone to the interior parts of the forest and done severe *tapasya* to Lord Shasta to give them a son who would defeat Udayan and restore the temple to its former glory. Ayyappan was their son. This was the strange story that had been written on the palmyra leaf. Even though they had been longing to see their son, they had not dared to approach the palace all these years. But when they heard that he had been sent to the *gurukulam* for his studies they went there and told him the whole story. Their happiness at seeing their beloved son can well be imagined. When it was time for him to leave the *gurukulam*, Maya Devi wrote the whole story on a palmyra leaf and gave it to Manikandan to give to the king. When he read the incredible tale, the king realized that the boy was his nephew and indeed the heir apparent to the throne and thus he had no qualms about adopting him. In Kerala the kings belong to the Nayar caste who follow the matriarchal system by which all property is inherited by the daughters. The king's sister's eldest son inherits the title and not his own son so Ayyappan was indeed the rightful heir to the kingdom of Pandala.

The whole mystery of his birth was now cleared and the king looked closely at his dear sister but could barely recognise her. He had seen her in the flower of her youth dressed in all the finery of a princess. Now she was clad in rough homespun. The hard and austere life that she had led made her look much older than her years. Her hair was grey and her face lined but the glow of spirituality on her face made it striking. They both came forward and knelt in front of the king. Maya Devi asked for his forgiveness for having disappeared without a word but of course she had been the helpless victim of fate. The king wiped her tears and told her that he was deeply grateful to her for having given Manikandan to him. After the happy reconciliation, his sister and brother-in-law urged the king that the installation of the idol should be done on the forty-first day of Mandala, which was the first day of the Malayalam month of *Makara* – January 14th. They told him that this was the day on which Manikandan had been born. The date also marked the termination of the forty-one day vow that Ayyappan had made his army undertake.

Ayyappan declared that everything was ready for the installation and he had come with the express purpose of escorting the king to Sabarimala. He advised him to bring all the jewels he had made for the Crown Prince. They reached Sabarimala on the 1st of *Makara* and found that the temple construction was over. The chief priest was ready to install the idol. The king went and kept the casket containing the jewels on the steps of the sanctum.

Ayyappan was standing just behind the priest on the eighteen steps. Vavar and Kochu Kadutha stood behind him. He lifted the conch to his lips and brought out the sound of the cosmic *aumkara* (sound of *Aum*). Everyone was thrilled. The priest sprinkled him with holy water. He then entered the sanctum sanctorum with the idol in his hands. He looked carefully at the idol and then turned back and bowed to Ayyappan who was standing just outside the door. All the devotees who were present saw Ayyappan bathed in an uncanny golden light. He turned round and showed his hand in the *abhaya mudra*, the gesture denoting fearlessness. For the last time he looked at them with his lotus eyes brimming with love and his unforgettable smile which drenched them in bliss. Just then there was a flash of lightning that blinded everyone. All of them started chanting, *Swamiye Sharanamayyappa!*

When their eyes started to function again they saw that neither Ayyappan nor the priest were to be seen any more.

No one saw Ayyappan again in the form of Manikandan. However they saw the golden idol inside the temple glowing with a supernatural radiance. It was adorned with all the paraphernalia of the crown prince that had been brought by the king. Ayyappan had promised his father to show him this sight and indeed it was a glorious spectacle. The king stood with folded palms, unable to utter a word, with tears streaming from his eyes. It was six o'clock, time for the evening *arati*. Another priest entered the sanctum and lit the lamps for the *arati*, which the devotees had been doing to Ayyappan in person for forty-one days during their journey. Exactly at that time the devotees who turned round to look at the eastern horizon gasped in astonishment. Far away on Ponnambalam hill a huge, blazing bonfire could be seen. The sages were worshipping the Taraka Brahman in their own fashion. As the sky darkened the star *uttram* was seen to be glowing brightly in the eastern sky. The fireflies fluttered around providing their own *arati* to Bhootanatha, the Lord of the Universe. The peacocks that had been hiding in the forests came forward and spread their glorious plumage and danced for the Lord. The eagle that had been following them for so many days came down to the ground and bowed to the Lord and then slowly rose up into the air again. How fortunate were those who had accompanied Ayyappan and witnessed these miracles! They felt waves of bliss flowing over them.

With tears streaming down their cheeks, they started chanting the sacred *mantra, Swamiye Sharanamayyappa*. Louder and louder they chanted until the hills resounded with their reverberating cries. Their hearts were filled with Ayyappan's form and their minds with the great truths he had taught them. Their chants floated down to the Pampa. The river caught these vibrations and started to dance and gurgle with joy. Pampa – the beloved of Ayyappa! What scenes have you not seen! The miracles which take place every year at this sacred spot are a vivid reminder to his devotees that he is ever present and ever watchful of their welfare.

Thus, Dharma Shasta incarnated himself in order to save his land from the grip of *adharma* and restore the temple. For hundreds of years mystics and *sadhu*s living in these forests reported seeing a young boy riding through the jungle seated on a magnificent tiger.

Bootanaatha-Sadaananda
Sarvabootadhayaabara,
Raksha Raksha Mahaabaaho
Shaastre' Thubhyam Namo Namaha!

"I bow to Lord Shasta,
The Lord of all creation ever filled with bliss.
Save me O mighty armed!
Thou who art filled with compassion for all creatures."

— *Shasta Panchahshara Stotram*

Swamiye Sharanamayyappa!

"All types of religious observances or giving of charity,
Will not give you liberation without having knowledge of Brahman."

— Adi Shankaracharya

Bhayanashanaaya Namaha!

CHAPTER TEN

SABAREESHA

Makara Sankranti

Sakala-loka namaskrita-paadukam,
Sukritu-vaasaka Sajjana-modakam,
Sukrita-bhaktajanavana Bhikshakam,
Hariharatmajam-iswaramaashraye.

I take refuge in the son of Shiva and Vishnu,
At whose feet the whole world bows,
Who is the delicacy relished by all noble souls,
Who is goal of all fortunate devotees.

— *Aashrayaashtakam*

Since the Lord is a celibate *Brahmachari* during his sojourn at Sabarimala he does not wear any of his princely ornaments. He wears only a dark blue loincloth. He sits on his haunches, in the most difficult of *asanas*, knows as *pattabandha.* The right hand shows the *chinmudra*, which is formed by touching the tip of the forefinger to the tip of the thumb. His left hand hangs loosely over the left knee. This is his usual posture but as we have seen, to please his father he had promised to wear all the gorgeous ornaments, which the king had made for him, on the day of *Makara Sankranti* and for the next seven days.

These ornaments are kept in safe custody in the palace of the king of Pandala and are carried by his servitors to the temple on the evening of the day of *Makara Sankranti.* Ayyappan allows himself to be adorned with these jewels on that day. They remain on him for the next seven days so that all who come may have *darshan* (vision) of this glorious sight. Many, many miracles take place on this day and also on the previous days when the jewels are being brought.

Three days prior to *Makara Sankranti*, the procession carrying the precious caskets containing the sacred ornaments and also other paraphernalia needed for the special *pujas* at Sabarimala, starts its long trek from Pandala. The ruling monarch never goes. It is said that the sight of the king of Pandala would remind him of his father and Ayyapan's idol would spontaneously rise up to greet him. The heir to the throne is the one who goes with the procession. Once he becomes the king he never makes the journey. Since the kings of Kerala follow the matriarchal system, the heir to the throne is always the nephew of the king and never his own son.

The procession usually starts on the 12th of January. At four in the morning the ornaments and sacred relics are taken out of the boxes from the Srampickal Palace where they are kept in safe custody, and moved to a temple close by. Here they are kept for public view. This is a great boon for devotees who are not able to make it to Sabarimala for the festival. Thousands queue up to see these holy relics. At about one in the afternoon a *brahminy* kite, with the white marking on its neck, which is a sign of Lord Vishnu's vehicle, the Garuda, makes its appearance out of the blue and slowly starts circling the temple in which the ornaments are kept. The pilgrims anxiously scan the skies. As soon as the kite is sighted everyone is jubilant and shout in ecstasy and start chanting the Lord's name with increasing fervour.

This is a yearly miracle and the kite keeps circling over the heads of the runners as they carry the caskets, right up to the Sabarimala temple. It goes ahead of them in the last lap and is seen to be slowly circling the temple and waiting until the procession arrives. It is believed that Lord Vishnu seated on the Garuda follows his son's ornaments throughout the way.

After the kite is sighted, the reigning king arrives with the sword of Ayyappan and offers *vibhuti* (sacred ashes) to all the bearers and to his nephew whom he has chosen to accompany the procession. The delegation of authority and responsibility to his nephew is symbolised by the formal handing over of the sword. After this the caskets are closed and taken out by bearers who are specially deputed for this purpose.

The moment of departure is marked with frenzied shouts of *Swamiye Sharanamayyappa!*

Crackers go off as the prince climbs into his palanquin. Far above the madding crowd the kite hovers, totally oblivious of the din and clamour below! This is truly the fulfilment of the vow made by Ayyappan to his beloved father, Rajashekharan.

The procession takes the age-old route through villages, forest tracks, across rivers and up and down hills. The prince is accorded a formal reception at all the villages that they pass. The tribals also come to pay their respects. The route throngs with people who are eagerly waiting for a glimpse of the divine procession and hoping to get some of the blessed ashes from the prince. After scheduled halts at Ayroor and Laaha, the procession reaches Pampa on the third day, which is always the first day of the Malayalam month of *Makara* – 14th January. The prince and his aides now go to the Rajamandapam (king's residence) that is near the Pampa Ganapati temple and stay there for three days.

The procession carries on through the traditional forest route up the Neeli Hill to the *peepul* tree known as Saramkutthi. It reaches this place on the evening of the third day after starting. The temple officials now come to escort the precious casket up to the eighteen steps. The kite keeps hovering above the temple until this moment.

The chief priest comes down the steps and receives the casket containing the ornaments and goes into the sanctum sanctorum and closes the door. He spends about twenty minutes adorning the Lord with all his splendid jewellery as befitting the Crown Prince of Pandala. At the time of *arati*, which is normally around 6.30 p.m., depending on the light, the door of the sanctum sanctorum is flung open with a flourish and all those who are fortunate enough to have reached there at the correct time, are able to see the Lord in all his splendour. Of course now thanks to modern technology thousands can watch this special moment on the TV. The main priest now does the *arati* (*deeparadhana*) or waving of many types of lights and finally camphor in front of the deity.

The "Makara Jyoti" is another miracle that occurs every year. Synchronising with the *arati* in the temple, a fire springs up far away in the distant hills of the east. To this day no one knows how this appears at exactly the same moment as the *arati* in the temple. It is said that the sages on the mountain known as Ponnambalamedu light the *jyoti* to honour the Taraka Brahman or Bhootanatha. Thousands of devotees flock to the temple on this day to witness this recurring miracle for themselves. The occasion is also marked by the appearance of the star *uttram* in the eastern horizon. Now of course millions, seated comfortably in their homes in front of the TV, can also witness it. The ornaments remain on the Lord for seven days and countless people come for *darshan*.

The prince, who accompanied the procession, had stayed back in Pampa as we have seen. He arrives at the temple on the third day of *Makara*. The officials escort him from Saramkutthi up to the eighteen steps. Here he is met by the chief priest and escorted up the steps to the temple where he worships the Lord. At Sabarimala the prince stays at the Rajamandapam (king's residence) near Maalikappuram. He carries the sword, the symbol of authority and supervises the various *pujas* and receives special *prasadam* from the chief priest.

On the fifth day, the idol is anointed with sandal paste. On the sixth day, a special *puja* known as *guruti* is done for Maalikappuram. After this the prince moves to a room close to the eighteen steps. On the seventh day he returns to Pandala. Before he returns he is allowed to enter the sanctum sanctorum to take leave of the Lord. Even the chief priest moves out of the sanctum and leaves the prince alone with the Lord. It is a most moving scene and is the vindication of the promise made by Manikandan to his father, King Rajashekara, that he will give private audience to him every year in all his glory. No one knows exactly what transpires within the sanctum but the prince is bathed in a divine glow when he comes out. After a few minutes the priest returns and seeks permission from the prince to close the temple for the season. He then closes and locks the door and solemnly hands over the key to the prince in a symbolic gesture that re-establishes the rights of the Pandala family over the shrine of Sabarimala. The prince of course considers himself to be only a vassal and accepts the keys and the ornaments most reverently before he returns to Pandala. The procession winds its way back exactly as it came and the jewels are kept back in their caskets for another year.

Patram pushpam phalum toyam,
Yo me bhaktya prayachati,
Tad-aham bhaktiyupahritam
Ashnaami prayataatmanaha!

"I am happy to accept the loving gift of a pure soul,
Offered with devotion—
Be it a leaf, a flower or fruit or even a drop of water."

— *Srimad Bhagavad Gita*

Swamiye Sharanamayyappa!

"I am not the body or the mind or the intellect or the senses
I am not the ego or prana or the subtle essences,
I am the Supreme Consciousness – I am That, I am That."

ॐ

ॐ

Janmaheenaaya Namaha!

CHAPTER ELEVEN

SRIKANTA

Pilgrim's Progress

Api chet suduraachaaro,
Bhajate maam ananyabhak
Sadureva sa manthavya
Samyagvyavasito hi saha.

Even a most degenerate person
Who worships Me with exclusive devotion,
Should be considered righteous,
For he has made a right decision.

— *Srimad Bhagavad Gita*

The pilgrimage to Sabarimala is a most unusual one and has a deep esoteric meaning. It is a symbol of the pilgrimage undertaken by every embodied soul (*jivatman*) that ends only with union with the Supreme Soul (*Paramatman*). The external journey is only a symbol of the inner process. If the pilgrim has intense faith and devotion every step on the physical path will remove some obstacle in his spiritual progress and draw him nearer to the goal. A person, who faithfully goes on this symbolic pilgrimage year after year, will discover the truth that underlies it. He will come to realise the reality of the Lord's advice, *sarva dharman parityejya, mamekam sharanam vraja.* "Surrender all your earthly duties to me and have recourse to me alone! I shall absolve you from all sins and give you liberation!"

The *jivatman* roams round in this world, birth after birth in order to fulfil his physical desires. He runs after many material objects thinking that they will give him perfect happiness. At the end of his life he realizes that none of these ephemeral things have brought him the bliss for which he has been longing. At last he comes to realise that God is the most desirable object. Everything else can only give temporary satisfaction. It is only God who can give us bliss. Unknowingly we have been searching for Him. When this realisation dawns our lesser desires will vanish to be replaced by the one all-consuming wish to attain union with the *Paramatman*. This is the transformation, which is wrought in the mind of the devotee who undertakes the pilgrimage to Sabari with all sincerity.

The *atman* or soul is ever free and never bound by the rules and regulations of *maya*. Once it realises its unity with the Supreme, none of the duties of the world can attach it. These rules can only bind one who thinks himself to be a puny mortal. Once the devotee shakes off these bonds and experiences his unity with the Supreme, the lower duties can no longer bind him. Then he tastes the freedom of the divine and carries out his duties as an instrument of the divine without caring for any personal gain. This is the advice given by Lord Krishna to Arjuna in the *Bhagavad Gita*. The pilgrimage to Sabarimala is the physical expression of this advice.

The forty-one day vow is absolutely necessary for the serious devotee, who has understood these esoteric truths. It has to be strictly followed by those who want the full benefit of the pilgrimage. All the rules to be observed by the pilgrims had been detailed by Ayyappan himself. The austerities that he prescribed are of utmost importance since they constitute the foundation by which the changeover is made from the mortal into the immortal. This discipline is compulsory for one who wants to shed all material attachments. The result of the pilgrimage depends entirely on the intensity with which we carry out these observances and the unassailable faith that drives us. Total surrender to the will of God is called for with no giving in, to the demands of our individual egos. This alone will enable us to slowly withdraw our mind from the impermanent world and fix it on the only permanent substance – the Brahman. If we cannot do this it would be a mere farce. A safe return from the pilgrimage is not the criterion by which to judge the success of the trip. It should be judged by the amount of change that has been wrought in our individual psyche.

Unfortunately in this age of fast cars and instant foods many people forego these vows and try to make the period shorter but even the modern pilgrim has to do a minimum time of at least one week before going. The correct route to take, which was the one taken by Ayyappan himself, is through Erumeli but again in this age when people want instant enlightenment, pilgrims take a car up to the Pampa River so that they need to walk only eight miles up the Neeli Hill before they reach the shrine which is perched on top of the hill. Obviously these people do not know the esoteric meaning of this amazing pilgrimage or else they have conveniently chosen to forget about it and go only for the sake of some adventure.

All newcomers have to be initiated into the rites by someone called a Guruswamy. The Guruswamy is one who has been going to the temple on a yearly basis for at least eighteen years in succession. Every year, the devotee breaks a coconut on one of the eighteen steps leading to the temple. The first year he breaks it on the first step, the second year on the second step and so on. One who has completed eighteen years breaks his coconut on the eighteenth step and is given the honorary title of "Guruswamy" or one who is qualified to guide newcomers. The one who has completed eighteen years is asked to plant a coconut tree in some place.

The vow to Sabarimala commences when the devotee dons the *mala* or necklace of *tulasi* or *rudraksha* beads. This rite has to be performed by a Guruswamy at some temple. A good day has to be chosen for starting the vow. Saturdays are considered to be the best, failing which he can choose a day on which the star known as *uttram* is in ascendance. This was the star that was in ascendency on the day on which Ayyappa was born. On the morning of the auspicious day, the pilgrim has to take a bath in a river or tank if possible and then don a black *lungi* or loincloth. He then goes to an Ayyappa temple along with the Guruswamy. The Guruswamy recites a number of *mantra*s and then puts the *mala* or bead chain with a locket of Ayyappan, round the disciple's neck. By this act he forges a solemn pact with Ayyappan to follow all the rules that he himself had laid down for the young brigade, which had followed him at the time of the crusade to Karimala.

The wearing of black and the *mala* is a signal for the devotee to withdraw from all social activities. He leads a strictly disciplined life. He has to get up at 4 a.m. and take his bath and go to a temple. He cannot drink or eat anything until he has taken a few sips of holy water from the temple. He has to spend the rest of the day in prayer, meditation and other activities of a spiritual nature.

Those who have to attend office may do so but they should stick to their work and not spend time in idle gossip. After work they should return to the house and take a bath and go to a temple or do some *pujas* or conduct *bhajans* (group singing) in their own houses.

One may wonder at the importance of wearing black, dark blue and saffron robes. All these colours have esoteric meanings. Blue is the colour of the Infinite and it is what Lord Ayyappan wears. Saffron is the colour of fire and renunciation while black denotes death. The pilgrim going to Sabarimala is dead to the world of sensual enjoyments and that is why he wears black. Colours have the ability to change the mental mould of the pilgrim so they have to be accepted as part of the discipline.

Celibacy is one rule that has to be strictly followed. It has to be followed both in mind and body. A man who lusts after a woman mentally is as guilty of breaking his vow as one who actually consorts with her.

From the day he dons the *mala* the devotee is not allowed to share a room with his wife. This is one of the reasons that young women are not allowed to go to the temple at this peak season. The minds of men are weak and it is possible that the sight of a young and attractive woman may make them veer from their vow mentally if not physically.

There are many other sacrifices that the pilgrim has to make. He is not allowed to eat any non-vegetarian food. Even onions and garlic are to be eschewed. Food plays an important part in the observance of all austerities and the pilgrim would do well to observe these restrictions strictly since they will help him to control his appetite in other ways. *Sattvic* food will help the pilgrim to stick to his vow of continence. The quantity should also be restricted to the minimum required for maintenance of the body in a healthy condition. Ideally all the family members should also follow these rules so as to help him keep his vows.

Whatever temple he goes to, he repeats the magic *mantra* of Ayyappa, *Swamiye Sharanam en Ayyappa*! For those forty-one days he does not discriminate between different gods or even between different people. He sees only Ayyappan everywhere. Ayyappan takes total possession of him so that he exists in Ayyappan and Ayyappan in him. In other words, his personality is totally merged with Ayyappan, so that he has no individuality any more and no ego. Those who have taken this first step now call and recognise each other only by the name of Ayyappan or *swami*. They dress alike, look alike, talk alike and perhaps even think alike. Until we accept God's law of equality and try to see the One in us as well as in all others we will not be able to rise above the lower ignorant consciousness of mind and body and realise the eternal *dharma*.

This is one of the amazing things about the pilgrimage to Sabarimala. For forty-one days every pilgrim becomes a yogi and follows the rules set down for a yogic way of life. Ayyappan had hoped that by living such a disciplined life for forty-one days the devotee would get a taste for it and give up his usual vain existence of running after sensual pleasures.

However, the human being is capable of twisting every rule to his own advantage and we see many pilgrims wearing black who rush to the nearest hotel and order drinks and non-vegetarian food, the moment they come down from the hill.

Every devotee is supposed to practice all the three yogas – *jnana, karma* and *bhakti*. He has attained the height of *jnana* for he sees only the Supreme as personified in the form of Ayyappan, everywhere. The only *karma* or work required of him is to reach the sanctum of Ayyappa and surrender at his holy feet. He has no ego left since his mind and heart and intellect are filled with the form and name of Ayyappan alone. Ideally he is a perfect blend of *jnana, karma* and *bhakti*. Total surrender is something that is stressed in all forms of devotion so the devotee constantly repeats the *mantra, Swami Sharanam, Ayyappa Sharanam*! "I surrender to thee for thou alone art my protector." His mind is filled with thoughts of Ayyappan alone and thus he has no time for idle speculation. Having surrendered to Ayyappan, he has no worries for he knows that Ayyappan will take care of him.

Lord Krishna tells Arjuna in the *Bhagavad Gita*, "I will myself look after the needs of one who thinks of me constantly."

The sixty-sixth verse of the eighteenth chapter of the *Bhagavad Gita* is given great importance in the Ayyappa cult. Ayyappa is the *avatara* of Dharma Shasta so he is the upholder of *dharma*. In that particular verse at the end of his discourse to Arjuna, Lord Krishna says, "Surrender all your *dharmas* (duties) to me and depend only on me. I give you my solemn word that I shall deliver you from all sins and grant you final liberation."

This verse is to be seen in all Ayyappa temples because this is exactly what he also says. He is the upholder of *dharma* or righteousness and therefore he can give reprieve to even those who might not have upheld it all their lives but who have now surrendered their all to him. The Ayyappa *bhakta*s have no mind of their own any more and therefore they are not liable to take the responsibility for any of their actions. Their level of perception has gone beyond the intellect and its limitations. Duality dissolves as the ego starts to melt in the fire of devotion, which is ignited in their hearts. Ayyappan's form alone fills their hearts and minds. They have become mere puppets in his hand. He guides them, he leads them and finally they reach him alone.

All their five senses are turned to him. They see Ayyappa, hear Ayyappa, touch, smell and taste Ayyappan alone. They have no other desires. They have given up all their worldly *dharmas* and requirements and have only this one desire left – to attain him and become united with him! Ideally this should be the true state of all those who have donned the *mala* and the black robe. They may have different names in their normal lives but for those forty-one days they are walking replicas of Ayyappan! If they are able to keep up this *bhava* (mental state) throughout the rest of their lives there is no doubt that they would attain liberation. This is what Ayyappan hoped and this is why he insisted that this vow had to be observed by all those who wanted to visit him!

The constant repetition of the *mantra* of Ayyappa somehow has the effect of bringing about a deep inner peace. All the worries that beset the devotee before he donned the robe vanish into the absolute security of being protected by Ayyappan at all times.

Normally the actual pilgrimage starts about a week before the date kept for reaching the shrine. Of course this was necessary when pilgrims climbed by the forest route. The previous evening there is a ceremony performed by the Guruswamy called *kettu-nira*. The *kettu* is a bag, which the pilgrim has to carry on his head throughout the journey. The pilgrimage is complete only when the front portion of the bag is emptied at the temple. The bag is made out of black cloth and has two compartments. The offerings to the Lord are to be taken in the front compartment and personal requirements at the back. The

list of offerings is standardised and compulsory. A coconut is a must. One
of the eyes of the coconut is gouged out and the water drained. It is then
filled with pure cow's ghee. It is corked firmly and pasted over with some
sticky material so that it will not leak. In the symbolic journey of the soul towards
the Supreme, the soft eye of the coconut represents the spiritual eye of the
human being, the ghee is his *atman* and the outer shell his body. Apart from
the symbolic coconut, this compartment should also contain raw rice, popped
rice, sandalwood pieces, betel leaf, turmeric powder, pepper corns, bananas
and a few coins, all of which are to be offered at the temple.

The rear compartment contains whatever the pilgrim might need on his
journey. His needs have to be reduced to the bare minimum. This part of
the bag represents his *prarabda karma*. These are the good and bad results of
our actions or *karmas* of a previous birth, which have propelled us into this
life and which have to be exhausted before we get liberation. This *prarabda
karma* is something which has been brought about by our own desire-prompted
actions of a previous birth, and therefore the contents of the rear compartment
will be quite different for each individual. We have to be careful not to acquire
more *karma* during the journey of our life. If we keep on acquiring more we
will have to take more births in order to exhaust them. Thus we will never
reach our destination, which is the Divine. Since the pilgrimage to Sabarimala
is symbolic of the pilgrimage of life, we will find that this part of the bundle
keeps getting exhausted en route until it is totally empty by the time the temple
is reached. This denotes that our desires that have been induced by our previous
actions have been exhausted on the way. What remains is only the front portion
of the bag with the ghee-filled coconut, which signifies our body and our *atman*.
Thus we see that the contents of the front part will be exactly the same for
everybody.

Throughout the time when the Guruswamy is filling the two compartments
all those present have to keep chanting, *Swamiye Sharanam Ayyappa!* When the
ceremony is over the Guruswamy puts the *irumudi* or bundle on the head of
the disciple. He carefully ensures that the compartment containing the offerings
come to the front of the head. The *irumudi* should never be kept on the ground
until we reach our destination, which is the temple! Of course this is not always

possible so we can hang it on some hook or a branch of a tree when we sleep or when we go to the toilet. The pilgrim is also allowed to carry a staff in his hands to help him over the difficult terrain in the mountain. One who goes for the first time is known as a *kanni swami*.

The coconut as has been said before symbolises the human body. It has three eyes. Two of them stand for the mind and intellect and the third is the spiritual eye that is opened by the Guruswamy so that we can perceive the reality of the Brahman towards which we are proceeding. The hard outer shell is the ego, the sweet kernel is the mind saturated with love for the Divine and the ghee is the *atman* or the divinity within us. This ghee is poured over the idol of Ayyappan at the end of the journey. This act is symbolic of the union of the *jivatman* with the *Paramatman* – the embodied soul with the Supreme Soul.

Kshipram bhavati dharmatma,
Shaswat shantim nigachati,
Kaunteya pratijaaneehi
Na me bhakta pranasyati.

"Such a person will soon turn into a soul of righteousness,
And attain everlasting peace.
O Arjuna! I give you my solemn pledge,
My devotee shall never fall."

— *Srimad Bhagavad Gita*

Swamiye Sharanamayyappa!

ॐ

Swamiye Namaha!

CHAPTER TWELVE

SARANAGATI

The Holy Trek

Manmana bhava madbhakto,
Madyaaji maam namaskuru,
Maamevyshasi yuktvaivam,
Atmaanam matparaayanam

Fill your mind with Me,
Worship Me and make obeisance to Me,
Consider Me as the supreme goal,
Be in constant communion with Me,
And you will undoubtedly come to Me.

— *Srimad Bhagavad Gita*

The evolutionary journey of the *jivatman* starts when it dons the human body and gets born in a human womb. It ends only when it reaches its goal, which is the *Paramatman* or the Supreme Soul. This might take one life or many lifetimes but it will never end till the goal is reached. The pilgrimage to Sabarimala is meant to hasten the progress of the *jivatman* towards this goal. It starts when the *irumudi* is filled and placed on the head of the pilgrim by the Guruswamy. The devotee keeps chanting the *mantra, Swamiye sharanam en Ayyappa* —"Ayyappa I take refuge in you!" After this he leaves his house and does not look back at his house or parents or wife or children. His mind is fixed with single-pointed concentration on Lord Ayyappan. He has no thoughts of the life he has left behind.

The Guruswamy will accompany him and give him all directions as to how he should behave and the route he should take and so on. The disciple has to give a *dakshina* or a monetary offering to the Guruswamy eight times during the course of the pilgrimage. The first offering is made when the Guruswamy puts the *mala,* or rosary round his neck, next when he dons the black clothing, then at Erumeli, at the beginning of the trek into the forest, then after the dip in the Azhutha River, after the dip in the Pampa, after descending the eighteen steps and finally when he reaches home and the Guruswamy takes off the *mala* from his neck.

The trek via Erumeli is the most dangerous and is the one that should be taken by all those who go up for the first time. It is supposed to be the most sacred path since it is the route which Ayyappan himself took when he led the first crusaders. The distance from Erumeli to the temple is about forty-five miles and has to be done on foot. Erumeli is the last stop for all vehicles. Normally it is a small, sleepy town but during the pilgrim season its population of a thousand or so swells to three or four lakhs, all of them clad in black, blue or saffron! Even the shopkeepers wear these colours. There are no ordinary people in this town any more – only Ayyappans! The air is rent with ecstatic shouts of *Swamiye sharanam en Ayyappa!* To be present there at this time is a most thrilling experience. At Erumeli the temples of Dharma Shasta and the mosque are found close to each other. All pilgrims have to pray at both places before proceeding to Sabarimala.

The devotees stay the night at Erumeli and take part in a strange ceremony called *petta-thullal.* This is a most interesting sight. Thousands of pilgrims smear their body with different colours and start dancing from the Karuppuswami temple to the Shasta temple where the idol of Shasta is in the form of a hunter. Drums keep time to the dancing. The dancers appear to be in a state of bliss and dance in wild abandon totally unaware of their dignity or their status in life. Despite the crowds who are dancing in this state of ecstasy, there has been no incidence of any accidents since Ayyappan is said to be dancing with them. This is the spot where the carcass of Mahishi fell and he danced on the carcass. The dancers honour this event which esoterically speaking is the victory of good over evil. This is the first step in the shedding of our worldly egos. Most sophisticated people feel some shame in painting their bodies with colours and dancing to the beat of drums. This is the acid test that Ayyappan gives us at the start of the journey. Can we totally free ourselves of our body consciousness and dance with abandon without criticizing and questioning the necessity for taking part in this barbaric custom!

After this the pilgrims change their clothes and go to the Shasta temple to ask his permission to tread the holy hill of Sabari.

Some pilgrims approach Sabarimala from the beautiful Krishna temple at the place called Ambalapuzha. They are accompanied by an eagle, which follows them in slow circles above their heads. Krishna himself is said to follow the progress of the pilgrims to Sabarimala. This phenomenon is seen every year. Pilgrims coming from different directions meet at various points.

From Erumeli the pilgrims set out barefoot through the jungle. First they have to traverse across a green meadow dotted with the small huts of the workers in nearby plantations. Three kilometres away they reach a small canal called Perur Thodu from where the actual ascent starts. Those who reach there by dusk have to camp there for the night. The next morning it is wise to get an early start. The track is lined with bushes on both sides with occasional trees. The rising sun burns into the backs of the pilgrims and the stones bite into their feet but all this is part of the progress of the pilgrim in the journey of life. "Stones and thorns are carpets for our feet," is what the pilgrims chant. There is no proper track and one has to follow the trail laid by dried rivers, crossing boulders and rivulets on the way.

Six kilometres from here they reach the place known as Kallaketti. This is the place where Lord Shiva is supposed to have tethered his bull (*kaalla*) when he went down to watch Ayyappan dancing on the carcass of Mahishi, thus liberating her from her curse. Another two-and-a-half kilometres from here they come to the Azhutha River where the pilgrim has to take a bath and pick up a stone from the river. This stone is to be deposited on top of the hillock known as *kallidum kunnu* which literally means the hill where one puts a stone. As recorded in the story of Ayyappan, after killing Mahishi, Brahma had asked him to dig a pit and throw the carcass into it and cover it with stones to prevent it from growing.

Azhutha River is not very big but it is deep with steep banks. Sunset time is unforgettable. Pilgrims from different places meet at this point and make their camps. They cook their food to the chanting of Ayyappan's *mantras*. There is a feeling of total involvement and unselfishness and everyone is eager to help anyone who needs it. Little lamps are lit on both sides of the river and cast their glow on the waters. Many people bring musical instruments and these add to the beauty of the chanting and singing. Some pilgrims rest for the day and then make an early start. They cross the river and climb the Azhutha Mountain on a trackless path covered with boulders, gnarled roots of giant trees and creepers. This is a very stiff climb and pilgrims climb slowly, in single file, one after the other, supported only by the name of the Lord. Even when they reach the top they can't afford to rest for more than an hour or so. They have to make the even more hazardous descent through a dense forest into which sunlight does not penetrate. The ground is damp and slippery and the air is rent with the cries of birds and wild animals. Very often they come across elephant trails covered with dung. It is only the grace of Lord Ayyappan that can save the pilgrims from the charge of a wild elephant.

The track now goes between the two mountains, Azhutha at the back and Karimala in front. It ends in another canal called Karimala Thodu, which is the only watercourse in the district, and therefore extremely dangerous since all animals including tigers, leopards and elephants come here to drink water in the early morning. Some pilgrims who are totally exhausted, camp here for the night even though it is very risky.

From this place one goes to the Injipara fort and then to Mukkazhi temple. They have to take a bath in the Puthusseri River before they attempt the next ascent of the notorious Karimala Mountain, which is the most difficult of all. It has to be climbed in a zigzag fashion. One of the Sanskrit names for elephant is *kari* and this mountain is noted for its wild elephants. The climb can only be done in painful stages. Right on top is a spring so most pilgrims halt here for the night.

The next morning they start on the even more perilous descent. A single false step may end in disaster since the fall down the steep precipice spells instant death. After this terrible trial, they come to the long-awaited Pampa River.

In the *Ramayana*, it is said that Rama and Lakshmana were delighted when they reached the Pampa. Modern pilgrims also rejoice at the sight of the holy river. Everyone runs to take a dip as it is considered as holy as the Ganga. Sri Rama's footprints are seen here. Ayyappan is supposed to have performed a special *puja* here for the departed souls of the warriors who had fallen in the fight with Udayan. Many people make similar offerings to their departed ancestors at this place. Pilgrims set up their camps and some even rest for a few days delighting in the ambience of this beautiful spot. The lovely Pampa meanders its way through dense forests containing many medicinal plants and hence it is said that those who bathe in its waters feel most refreshed. This is the spot where King Rajashekhara saw the baby, Manikandan, so it is indeed a most holy spot. After having spent many nights in the open under the starry skies, listening to the muted roars of tigers and leopards, the pilgrim feels as if he has reached a safe harbour when he camps on the banks of the Pampa. Sunrise and sunset here are glorious sights. Long golden streaks dart across the sky and chase away the darkness, heralding the approach of dawn.

The short equatorial twilight suddenly changes to pitch darkness when the sun sets. Now come the little lamps like so many fireflies casting their flickering shadows on the banks. Many people like to spend a few days at this idyllic spot.

The day before *Makara Sankranti* or the first day of the month of *Makara* when the temple opens, is the day when the festival of lights takes place on the Pampa River. The Lord is supposed to be present at Pampa on this day. The pilgrims float small boats made out of leaves in which little lights and flowers are placed, down the river. Each boat carries a wish. There is a big feast on the banks of the river on this day.

On the first day of *Makara* the pilgrims pray at the temple of Ganesha where their bundles have been kept for the night. They beg him to allow them to go up the hill and have *darshan* of the Lord without any difficulty. The prince from the royal house of Pandala is present there on that day and pilgrims have to pay their respects to him and receive the sacred ashes from him before proceeding. The eight miles from the banks of the Pampa River to the eighteen steps leading to the altar are steep but devotion is at its peak and this is what keeps them going. They sing the same ditty sung by Ayyappan's crusaders, *kallum mullum, kaalikku methai* "These stones and thorns are a carpet under our feet!"

The final mountain is known as "Neeli Mala" and is the most difficult climb of all. It is very steep and slippery and appears more difficult than Karimala. They have to pass between the hills known as Appachi and Ippachi. These are very steep and used to be covered with dense forest. Unfortunately the forest has been cleared now and concrete steps made to facilitate the climb. Much of the magic of this climb has gone with this modernization. There is an old custom of throwing some sweet balls on either side of the path during the climb to ward off evil elements.

At last after completing this they reach the place known as "Sabari Peetham" where Manikandan gave salvation to the old tribal woman called Sabari. From here there is a beautiful panoramic view of deep ravines, green valleys and lofty mountains. The Ponnabalamedu which was the golden temple created by the *rishi*s by the power of their *tapasya* is just opposite. The pilgrims however are agog to reach the temple and most of them have no inclination to stand and gaze at the natural beauty that surrounds them.

From here it is only a half hour walk on fairly level ground till they reach the place known as "Saramkutthi". This is the spot where Ayyappan's arrow fell and the king had marked it. There is no peepul tree there now but this is indeed sacred ground since that was the place chosen by Ayyappan. Those who carry staffs are supposed to deposit them at this place. They are not allowed to carry them to the temple. The eighteen steps and the golden flagstaff are visible from here. Naturally pilgrims rush forward to climb the steps. They are in a desperate hurry to reach the steps. They have reached the end of their journey where the Lord is waiting to receive them.

The air is rent with frenzied shouts of *Sharanam en Ayyappa*! The hills become a concert hall where the sounds of the *mantra*s, the ones who repeat it as well as those who listen to it are joined together in a glorious symphony of ecstasy impossible to describe. Only those who have experienced this can know the magic of those moments. It is a convention that from here to the temple until one gets *darshan* of the Lord, the *irumudi* should be kept on the head, however long the queue and however lengthy the wait.

The temple is at a moderately high level and one has to climb the eighteen steps in order to have *darshan* of the Lord. Only those who have observed a strict forty-one day vow and who are carrying the bundle on their heads are allowed to climb the eighteen steps. Others have to go by the back way. The police keep a strict vigilance to see that no one who is not carrying the *irumudi* on his head is allowed to climb the steps. But this is only an external sign. No one can guess the number of days of austerity, which each person has followed. This is a secret between the pilgrim and the Lord. One can cheat others but not the Lord!

When they reach the bottom of the steps the pilgrims prostrate still clutching their *irumudi* tightly on their heads. Who can describe the ecstatic state of their mind when they reach those sacred steps? Tears of joy stream down their eyes and they are rendered speechless. The arduous trek and the long wait were well worth the effort. As mentioned earlier, pilgrims have to break a coconut on one of the steps depending on the number of years that they have been coming. Those who are coming for the first time have to break the coconut on the first step. It is said that Maallikapurathamma waits anxiously at the bottom of the steps and watches carefully to see if there is any newcomer to the temple. Ayyappan had promised her that he would wed her in that year in which no new pilgrim came to the temple! Needless to say every year, she goes back to her own shrine, disappointed!

Time is precious and there are thousands straining for a glimpse, literally treading on the toes of those standing in front of them, so nobody can afford to linger but have to keep moving. First they have to do a circumambulation of the temple. They visit the shrine of Ganesha first, then Kartikeya and finally stand enraptured before the form of Ayyappa. Here the coconuts are broken and the ghee poured over the idol. The state of exaltation of those who have done the total vow of forty-one days and experienced the hardships of the dangerous climb from Erumeli and eventually climbed the eighteen steps to stand face to face with the Lord of their hearts, can hardly be put into words.

There is a pit on top of the steps where pilgrims throw the camphor that they have brought. During that one week this bonfire of camphor can be seen burning day and night casting its sweet fragrance around and purifying the air. Such a sight can never be seen anywhere else. The temple is comparatively small and its precincts can hardly accommodate more than about two thousand people and it is a real miracle that on the occasion of the *Makara Vilakku*, more than a million people are gathered there and no one returns without having *darshan* of the Lord.

After this the pilgrims go to the temple of Maallikapurathamma, the *Shakti* of the Lord, to get her blessings. Then they wait for the glorious *deeparadhana* or *arati* at 6 p.m. at the temple. Those who are fortunate enough to be there at that time are also able to witness the *Makara Jyoti* which is a light of indescribable splendour which is simultaneously seen in the north-east corner of the horizon. Some say that it comes from Ponnambalamedu where the gods and *rishi*s congregate to worship the Lord on this auspicious day and time. Others say that this light is Dharma Shasta who reveals himself in the form of light on the mountain known as Kanthamala.

After receiving the *prasadam* (remains of offerings) the pilgrims go down the eighteen steps, carefully walking backwards so that they don't show their backs to the Lord. Many of them return the same night and by the same route. Others return via Mount Estate and Vandi Periyar. A person who has once experienced this amazing pilgrimage is never the same again. A dramatic change occurs in his psyche and he is forced to realise the ephemerality of human life and the futility of human endeavour without the help of God! Of course this applies only to those who have faithfully observed all the observances as decreed by Ayyappa! Even those who go with the mind of a tourist cannot help but be impressed by the miracles that take place there.

ॐ *Dhrityaa yayaa dharayate,*
Manapranendriyakriyaha!
Yogena-vyabhichaarinya,
Dhriti sa Partha saatviki.

"The unswerving firmness by which one controls the functions of the mind, breath and senses through yoga, is said to be sattvic."

— *Srimad Bhagavad Gita*

Swamiye Sharanamayyappa!

ॐ

Brahmane Namaha!

CHAPTER THIRTEEN

DHARMAATMA

Esoteric Eighteen

Samoham sarvabhuteshu,
Na me dweshyosti na priyaha!
Ye bhajanti tu maam bhaktya,
Mayi te teshu chapyaham.

I am the same to all beings.
There is none hateful or dear to Me,
However those who worship Me, with undeviating devotion,
Always abide in Me and I am always present in them.

— *Srimad Bhagavad Gita*

The shrine of Ayyappan at Sabarimala is on a remote peak on the Neeli Hills but despite the difficulties of approaching it, about four to five million people are drawn to it every year and the number keeps increasing. The temple opens only a few times in a year. It is kept open for the first week of every Malayalam month and then for the Mandalam festival that lasts for forty-one days from the November 15th to December 26th. Then it closes and opens again on the 1st January and remains open till the 14th January, which is the day when the famous *Makara Jyoti* is seen on the opposite hill known as Ponnambalam and the day on which the deity is adorned with the jewels brought from Pandalam by the representative of the reigning king. It also opens for the Kerala New Year known as Vishu on April 14th, which corresponds to the vernal equinox.

This temple unlike many others in Kerala is open to people of all religions. Muslims and Christians alike visit the temple. However, women above the age of ten and below the age of fifty-five are not allowed to enter especially during the main festival days. That is to say they can enter only before puberty and after menopause. The original reason was that no young woman could ever hope to observe the full forty-one day vow on which Ayyappan had insisted. They were sure to get their monthly period at least once during that time and thus there would have been a break in their vow. In Kerala it is forbidden for menstruating women to enter a temple or perform any *puja*. This was the main reason that young women were debarred from going to Sabarimala. The other reason was that they might prove a temptation to the male pilgrims who had been strictly adhering to their vow of celibacy for forty-one days. Of course considering the fact that even the men have waved these forty-one days, and people are able to go up and return within a few days, this regulation can surely be over-ruled but since we still live in a male-oriented society, this is one rule that is strictly observed by the temple authorities most rigidly! However, women can take pleasure from the fact that there are some temples in Kerala where only females are allowed!

Even in ancient times during the pilgrim season no tigers were found around the hill. But on the other hand there are many stories of how those who had flouted the rules of the forty-one day vow, especially the one pertaining to celibacy, were found to be missing during the hazardous trek up the mountain.

The path taken by the earth round the sun is elliptical. Twice a year the sun touches the farthest points of the ellipse. At these two times its distance from the equator is farthest. From the 14th of January onwards the sun starts its journey to the north and thus this day is known as the winter solstice. The six months of the year starting from January 14th to July 14th is known as *uttarayanam*, or the day of the gods. The sun starts its northward journey from January 14th and people in the northern hemisphere start to experience summer. This day is known as *Makara Sankranti* and is a very special day for all Hindus and is celebrated all over India. In Sabarimala this is the day on which the divine *jyoti* is seen and a star rises on the eastern horizon. This is a yearly event that is witnessed by millions of people.

There are eighteen steps leading to the temple, which have a great esoteric importance. In no other place have the steps to a temple been given such great importance. Manikandan had told his father that the entrance to the temple should be up eighteen steps. The king had immediately asked him for the esoteric significance of the steps and this is what he had told his father.

These steps represent the eighteen *tattvas* or traits, which go to make up the human personality. These are the *indriyas* or five senses, the eight *ragas* (*kama, krodha, lobha, moha, mada, matsarya, mamta* and *abhimana*, which are the primary emotions), the three *gunas* (*sattva, rajas* and *tamas*), and wisdom and ignorance (*vidya* and *avidya*).

Some other interpretations are also given. It is said that the steps stand for the eighteen types of *sadhana* that are necessary for the seeker before he can reach the Ultimate. These steps are beautifully explained in the eighteen chapters of the *Srimad Bhagavad Gita*. The climbing of these steps denotes that the pilgrim has actually completed all the spiritual practices given in the eighteen chapters. As we climb the eighteen steps that symbolise the eighteen *tattvas* the embodied soul transcends these within its body, thus enabling the *atman*, which has been covered by these veils of *maya*, to be revealed in all its glory. Such a person begins to shine with the light of the divine and as he performs the final act of pouring the ghee over the idol, he becomes one with the godhead embodied therein. Let us study the eighteen chapters of the *Gita* in order to find out how they can be connected with the pilgrimage to Sabarimala.

The first chapter of the *Gita* describes the confusion and indecision in the mind of the seeker (Arjuna) and his surrender to the Guru (Krishna). This is exactly what transpires between the pilgrim to Sabarimala and the Guruswamy.

In the second chapter Krishna describes the path and also gives a pen portrait of the *sthitaprajna* or the enlightened man. Again in the second step of the pilgrimage, the Guruswamy describes the path to be taken and what is to be expected of a person after he dons black and wears the *mala*.

In the third chapter, Krishna describes to him the yoga of action (*karma*). Next the Guruswamy tells him the meaning of *karma yoga* and how he has to follow this path during the forty-one days.

In the fourth chapter he describes to him the relationship between *sanyasa* and *karma*. The Guruswamy explains this very topic to the pilgrim. The fact that even though he is not a *sanyasin*, he has to be a *karma yogi*.

The fifth chapter gives the difference between *karma yoga* and *karma sanyasa*. The Guruswamy points out this difference to his disciple.

The sixth chapter gives the method of meditation and how to control the mind. The Guru gives a method of meditation to the pilgrim by which he thinks only of Ayyapan and is thus able to control his mind.

The seventh chapter shows us the difference between knowledge and discrimination. The true Guruswamy tells the disciple to discriminate between right and wrong behaviour.

The eighth chapter gives us the yogic technique of dying, what paths are taken by the departing yogi and so on. Ayyappan told his brigade not to be frightened of death since they were fighting for the sake of righteouness, so also the Guruswamy tells the pilgrim not be frightened of undertaking this rigorous bodily vow.

The ninth chapter gives us the supreme secret of how God is to be found everywhere and how to direct our minds to him all the time. Ayyappan had told this truth to his original brigade – that God is found everyhere and therefore they should love all.

The tenth chapter is called *vibhuti yoga* where the Lord gives examples of his presence in everything both animate and inanimate. The Guru tells his disciple to recognise God in everything.

The eleventh chapter gives us a glimpse of the cosmic person. Everything in the world is shown to Arjuna within the body of Krishna. The first crusaders did indeed see in Ayyappan, the cosmic person.

The twelfth chapter gives the yoga of devotion or *bhakti*. This is the greatest teaching – that of devotion or *bhakti* to Ayyappan.

The thirteenth chapter is highly scientific and gives us the relationship between the field of our perceptions and the knower of the field. This is actually a fact that has been proved by quantum physics.

The fourteenth chapter describes the qualities of one who has risen above the three *gunas* of *sattva, rajas* and *tamas*. This is a very important chapter and the person who wants liberation has to learn to go above the three *gunas*.

The fifteenth chapter gives a beautiful description of the Supreme Person, the Purushottama. The devotees of Ayyappan see in him, the supreme Purushottama.

The sixteenth distinguishes between noble and demonic characteristics. The devotees learn to recognise these traits in themselves.

The seventeenth tells us about the different types of faith that drive us to act in certain particular ways.

The eighteenth is a summary of the whole discourse of the *Bhagavad Gita*. At the end of it Krishna gives the famous verse that is inscribed in all the Ayyappa temples –

Sarvadharman parityajya, maamekam sharanam vraja,
Aham twa sarvapaapebhyo mokshayishyami ma shucha.

"Surrender all your duties to me and have recourse to me alone,
I shall absolve you from all sins and grant you eternal salvation!"

The devotee renounces everything into the capable hands of God who makes a solemn promise to guide him or her through the travails of worldly life and give her liberation. All Ayyappa devotees believe that this is a direct reference to Dharma Shasta who has given us once again the importance of following our *dharma* as well as of abandoning them into his hands. Liberation is not possible for the human soul without total surrender. This is the gist of the teaching of the *Bhagavad Gita* that was reiterated by Ayyappan.

With every step that he takes, up the eighteen steps leading to the sanctum of Lord Ayyappan, the devotee reiterates one of the eighteen truths of the eighteen chapters of the *Bhagavad Gita*.

Inside the temple, Ayyappan sits there in the unique *yogasana* known as *pattabandha*. His right hand shows the *chin mudra*. This *mudra* is indicative of the great Upanishadic dictum – "That thou art." The tip of the forefinger touches the tip of the thumb, thus indicating the great truth that the *jivatman* (embodied soul) is one with the *Paramatman* (the Supreme Soul). He blesses everyone who approaches him with faith, in silence. He is ready to give them what they desire but they have to ensure that they deserve it. They become fit recipients for his grace by following the steps of the forty-one day vow with all sincerity and dedication.

There are three other famous temples to Dharma Shasta in Kerala. These are Aryankavu, Achankovil and Kulatupuzha. These three along with the Sabarimala temple are all said to have been installed by Parashurama.

The idol at Aryankavu is that of a young boy seated on an elephant with his left leg hanging down and the right bent and kept across the left knee. On his right side is his wife Prabha and on his left his father, Lord Shiva. Girls who want to get married get a thread from the temple that has been blessed and kept in Shasta's hand. They tie this round their neck and very soon they will get suitable husbands!

At Kulatupuzha the idol is again that of a young boy. It is below the ground level and thus the Shasta here is said to be very powerful. Those who are beset with all sorts of ailments come here and feed the fish in the river and get cured of their diseases. This particular offering is especially beneficial for those who have huge moles and other disfiguring skin eruptions.

In Achankovil, Shasta is seen with his two wives Poorna and Pushkala on either side. This temple has two *pujaris* (priests) and is famous for curing all types of snakebites. Regardless of the time of day or night, the temple doors have to be opened to render aid to one who has been bitten by a snake. No other temple will open its doors once they have been closed for the day.

Prasadam (offerings) from inside the temple is given to the patient and invariably they get cured.

There is an interesting story connected with this temple. Shasta's wife Pushkala is supposed to have come from the community of the Saurashtrian Brahmins. In ancient days, Saurashtra was noted for its silk weaving industry and many traders came with silk *saris* to the state of Travancore where they could sell their wares. Once, one such trader came along with his daughter – Pushkala. He reached Achankovil at night and spent the night at the temple. Next morning when he was ready to start, his daughter begged to be allowed to stay on there. The priest supported her and told the father to leave her in his custody. Since he had to pass through a dense forest, the father agreed. The girl was intensely devoted to Shasta and spent her time praying and singing to the Lord.

When the trader was returning through the forest, he was terrified to see a huge elephant charging at him. He cried out to Shasta to save him. Immediately a hunter appeared and made a sign to the elephant. To the trader's surprise the elephant quietly turned round and walked away. Naturally he was overwhelmed at his miraculous escape and presented a beautiful silk scarf to the hunter who immediately accepted it. He wound it round his neck and asked the man.

"Now how do I look?"

The trader replied, "You look like a bridegroom!"

The hunter laughed and said, "In that case will you give your daughter in marriage to me?"

The trader replied, "You have saved my life and that of my household. I will be honoured to give my daughter's hand to you."

The hunter bowed and promised to meet him at the temple the next day.

The trader returned to Achankovil and found his daughter in deep meditation. She was not at all inclined to return home with her parent. In the meantime the *pujari* of the temple had a strange dream the previous night, which he narrated to the trader.

"I had a dream in which Shasta came to me and told me that he had married Pushkala, your daughter, who you left in my custody. He told me to open the front door and I would find you at the doorstep. Here you are exactly as I was told. Now let us open the door of the sanctum and see if we will find your daughter inside."

The astonished trader accompanied the *pujari* to the sanctum. When the priest opened the door, his eyes was blinded by the blaze of lights inside. An idol of his daughter, Pushkala was to be seen next to Shasta and to his utter amazement the trader saw that the silk scarf, which he had presented the hunter the previous day, was now wound round the neck of the idol of Shasta. He realised that the hunter who had saved him was none other than Lord Shasta.

At the same time, the king of Travancore had a dream in which he was requested to go to Achankovil along with his retinue with all preparations for a wedding. Shasta came to him in the dream and told him that he had married the daughter of the Saurashtrian trader. In future he decreed that the reigning king of Travancore should go every year to Achankovil, carrying presents for the bride and treat the trader and his family as their son's in-laws. The king did as commanded and the marriage was celebrated according to the Saurashtrian rites.

This custom continues to the present day. The marriage ceremony of Shasta and Pushkala is celebrated for eleven days. People from Saurashtra come to

Achankovil as representatives of the in-laws of the son of the king of Travancore. A portrait of the king is kept in the wedding hall and the ceremony is celebrated according to the Saurashtrian tradition.

The stories of Ganesha, Kartikeya and Shasta are all parts of Puranic literature and they cater to the multifaceted intellect of the human being who craves for different expressions of the godhead.

It must be noted that Hindu gods are not mere symbols. They are spiritual beings. Prophets and mystics have seen and heard and been influenced by them. They exist in a non-physical, microcosm. Hundreds and thousands of *devas* do exist and they can exist in a tiny space in this physical world. During *puja* the priest, if he is intuitive, can establish a contact with them and open up a channel of communication. He can enable the physical microcosm of the devotee to open into the macrocosm of the *devas*. Even without the mediation of a priest it is the personal experience of all true devotees that the deities whom they have worshipped faithfully have always helped them in times of need. The stories of the three sons of Shiva are meant to encourage everyone to approach these deities with the right attitude of devotion and surrender and experience for themselves the bliss of being in constant touch with the divine as expressed in these forms. The promise made by Lord Krishna to Arjuna in the following verse from the *Bhagavad Gita* is only a model of the promise made by every deity, be it Ayyappan, Kartikeya or Ganesha that they will protect and look after the needs of their devotees.

Ananyath chintayanto mam,
Ye jana paryupasate,
Tesham nityabhiyuktanaam,
Yogakshemam vahamyaham

"I will personally take care of every need and safeguard the possessions
Of those who are in constant communion with me,
Who think of me alone
And make me the sole object of their worship."

— *Srimad Bhagavad Gita*

Swamiye Sharanamayyappa!

IN PRAISE OF THE SONS

By Vanamali

In the supermarket of the world,
I search for gods,
One by one they come to me,
And offer me their goods.
I search for one face alone,
I seek one form alone,
Why does he not come – that formless one?
I see a glimpse in a lightning streak,
In the crescent moon caught in a net of leaves,
His voice in the thunderous cloud,
In the sweet murmur of the Ganga,
Can one capture the southern breeze?
Can one hear the unsung song?
Yet have I sinned,
In capturing Thee on paper,
Time and time again,
Enfolding Thee in the bonds of a book
Thou boundless One!
Forgive me,
This ignorant soul,
My love is my only reprieve
For I have loved Thee in Thy infinite forms,
Thou formless One!
Again and again have I caught Thee,
Enfolded to my breast within a book.
Here one more page,
One more book,

I crave Thy indulgence my Lord,
I place this at Thy feet,
My humble token,
Given to me by Thee!

Listen O! Listen! Thou big eared one!
Catch me with Thy trunk as I fall,
Prod me with Thy hook if I fail,
Feed me a modakam when I please,
Then will I break a coconut for thee!

How will you catch me if I do not fall?
How will you help me if I do not fail?
How will I find you if I do not seek?
How will I hear you if I close my ears?

Thy gaze is in the mote shining in the sun,
Thy voice is in the brook, meandering in the mud,
Thy form, in my mind wound like a trunk round my heart.

O Kumara of beauteous face!
Mounted on a peacock,
The thousand eyes on its tail,
Cannot drink in your exquisite beauty.
Your six faces look at me from all sides,
East, west, north, south, above and below
Guide me; guard me with or without my will.

A fool am I – a terrible fool!
Who cannot see you in the All
In the small,
In the mighty, in the minute,
In the beauteous peacock,

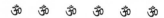

And the snake beneath its feet.
O Lover of Valli!

Did you not come for me as you went to her?
Did you not snatch me from the grasp of my greedy relations?
As you snatched her?
With twelve eyes do I look at Thee,
Obliquely – in silent adoration,
With twelve arms embrace Thee!
O six-headed son of the Krittikas
Kartikeya! Beloved of Valli!
Beloved of Vanamali!

ॐ   ॐ   ॐ   ॐ   ॐ   ॐ

When have I failed Thee?
Always or never?
When have you failed me?
Always or never?
Is there no end to this game?
Without a name.
If this be Thy game
How terrible Thy reality!
Can my desire be made into Thy will?
Or better still
Can thy will become my desire?

ॐ   ॐ   ॐ   ॐ   ॐ   ॐ

I know what is dharma yet I cannot follow,
I know what is adharma yet I cannot avoid,
O Hari Hara Putra!
Amazing son of Hara and Hari!
Lead me on the path of dharma,
Guard me from the curse of Mahishi,
The epitome of adharma!
Seated in my heart do thou guide me,
I'm only a puppet in thy hands.

Why do I love Thee and how,
When do I hate Thee and why?
Why do you hold me and set me free?
Why free me, if only to bind?

Inexplicable is Thy game,
Inexplicable Thy nature
O sons of Shiva!
Release me from Thy lilas!

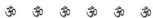

Groping in the darkness of ignorance
I search for the unknown,
Delving into the depths of unchartered seas,
I look for precious pearls.
Some find dirt, others fish
But I have found the most rare coral of inexplicable beauty.
Thee have I found my beloved,
In a thousand forms, with a thousand names,

This my sahasranama to Thee,
My garland of wild flowers,
I place at Thy feet
Do Thou accept,
And bless this scribe,
Along with those who choose to read.

Mantra heenam kriya heenam bhakti heenam Sureshwara,
Yad pujitam maya deva paripoornam tadastu te,
Aparaadha sahasraani kriyante hanisham maya,
Dasyoham iti mam matwa,
Kshamaswa Purushottama.

I beg of you to make this puja of mine perfect
Despite the mistakes I have made in the chanting of the mantras,
And the accompanying actions,
Consider me as thy slave and forgive me O Purushottama!
For all the mistakes I keep committing all the time.

Thus ends the final chapter on the Sons of Shiva. Another flower in thy garland O Vanamali!

Hari Aum Tat Sat

GLOSSARY OF SANSKRIT TERMS

abhaya mudra	The sign of fearlessness
abhimaana	pride
abhishekam	ritualistic bathing of the deity
adharma	non-righteousness
adiyantra	the first of the mystic drawings
advaita	non-dual; philosophy of non-dualism
advaitic	non-dualistic
aganya	incalculable
ahamkara	ego
ahamtwa	egoism
aiswarya	auspiciousness; wealth
ajam	unborn
akasa	ether; first of the five elements
amrita	nectar of immortality
anadi	without a beginning
ananda	bliss
anjana	type of black stone
ankusa	hook used to control elephants
apsaras	celestial dancers
arati	waving of lights before a deity
artha	wealth
asanas	yoga postures
ashrama	spiritual sanctuary
asti	beingness
astra	weapon
asuras	demons
asuric	demonic

atman	soul or inner spirit
Aum	the primeval sound
aumkara	sound of *Aum*
avatara	incarnation
avidya	ignorance
bala	small boy
Bauddhas	followers of Buddha
bhagas	special qualities of a god
bhajanas	spiritual songs
bhakta	devotee of god
bhakti	devotion
bhakti yoga	the yoga of devotion
bhasma	ashes
bhava	attitude
bhogam	food
bhutas	elemental spirits
bija mantra	seed *mantra*s
bindu	dot
brahmachari	one who practises continence
brahminical	pertaining to Brahmins
buddhi	intellect
chakra	wheel; psychic whorl of energy
chaturthi	4th day of the lunar fortnight
cheena-charam	Chinese salts and chemistry
chinmudra	mystic sign made by touching the thumb with the tip of the forefinger
chintamani	jewel of plenty
chit; chid	consciousness
chitta	super conscious aspect of the mind
daityas	demons
daityasena	army of the demons

Dakinis	set of malevolent mother goddesses
dakshina	fee to be paid to a priest or *guru*
danda	rod
darshan	auspicious sight
deeparadhana	waving of lights before deity at sunset; same as *arati*
devanagari	language of the gods; Sanskrit
devas	gods
devasena	army of the gods
dharma	cosmic law of righteousness
dharmic	pertaining to *dharma*
Dhruva	young boy who did *tapa*s to Lord Vishnu
dhumraketu	comet
dhyana	meditation
dhyana sloka	verse for meditation
doshas	negative tendencies
Ekam sat	truth is one
eruma	female buffalo
gaja	elephant
gaja mukha	face of an elephant
gajam	elephant
gam	seed *mantra* of Ganesha
Ganapatya	sect who worship Ganesha
*gana*s	elemental forces
gandha	smell
gandharvas	celestial singers
ganya	that which can be counted
gayatri	a vedic metre; name of the sun goddess
ghat	a safe place for bathing in the river
ghee	clarified butter
gotra	clan in which a Brahmin is born
grihas	planets

ॐ

guha	cave
gunas	the three strands of nature: *sattva, rajas, tamas*
Guru	spiritual perceptor
gurukula	house of the guru which serves as a school
guruti	special ritual for the goddess
hastimukha	elephant-faced
hreem	seed sound of the goddess
Hum	an explective
hutavaha	born of fire
iccha Shakti	the power of desire which creates
Ida nadi	astral tube, which lies to the left of the spine
indriyas	sense organs
irumudi	bundle kept on the head of the pilgrim to Sabarimala
Itihasas	epics
japa	continuous repetition of a *mantra*
japa-mala	rosary used for *japa*
jivatman	embodied soul
jnana	wisdom
jnana Shakti	knowledge of the process of creation
jnana yoga	yoga of knowledge
jnanastra	weapon of knowledge
jnanendriyas	sense organs of perception
jujutsu	one of the martial arts of Japan
jyoti	light
jyotirlinga	a self-manifested *linga* of Shiva
kaalla	Malayalam word for bull
kaama	desire; lust
kalari	place where the martial arts of Kerala were taught

kalaripayattu	martial art of Kerala
kallidum kunnu	hill of stones
kallum mullum, kaalikku methai	stones and thorns are a carpet for our feet; one of the ditties sung by the devotees to Sabarimala
kalpa	an epoch or age of Brahma, the creator
Kama	god of love
kamandalu	special water pot carried by *sanyasis*
kanni swami	a new devotee to Sabarimala
karate	Japanese martial art
kari	Sanskrit name for elephant
karma	action and reaction
karma sanyasa	renounciation of action
karma yoga	the technique of action
Kaumaras	sect who worship Kartikeya
kavadi	bow-shaped structure carried by devotees of Kartikeya
kaya	body
kaya kalpa	special pill for prolonging life
kettu-nira	ritual for the devotee to Sabarimala
kirti	fame
koans	mystic Zen sayings
kriya Shakti	ability to create
krodha	anger
ku	prefix to denote something bad
kusa	type of grass
Kushmandas	evil spirits
kutarka	illogical arguments
lakh	hundred thousand
lila	cosmic play
linga	sign; phallic symbol of Shiva
lobha	greed

loka-samgrahamevaapi	for the good of the world
lungi	piece of cloth tied round the waist
mada	pride
Maha Maya	the great illusion; name of the goddess
Mahatmya	book describing the greatness of something
Mahayogi	the great yogi
mahisha	male buffalo
mahishi	female buffalo; spouse
makara jyoti	light which appears in Sabarimala on the first of the month of *Makara*
makar sankranti	14th January
mala	garland
mamta	the feeling of "mine"
mandala	mystic design; forty-one days
mantra	mystic sound
mara	to kill
matsarya	competitive spirit
maya	illusion
mayura	peacock
modakam	round sweet loved by Ganesha
moha	desire
moksha	liberation
mridanga	type of drum
mudra	mystic sign
mukkuruni	huge vessel for cooking a huge *modakam*
Muladhara	*chakra* at the base of the spine
Mulamantra	the first *mantra*
muni	a realised saint
murti	idol
nada	sound of creation
nadis	astral tubes of energy
naga puja	ritual done to propitiate snakes

Namaste Ganapathaye	obeisance to Ganapathy
nara	human being
nath sadhus	ascetic sect
navapashanam	nine toxic substances
nayaka	Lord; father
nirguna	without qualities
nitya brahmachari	eternal celibate
nivritti	path of knowledge
niyama	rules of conduct
nrittya	dance
ojas	spiritual radiance
palam nee	you are the fruit
pallikettu	first time on the pilgrimage to Sabarimala
Paramatma	supreme soul
parashu	axe
pattabandha asana	yogic posture in which Ayyappa sits
petta-thullal	special dance done by devotees of Ayyappa
phala	fruit
phalguni uttram	one of the twenty-eight stars
pingala	astral tube on the right side of the spine
pradakshina	circumambulation of deity
Prakriti	nature
pralaya	cosmic flood
prana	life breath
pranava	sound of *Aum*
pranava-swaroopa-vakrathunda	Ganesha in the form of *Aum*
prarabda karma	consequences of our past *karmas*
prasadam	left-overs from offerings
pretas	ghosts
puja	ritualistic worship of a deity
pujari	priest
puranas	books of mythology

puranic	mythological
Purusha	the supreme soul
Purusharthas	four goals of life: *dharma, artha, kama, moksha* (desire for righteousness, wealth, pleasure and liberation)
ragas	different types of melodies
raja yoga	method of stilling the mind as given in the *Patanjali yoga sutras*
rajas	one of the three qualities of Nature: passion, energy, desire
rajasic	passionate, energetic, restless
rajasika	having all the qualities of *rajas*
rakshasas	cannibalistic tribe which existed in India, demons
Rig Veda	The first of the four Vedas or scriptures
rishis	sages having great powers
rudraksha	seed of a tree worn by Shiva and his devotees
sadhana	spiritual practices
sadhus	wandering monks
saguna	having qualities
samadhi	super conscious state
samsara	transmigratory world
Sanatana Dharma	name of Hinduism; the ancient law of righteousness
sanyasi	renunciate
sapta rishis	seven sages
saptamatrikas	the seven celestial mothers
saptayugas	seven epochs
sara	essence
sarpa dosha	curse of the serpents
sat	existence
sattva	first of the three qualities of Nature; harmony; balance

sattvika	harmonious, balanced
Shaiva	pertaining to Shiva
Shaivites	followers of Shiva
Shaktas	sect who consider the goddess as the Supreme Reality
Shakti	power; energy of the goddess
Shanmata	six-fold system of worship, created by Adi Shankara of the six major gods
saara	essence
shaara	type of reed
sharanam	surrender
shasti	6th day of the lunar calendar
shat-kona yantra	mystic figure in which two triangles intersect
shikar	peak; the crown of a building
Shodashopachara puja	ritual making use of 16 types of offerings
shoucha	purificatory acts
Shouraya	worshipper of the sun god – Surya
Shree; Sree; Sri	Name of Lakshmi; auspiciousness
siddhas	perfected beings
siddhi	supernormal power
siddhi mantras	*mantras* to give such powers
sloka	verse
snana	bath
sruti	collective name for the Vedas
sthalam	place
sthitaprajna	an enlightened person; one of steady intellect
sukhasana	easy posture of sitting with feet tucked under the thighs
sutras	aphorisms
svaha	*mantra* for invocation of Agni
swara	pitch of the voice
swarupa samadhi	apparent death of the body
swastika	esoteric symbol of the Supreme
swayambhu	self created

tamas	one of the three qualities of Nature; darkness, ignorance; inertia
tamasic	lazy, dull
tanaya	son
tanmatras	subtle elements
tantric	pertaining to Tantra or the esoteric method of worshipping the divine as the goddess
tantrism	the worship of the divine as the goddess
tapas; tapasya	austerities for gaining spiritual benefits
tapaswini	lady ascetic
Tat twam asi	"That thou art"; esoteric mantra of the Upanishads proclaiming the unity of the human being with the infinite spirit
tattvas	the elements
teertham	holy water; holy river
tejas	spiritual light
termas	sacred Tibetan texts clothed in mystic language
theerthankaras	Jain saints
til	sesame seed
tilaka	dot on the forehead of Hindus
trisula	three-pronged weapon of Shiva
tulasi	the holy basil
urumi	the snake sword worn round the waist in ancient Kerala
uttarayanam	six months of the year from January 14th to July 14th
uttram	star on which Lord Ayyappa was born
vairagya	dispassion
vaishnavites	worshippers of Vishnu
vajra	thunderbolt
valli	creeper
vanamala	garland of wild flowers
vara	boon

varaha	boar
vasanas	inherited tendencies
vata	the wind element in our body
vriksha	tree
vayu	air
Vedas	ancient books of the Hindus; 4 in number
Vedic	pertaining to the Vedas
vel	spear; lance
vibhuti	ashes
vidya	knowledge
vighna	obstacle
vi-nayaka	one without a father; name of Ganesha
Vinayakas	followers of Ganesha
vipra	Brahmin
viveka	discrimination
Yaga; Yajna	fire ceremony
yakshas	celestial guardians of wealth
yama	rule of conduct
yang	chinese name for the masculine force
yantra	mystic diagram
yin	chinese name for the feminine force
yoga	activity which will unite us with the Supreme
yogasana	yogic postures
yoginis	female yogis
yogi	an adept in yoga
yuga	an epoch

GLOSSARY OF NAMES OF GANESHA

Ananta	The endless one
Anantarupa	One with endless forms
Dhumraketu	The terrible one
Ekadanta	One with only one tusk
Gajakarna	One with the ears of an elephant
Gajanana	One with the face of an elephant
Ganadyaksha	Chief of the ganas
Ganesha	Lord of ganas
Heramba	Protector of the weak
Kapila	One with a short stature
Lambodara	One with a huge belly
Maha Ganapathy	The great lord of the ganas
Phalachandra	One with the crescent moon on his forehead
Shurpakarna	One with pointed ears
Sumukha	One with a pleasing countenance
Vakratunda	One with a curled trunk
Vighnaraja	The king of obstacles
Vignesha	Lord of obstacles
Vikata	One with a crooked body
Vinayaka	One who is born without a sire; Lord of light

ॐ *Gam Ganapataye Namaha!*

GANESHA MANTRAS IN CHAPTER ORDER

ॐ Gam Ganapataye Namaha! The main mantra of Ganesha

ॐ Sri Ganeshaaya Namaha! Salutations to Ganesha

ॐ Vigneshaaya Namaha! Salutations to the Lord of obstacles

ॐ Anantaaya Namaha! Salutations to the one without an end

ॐ Sri Mahaganapathaye Namaha! Salutations to the great Lord of the ganas

ॐ Sumukhaaya Namaha! Salutations to the one with a pleasing face

ॐ Ekadantaaya Namaha! Salutations to the one with one tusk

ॐ Kapilaaya Namaha! Salutations to the short-statured one

ॐ Gajakarnakaaya Namaha! Salutations to the elephant-eared one

ॐ Lambodaraaya Namaha! Salutations to the big-bellied one

ॐ Vikataaya Namaha! Salutations to the strange-bodied one

ॐ Vighnarajaaya Namaha! Salutations to the Lord of obstacles

ॐ Vinayakaaya Namaha! Salutations to the one who is the Lord of Light

ॐ Dhumraketave Namaha! Salutations to the terrible one

ॐ Ganadyakshaaya Namaha! Salutations to the leader of the ganas

ॐ Phalachandraaya Namaha! Salutations to the one adorned with the crescent moon on his forehead

ॐ Gajananaaya Namaha! Salutations to the elephant-faced one

ॐ Vakratundaaya Namaha! Salutations to the one with a curled trunk

ॐ Shurpakarnaaya Namaha! Salutations to the one with pointed ears

ॐ Gam Ganapataye Namaha!

GLOSSARY OF THE NAMES OF KARTIKEYA

Agneya	Son of Agni
Agnibhu	Born of Agni
Dandapani	One who holds a staff
Devasenapati	General of the gods
Gangaputra	Son of Ganga
Gangeya	Born of Ganga
Guha	The cave-dweller
Kartikeya	Son of the Krittikas
Katargama	Name of Kartikeya in Sri Lanka
Krounchabheda	The destroyer of Krauncha
Kumara	The young boy
Mahasena	The great general
Muruga	The charming boy
Parvati Nandana	Beloved of Parvati
Pavakatmaja	Son of Fire
Pavaki	Born of fire
Shanmukha	Six-faced one
Sharavanabhava	Born in the forest of reeds
Shastipriya	Lover of the sixth lunar day
Shikhivahana	One who has a peacock as a vehicle
Skanda	One who slipped out
Subramanya	One who is worthy of worship
Sukumara	Handsome young man
Swaminathan	Teacher of his father
Umasuta	Son of Uma (Parvati)
Velayudha	One who carries a spear
Vishakha	One who was born on the star of that name
Yogeswara	Lord of yoga

ॐ *Sharavanabhava!*

KARTIKEYA MANTRAS IN CHAPTER ORDER

ॐ Sharavanabhava — The six-syllabled mantra of Kartikeya

ॐ Guhaaya Namaha! — Salutations to the secret one

ॐ Shanmukhaaya Namaha! — Salutations to the six-faced one

ॐ Subramanyaaya Namaha! — Salutations to Subramanya

ॐ Phalanetrasuthaaya Namaha! — Salutations to the son of Shiva

ॐ Tarakasurasamhaarine Namaha! — Salutations to the destroyer of Taraka

ॐ Krittikasunave Namaha! — Salutations to the son of the Krittikas

ॐ Shikhivahanaaya Namaha! — Salutations to the one who rides a peacock

ॐ Shaktidaraaya Namaha! — Salutations to the wielder of the Shakti weapon

ॐ Sukumaraaya Namaha! — Salutations to the handsome one

ॐ Amruthaaya Namaha! — Salutations to the immortal one

ॐ Abhayaaya Namaha! — Salutations to the one who grants fearlessness

ॐ Pavakatmajaaya Namaha! — Salutations to the son of Fire

ॐ *Sharavanabhava!*

GLOSSARY OF NAMES OF DHARMA SHASTA

Ayyan	Distortion of Aryan
Ayyanar	Lord
Ayyappan	Lord and father
Bhootanaatha	Lord of all creatures
Dharma Shasta	Wielder of dharma (righteousness)
Dharmatman	The soul of Dharma
Hari Hara Putra	Son of Vishnu and Shiva
Mahishimardaka	Slayer of Mahishi
Manikandan	One with a bell round his neck
Sabareesha	Lord of Sabari
Saranagati	The ultimate recourse
Srikanta	One with a beautiful neck
Taraka Brahman	The supreme Brahman
Vishwamohana	One who entices the world

Swamiye Sharanamayyappa!

AYYAPPA MANTRAS IN CHAPTER ORDER

Swamiye Sharanamayyappa	The most famous mantra of Ayyappa
ॐ Dharmashastaaya Namaha!	Salutations to the upholder of Dharma
ॐ Shivaputraaya Namaha!	Salutations to the son of Shiva
ॐ Mahatejase Namaha!	Salutations to the great light divine
ॐ Hariharasuthane Namaha!	Salutations to the son of Vishnu and Shiva
ॐ Shivapradaaya Namaha!	Salutations to the best of Shiva
ॐ Surotthamaaya Namaha!	Salutations to the best of the gods
ॐ Tejase Namaha!	Salutations to the one filled with divine light
ॐ Suraadakshaaya Namaha!	Salutations to the cleverest of the gods
ॐ Karunaabdaye Namaha!	Salutations to the compassionate one
ॐ Komalaangaaya Namaha!	Salutations to the one with beautiful limbs
ॐ Bhayanaashanaaya Namaha!	Salutations to the destroyer of fear
ॐ Janmaheenaaya Namaha!	Salutations to the one without birth
ॐ Swamiye Namaha!	Salutations to the Lord
ॐ Brahmane Namaha!	Salutations to the Brahman

Swamiye Sharanamayyappa!

BIBLIOGRAPHY

Glory of Ganesha	Central Chinmaya Mission Trust
The Shiva Purana	
Sri Ganesha	Sri Kant
Ganesh	B.K. Chaturvedi
Ganesha	Chitralekha Singh, Prem Nath
Kandar Anubhuti	N.V. Kartikeyan
Kartikeya	Shakti M. Gupta
Kumara Sambhava	Kalidasa translated by M.R. Kale
Subramanya Bhujangam	Adi Shankaracharya
Lord Ayyappan	Pyyappan
Sri Sabarimala Temple History	Balakrishnan Guruvayoor
Sharanaravangal	K.M. Keshvan Bhattathiri

Hari Aum Tat Sat